Immersed in Media

Imm ___ *Media* highlights the increasing significance of telepresence
in th ___ field. With contributions representing diverse disciplines,
this v ___ lelves into the topic through considerations of popular media
types ___ eir effects on users. Chapters in the work explain how the
expei ___ of presence can be affected by media technologies, including
televi ___ video games, film, and the Internet. They also discuss how
prese ___ perience mediates or moderates commonly studied media
effeci ___ as enjoyment, persuasion, and aggression. These discussions
are a ___ anied by overviews of the current state of presence research
and i ___ re. Ultimately, this work establishes the crucial role of tele-
prese ___ gaining a complete understanding of the uses and effects of
popu ___ lia technologies.

Cher ___ oanella Bracken (Ph.D., Temple University) is an Associate
Profe ___ the School of Communication at Cleveland State University. I ___ earch interests include psychological processing of media
conte ___ her work has been published in *Journal of Broadcasting*
and I ___ *ic Media, PsychNogy, Media Psychology*, and *Jounal of*
Com ___ *ion*. She is on the Board of Directors of the International
Socie ___ sence Research.

Paul S ___ h.D., Michigan State University) is an Assistant Professor
in th ___ of Communication at Cleveland State University. His
resear ___ its include video games, new media technologies, and
media ___ His work has been published in *Media Psychology,*
Journal of Broadcasting and Electronic Media, Communication
Research, and the book *Playing Video Games: Motives Responses and*
Consequences. He is a charter member of the International Society for
Presence Research.

Immersed in Media

Telepresence in Everyday Life

Edited by

Cheryl Campanella Bracken
and
Paul D. Skalski

Routledge
Taylor & Francis Group

NEW YORK AND LONDON

First published 2010
by Routledge
270 Madison Avenue, New York, NY 10016

Simultaneously published in the UK
by Routledge
2 Park Square, Milton Park, Abingdon, Oxon OX14 4RN

Routledge is an imprint of the Taylor & Francis Group, an informa business

© 2010 Taylor & Francis

Typeset in Sabon and Gill Sans by EvS Communication Networx, Inc.
Printed and bound in the United States of America on acid-free paper by Edwards
Brothers, Inc.

Library of Congress Cataloging in Publication Data

Immersed in media : telepresence in everyday life / edited by Cheryl Campanella Bracken
& Paul D. Skalski.
p. cm. — (Routledge communication series)
Includes bibliographical references and index.
1. Mass media—Technological innovations. 2. Telepresence. I. Bracken, Cheryl Campanella. II. Skalski, Paul D.
P96.T42I45 2009
302.23—dc22
2009029768

ISBN 10: 0-415-99339-3 (hbk)
ISBN 10: 0-415-99340-7 (pbk)
ISBN 10: 0-203-89233-X (ebk)

ISBN 13: 978-0-415-99339-5 (hbk)
ISBN 13: 978-0-415-99340-1 (pbk)
ISBN 13: 978-0-203-89233-6 (ebk)

Contents

Figures and Tables

Figures

Tables

Contributors

Renée A. Botta, PhD
Chair and Associate Professor
Mass Communication and Journalism Studies
University of Denver, USA
Renée A. Botta's (Ph.D., University of Wisconsin-Madison, 1998) research focuses on how we process and are affected by media; persuasion in media messages; the mediating role of message processing on media effects; international and intercultural health communication; family and peer communication about health and about health messages; health behavior change; and social marketing campaigns. Her work has been published in the following journals: *Journal of Communication, Communication Research, Communication in Healthcare, Health Communication, Sex Roles, Journal of Health Communication, Communication Quarterly, Science Communication,* and *Nursing Outlook.* She was a Fulbright Scholar studying communication about AIDS in Zambia from January through August 2003.

Nicholas D. Bowman
Assistant Professor
Media Studies
Young Harris College, Young Harris, Georgia, USA
Dr. Bowman's research focuses on individual's uses of and responses to different forms of entertainment media. His recent work has examined social facilitation processes in video game play as well as the role of user engagement in mood repair processes stemming from video game play.

Cheryl Campanella Bracken, PhD
Associate Professor
School of Communication
Cleveland State University, Cleveland, USA
Cheryl Campanella Bracken's general research area is the psychological processing of media with an emaphsis on studying media users'

responses to media form and content. She is a co-founder and Board Member of the International Society for Presence Research (www.ispr. info). Her work has been published in several journals including: *Journal of Broadcasting and Electronic Media, PsychNogy, Media Psychology,* and *Jounal of Communication.* More information about Dr. Bracken's research can be found at www.meme-dia.tv.

Laura Bright, PhD
Interactive Advertising Consultant
Austin, Texas, USA
Laura Bright's research focuses on interactive advertising in Web 2.0 environments, customization in online arenas, and consumer-generated content. Dr. Bright's work has appeared in the *Journal of Interactive Advertising, the International Journal of Electronic Business,* as well as several book chapters and academic conferences. More information can be found at: brightwoman.com.

Terry Daugherty, PhD
Assistant Professor
Department of Marketing
The University of Akron, Akron, USA
Terry Daugherty's research focuses on understanding consumer behavior and interactive marketing by examining how individual characteristics and media elements converge to effect both cognitive and behavioral outcomes. Dr. Daugherty's work has appeared in the *Journal of Consumer Psychology, Psychology and Marketing, Journal of Interactive Marketing, Journal of Advertising, International Journal of Internet Marketing and Advertising,* and the *Journal of Interactive Advertising,* among numerous others.

James Denny, MA
Adjunct Faculty
School of Communication
Cleveland State University, Cleveland, USA
James Denny earned his Masters degree in Applied Communication Theory and Methodology from Cleveland State University and has been teaching there since 2006. His research often focuses on the history, form and content of film and television. Other media interests include old-time radio, early video games, subliminal persuasion, and the history of rock 'n roll.

Harsha Gangadharbatla, PhD
Assistant Professor
School of Journalism and Communication
University of Oregon, Oregon, USA
Harsha Gangadharbatla's research focuses on new and emerging media, and social and economic effects of advertising. His publications have appeared in the (or are forthcoming) *International Journal of Advertising, Journal of Interactive Advertising, Journal of Computer-Mediated Communication,* and various other conferences.

Tilo Hartmann, PhD
Assistant Professor
Department of Communication Sciences
VU University, Amsterdam, The Netherlands
Tilo Hartmann has worked at the Hanover University of Music and Drama, the Annenberg School for Communication at University of Southern California Los Angeles, University of Erfurt, and University of Zurich. His research focuses on media-psychological aspects of media use (selective exposure, experience, effects), especially on media choice, social perceptions, presence, and behavioral effects. He is editor of the book *Media Choice: A Theoretical and Empirical Overview.*

Christoph Klimmt, PhD
Assistant Professor
Department of Communication
Johannes Gutenberg University of Mainz, Germany
Christoph Klimmt's topics of interest are media entertainment, videogames, media effects, new media technologies, and methods of communication research.

Evan A. Lieberman, PhD
Associate Professor
School of Communication
Cleveland State University, Cleveland, USA
Evan Lieberman is an experienced screenwriter, filmmaker, and director. He has taken part in the production of music videos, short films, and dramatic features. As an instructor, he has taught numerous courses covering all aspects of film, from history to production to acting to technical. He is a graduate of the American Film Institute.

Matthew Lombard, PhD
Associate Professor
Department of Broadcasting, Telecommunications, and Mass Media
Temple University, Philadelphia, USA
Matthew Lombard is a faculty member in the Mass Media and Communication doctoral program. He teaches introductory and advanced courses in media theory and research methodology, with emphases on survey, experimental and content analytic methods, and statistical analysis. His research centers on individuals' psychological and physiological processing of media presentations and experiences, with particular focus on the concept of (tele)presence, the illusion of being in and/or with people in a virtual environment. His work has appeared in journals including *Human Communication Research, Communication Research, Journal of Communication, Behaviour & Information Technology,* and *Journal of Computer-Mediated Communication.* He co-founded and is president of the International Society for Presence Research (ISPR; http://ispr.info) and moderates the presence-l listserv, a cross-disciplinary discussion forum related to presence theory and research.

Kimberly A. Neuendorf, PhD
Professor
School of Communication
Cleveland State University, Cleveland, USA
Kimberly A. Neuendorf is a Professor in the Media Arts and Technology Division at the School of Communication. Her recent published works include the highly acclaimed book, *The Content Analysis Guidebook* as well as the journal articles and conference papers *Tailoring New Websites to Appeal to Those Most Likely to Shop Online, Cosmopoliteness in the Internet Age, Cross-national Differences in Website Appeal: A Framework for Assessment, The Influence of Expanding Media Menus on Audience Content Selection, Obstacles and Openings to Presence in the Experience of Film,* and *Senses of Humor and Television Program Preference.*

Ashleigh K. Shelton, MA
Graduate Instructor
School of Journalism and Mass Communication
University of Minnesota, Minneapolis, USA
Ashleigh is a Ph.D. student at the University of Minnesota's School of Journalism and Mass Communication. She joined the program in the fall of 2007 after graduating summa cum laude and top of her class from the University of Minnesota Duluth. Her research focuses

on media effects, presence, video games, and social networking sites, and she also teaches courses on popular culture and media effects.

Paul D. Skalski, PhD
Assistant Professor
School of Communication
Cleveland State University, Cleveland, USA
Paul Skalski's scholarship focuses primarily on interactive entertainment and persuasion. His work has appeared in journals such as *Media Psychology, Journal of Broadcasting and Electronic Media,* and *Communication Research.* He teaches courses on video games, mass communication, new media, persuasion, and research methods and is currently serving as Graduate Program Director in the School of Communication at Cleveland State University.

Ron Tamborini, PhD
Professor
Department of Communication
Michigan State University, East Lansing, USA
Ron Tamborini is the Director of Doctoral Programs in the Department of Communication at Michigan State University. Ron received his PhD in Mass Communication from Indiana University. He teaches and does research in several areas of media effects. His recent work explores exposure to educational and entertaining content in traditional and new media. His entertainment research spans the psychology of comedy, suspenseful and violent drama, horror, tragedy, erotica, and sports. His new media research focuses on the experience of virtual and augmented reality. Independent of media effect, his research focuses on emotional behavior, especially fear/anger and their relation to human behavior.

Peter Vorderer, PhD
Professor of Communication Science and Scientific Director of Center for Advanced Media Research Amsterdam (CAMeRA)
VU University Amsterdam, The Netherlands
Peter Vorderer is a leading expert on the psychology of entertainment. He is co-editor of *Media Psychology.* His most recent publications include *Psychology of Entertainment* and *Playing Video Games: Motives, Responses, and Consequences,* both of which he has edited with Jennings Bryant and are published by Lawrence Erlbaum Associates. His research interests include media effects, entertainment, new technologies, and video games.

Eva L. Waterworth, PhD
Q-Life Group
Department of Informatics
Umeå University, Sweden
Eva Waterworth is a Docent in the Department of Informatics. Her primary research interests focuses on exploring the use of information technology to improve quality of life and creativity.

John A. Waterworth, PhD
Q-Life Group
Department of Informatics
Umeå University, Sweden
John A. Waterworth is a Professor of Informatics. His main research interest is in the design of interactive technology and its impact on user experiences.

David Westerman, PhD
Assistant Professor
Department of Communication Studies
West Virginia University, Morgantown, USA
David Westerman's research focuses on impression formation and entertainment experiences in online environments. His research has been published in *Human Communication Research*, *Journal of Computer-Mediated Communication*, and *Journal of Broadcasting and Electronic Media*.

Acknowledgments

I must acknowledge the support and patience of my family—my husband, Enda and my children, Ronan, Eamon, Fintan, and Siobhan—without you I would never have been able to complete this project.

CB

To my Mom, Sheila Jus

PS

Preface

This book is part of a set of two books addressing telepresence and related concepts concerned with the experience of media as "real" or non-mediated. This volume is specifically interested in how people experience telepresence (or presence) with communication technologies they use every day. It is the product of several years of research and academic discussion. A number of researchers, several who have authored chapters in the current text, found each other and started presenting their research together in panels at different conferences. Their common research interest was telepresence and popular media—the type of information and communication technologies (ICTs) that people use every day. These technologies include computers, television, video games, films, and handheld devices such as mobile phones. Part of the reason for this camaraderie was that these researchers represented a small group of people who were interested in studying the concept of telepresence and popular or everyday media.

At the time there was a lot of interest in the concept of presence but also a lack of attention amongst mainline presence scholars about how presence operates in daily life, since telepresence originally was concerned with highly immersive technologies that were not available to the general public. Much of the literature at this time was very technical or focused on emerging technologies such as virtual reality (VR). After several conferences, we started discussing being more organized and perhaps creating a "Presence and Popular Media" research group, to advance the study of telepresence occurring during the use of mass media technologies. One of the ways we felt we could promote our area of research was a book; thus, the idea for the present volume was born. This book is targeted towards researchers, teachers, and students who are interested in presence, telepresence, media, and the interaction between those areas.

A related and important impetus for this book was the profound changes in media that were occurring at the beginning of the 21st century, when the Presence and Popular Media group discussions began.

Digital technologies were sweeping the nation and the world, causing a radical alteration of the media environment in a very short period of time. The popularity of print media and landline-based telephony were on the decline, while computers, the Internet, and cellular technology were propelling toward mass adoption. Paralleling this growth were changes to more traditional electronic media such as film (including digital projection and 3D), television (most notably HDTV), and video games (including HD graphics and motion controllers). A common thread in these changes in the tapestry of popular media was that they were working toward "blanketing" media users with telepresence-type experiences. This book addresses the many advances in popular media that have recently occurred and their present and future implications for individuals and society.

It is the editors' hope that this volume, along with volume two (on telepresence theory and research), informs researchers, teachers, and students about the concept of telepresence. Specifically, our goal for this volume is to demonstrate that sensations of telepresence are not limited to highly immersive technologies, and that because of this people are experiencing such sensations on a daily basis. We also wanted to bring up-to-date the literature about the impact of telepresence sensations on media users. We strongly believe that media users desire such experiences, and the recent success of 3-D movies and other telepresence technologies in the United States and abroad is evidence of this. To paraphrase Matthew Lombard and Theresa Ditton (1997), telepresence is at the heart of all media experiences.

In addition to our colleagues and friends who contributed chapters to this volume, Cheryl Campanella Bracken would also like to thank the following people for their support before and during the preparation of this volume: Gary Pettey, Theresa Ditton, Betsi Grabe, Jennifer Snyder-Duch, Selcan Kayank, Leo Jeffres, Richard Perloff, Ryan Lange, Tom Gore, Bridget Rubenking, Amy Dalessandro, and Erika Gress.

Paul Skalski would also like to thank the following individuals for their inspiration, help, and support during the writing of this book: Leo Jeffres, David Atkin, Carolyn Lin, Richard Perloff, Sandi Smith, Chuck Atkin, Bradley Greenberg, Tim Levine, Stacy Fitzpatrick, Patric Spence, Ken Lachlan, Robert Brady, Leslie Deatrick, Tom Fediuk, Isa Botero, Jeff Stark, Craig Callander, Bettina Lunk, Kimberly Pride, Pete Lindmark, Mike Buncher, and Alysia Rogers.

References

Lombard, M., & Ditton, T. B. (1997). At the heart of it all: The concept of presence. *Journal of Computer-Mediated Communication, 3*(2). Retrieved October 1, 2009, from http://jcmc/indiana.edu/vol3/issue 2/lombard.html

Part I

Telepresence and Entertainment Media

Telepresence in Everyday Life

An Introduction

Cheryl Campanella Bracken and Paul D. Skalski

The goal of this book is to highlight the growth and importance of the concept of telepresence in everyday media use. Telepresence (or presence) is commonly defined as the "perceptual illusion of nonmediation" (Lombard & Ditton, 1997). The extent to which media users feel "in" a media environment or "with" mediated others has significant implications. Since various researchers introduced telepresence to the discipline of Communication, most notably Frank Biocca and Matthew Lombard (e.g., Biocca & Delaney, 1995; Lombard & Ditton, 1997; Biocca, 1997), attention to the concept has grown tremendously. Researchers investigating telepresence now herald from diverse disciplines (e.g., communication, psychology, computer science, philosophy, etc.), resulting in a large and diverse body of scholarly work. In 2007, Lombard and Jones identified more than 1,400 articles that addressed the concept. Even more impressive, the vast majority of this work came out in only the last 12 years.

How did we get to this point? During the 1980s, there was growing interest in perceptual realism and sensations of "being there" among media scholars. Marvin Minsky coined the term "telepresence" in 1980 to refer to the manipulation of remote objects through technology, and Sheridan (1992) broadened this definition (as "presence") to include the feelings people have while immersed in virtual environments such as those created through Virtual Reality (VR) technology. VR became a popular subject in the early 1990s and captured the attention researchers even outside of Computer Science. In the field of Communication, for example, Steuer (1992) conceptualized virtual reality in terms of vividness and interactivity. VR is a highly immersive technology and can elicit high levels of telepresence, making it the ultimate form of "being there" through media. It seemed for awhile that VR would take off as a technology and widely diffuse into homes. However, VR has still not successfully converted into an everyday form of media, nor does it show any signs of doing so. Although VR was viewed as an emerging technology in the 1990s (Biocca & Levy, 1995), the promise of VR has yet to be realized (Ebersole, 1997).

But a technological revolution has taken place since the 1990s, due to the rise of the digital age, and this has led to changes in everyday media like film, television, and video games. These technologies are rapidly expanding their potential to create sensations of telepresence. At the same time, the emergence of the Internet has revolutionized the use of computers, transforming them into a popular medium that converges features of all preceding media forms. Worldwide, people are now using media more than ever in history, as the following examples illustrate:

- There have been increases in box office sales at cinemas in the United States, the United Kingdom, and the Republic of Ireland (Barnes, 2008) resulting in $1.7 billion U.S.D. (1.2 billion Euros) in sales for the first two months of 2009 in the United States alone (Cieply & Barnes, 2009).
- Television viewing has increased to 5 hours per day in the United States (Gandossy, 2009). In the Europe, television viewing varies by country but has recently been at an average of 11.5 hours per week (Sandison, 2009).
- The United Kingdom averages 4.7 television sets per home (O'Neill, 2008). In the United States the average home has more TVs ($M = 2.73$) than people ($M = 2.25$) (Average Home, 2006).
- High definition television now exceeds 23% penetration in the United States (Penetration of High Definition, 2008).
- The number of individuals who use the Internet has increased from 16 million people (representing 0.4% of the world's population) in December 1994 to 1,574 million people (representing 23.5% of the world's population) in December 2008 (Internet World Stats, 2009).
- Video game sales reached $21.33 billion U.S.D. (14.6 billion Euros) in the United States in 2008 according to the NPD Group, up from $18 billion U.S.D. (12.3 billion Euros) the previous year (Sinclair, 2009). The industry experienced the most growth in the U.K., where software sales increased 26% in 2008 (NPD Group, 2009).
- The Middletown Media Studies report that Americans spend 11.7 hours a day, on average, with media (Papper, Holmes, & Popovich, 2004). This makes media use the number one life activity, even accounting for more time than sleeping (Finberg, 2005).

These figures demonstrate the enormous scale of media use around the world, in which telepresence undoubtedly plays a role.

This book highlights the importance of telepresence in considerations of popular media and their effects on users. While there are a limited number of books on telepresence, most deal with virtual reality systems and other highly immersive emerging technologies, instead of everyday media. Although there are various journal outlets publishing work on telepresence, the primary presence journal, *Presence: Teleoperators and Virtual Environments*, predominantly publishes articles focusing on applications of presence in computer science and virtual reality rather than work on the popular forms of media discussed in this text. Informed largely by traditions in the Communication, Media Psychology, and Media Studies disciplines, this book focuses on everyday electronic media technologies (e.g., film, TV, computers/the Internet, and video games) and commonly studied media effects (e.g., entertainment/enjoyment, persuasion, and effects of violent/sexual/frightening content, to name a few).

The unique contribution of this text, therefore, is that its chapters detail the impact of telepresence on popular media technologies and effects. The volume is intended to serve as a handbook on telepresence and popular media. It contains chapters by the most notable researchers on telepresence in their respective areas and will capture what we know about popular media and telepresence at the beginning of the 21st century.

One nagging issue we faced as editors of this book was, do we call the central concept "telepresence" or "presence"? While this may seem like a trivial or easy decision, it proved to be somewhat difficult due to discoveries during the course of this project. On one hand, seminal works such as Lombard and Ditton (1997) and Sheridan (1992) call the concept "presence," and this label has been dominant in the Communication literature. The primary organization of researchers studying the concept is also called the International Society for Presence Research (ISPR). On the other hand, the president of the organization, Matthew Lombard, has recently expressed some concerns about the term "presence" (Lombard, 2008). One major problem is that the word has been adopted by individuals and organizations who are not studying what the ISPR community is interested in, such as those who talk about religious "presence" with deities and spiritual forces. Adding "tele" suggests mediated presence, and for this reason we have decided to make "telepresence" our dominant term throughout this book (and in the title). But we allowed individual chapter authors to use "presence" or other related terms, since telepresence (or presence) is a complicated area of study that also includes subdimensions like immersion, involvement, realism, spatial presence, and social presence. The varying terms used to describe what we are interested in highlights the complexity of telepresence as an area of study, but the goal of telepresence researchers remains consistent—to capture an important and particular psychological experience of media technology users, whether it be their sense of feeling "in" a mediated environment or "with" mediated others, etc. The chapters in this book represent varying perspectives on the concept, offering a broad but rich take on the concept.

This book is divided into three parts. In the first section, the chapters address the role of telepresence in the experience of several popular media technologies, illustrated under "Popular Electronic Media" in Figure 1.1. The second section of the book addresses outcomes of experiencing telepresence, as represented in the column under "Common Media Effects" (see Figure 1.1). In the third section, the future of telepresence and popular media is discussed.

Specifically, on the technology side, Neuendorf and Lieberman discuss the history of film and the role telepresence has played throughout its history in chapter 2. The impact of television form and content is examined in chapter 3 by Bracken and Botta. In chapter 4, Westerman and Skalski discuss the ways in which computers can lead to telepresence in two main domains of study: Human-Computer Interaction (HCI) and Computer-Mediated Communication (CMC). The integral relationship between telepresence and video games is discussed in chapter 5 by Tamborini and Bowman, with a focus on how telepresence mediates the ongoing entertainment experience of gamers and an eye toward explicating processes that might moderate the personal and social outcomes associated with game play.

On the effects side, the impact of telepresence on the process of persuasion is discussed in chapter 6 by Daugherty, Gangadharbatla, and Bright. In chapter 7 Hartmann, Klimmt, and Vorderer discuss the impact telepresence has on the experience of media enjoyment. Skalski, Denny, and Shelton discuss a range of media theories and effects and

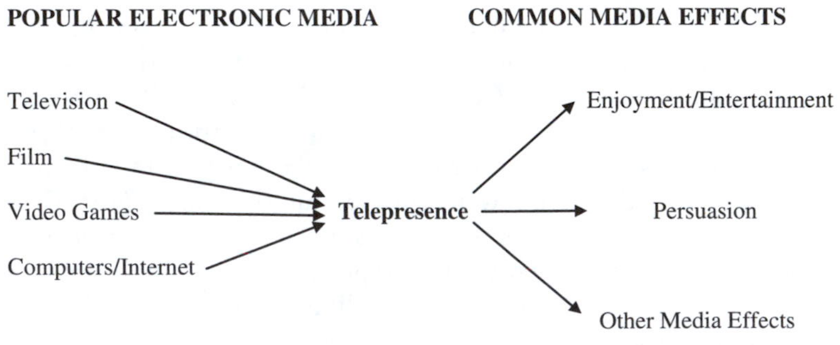

POPULAR ELECTRONIC MEDIA   COMMON MEDIA EFFECTS

Television

Film

Video Games → **Telepresence**

Computers/Internet

Enjoyment/Entertainment

Persuasion

Other Media Effects

Figure 1.1 The role of telepresence in popular media.

the influence of telepresence on such processes in chapter 8. Waterworth and Waterworth offer some theoretical possibilities about sensations of telepresence in the future in chapter 9. Lombard discusses the promise and perils of telepresence in the ever changing world of popular media in chapter 10. Lastly, in chapter 11, Bracken and Skalski present a conclusion that ties the chapters together and offers directions for future research. Ultimately, this text will establish the necessity of telepresence in gaining a complete understanding of the uses and effects of popular media technologies of the past, present, and future.

References

Average home has more TVs than people. (2006, September 21). *USA Today*. Retrieved May 19, 2009, from http://www.usatoday.com/life/television/news/2006-09-21-homes-tv_x.htm

Barnes, B. (2008, January 2). A film year full of escapism, flat in attendance. *New York Times*. Retrieved December 18, 2008, from http://www.nytimes.com/2008/01/02/movies/02year.html

Biocca, F. (1997). The Cyborg's dilemma: Progressive embodiment in virtual environments. *Journal of Computer-Mediated Communication, 3*(2). Retrieved March 8, 2009, from http://jcmc.indiana.edu/vol3/issue2/biocca.html

Biocca, F., & Delaney, B. (1995). Immersive virtual reality technology. In F. Biocca & M. R. Levy (Eds.), *Communication in the age of virtual reality* (pp. 57–124). Mahwah, NJ: Erlbaum.

Biocca, F., & Levy, M. R. (1995). *Communication in the age of virtual reality*. Mahwah, NJ: Erlbaum.

Cieply, M., & Barnes, B. (2009, February, 28). In downturn, Americans flock to the movies. *New York Times*. Retrieved May, 2009 from http://www.nytimes.com/2009/03/01/movies/01films.html

Ebersole, S. (1997). A brief history of virtual reality and its social applications. Retrieved March 29, 2009, from http://faculty.colostate-pueblo.edu/samuel.ebersole/vitae.html

Finberg, H. (2005). Our complex media day. *Poynter Online*. Retrieved April 20, 2009, from http://www.poynter.org/content/content_view.asp?id=89510

Gandossy, T. (2009, February 24). TV viewing at 'all-time high,' Nielsen says. Cnn.com. Retrieved August 26, 2009, http://www.cnn.com/2009/SHOWBIZ/TV/02/24/us.video.nielsen/

Internet World Stats. (2009). *Internet growth statistics*. Retrieved March 29, 2009, from http://www.internetworldstats.com/emarketing.htm

Lombard, M. (2008). *Presence and telepresence scholarship: Challenges ahead*. Keynote presentation at When Media Environments Become Real (WMEBR) conference, University of Berne, Switzerland.

Lombard, M., & Ditton, T. (1997). At the heart of it all: The concept of presence. *Journal of Computer-Mediated Communication, 3*(2). Retrieved March 9, 2009, from http://jcmc.indiana.edu/vol3/issue2/lombard.html

Lombard, M., & Jones, M. (2007). Identifying the (tele)presence literature. *PsychNology Journal, 5*(2), 197–206.

Minsky, M. (1980). Telepresence. *Omni*, June, 45–51.

NPD Group. (2009). 2008 video game software sales across top global markets experience double-digit growth. Retrieved May 2, 2009, from http://www.npd.com/press/releases/press_090202.html

O'Neill, B. (2008, January 17). Misery creep. *BBC News*. Retrieved May 19, 2009, from http://news.bbc.co.uk/2/hi/uk_news/magazine/7189947.stm

Papper, R. A., Holmes, M. E., & Popovich, M. N. (2004). Middletown media studies. *The International Digital Media & Arts Association Journal, 1*(1), 9–50.

Penetration of High Definition Television. (2008). The Nielsen Company. Retrieved May 19, 2009, from http://www.nielsenmedia.com/nc/portal/site/Public/menuitem.55dc65b4a7d5adff3f65936147a062a0/?vgnextoid=c5465e f5ad12e110VgnVCM100000ac0a260aRCRD

Sandison, N. (2009, April 8). European Internet consumption to overtake TV in 14 months. *BrandRepublic*. Retrieved on May 6, 2009, from http://www.brandrepublic.com/Discipline/Media/News/897321/European-internet-consumption-overtake-TV-14-months/

Sheridan, T. B. (1992). Musings on telepresence and virtual presence. *Presence: Teleoperators and Virtual Environments, 1*, 120–126.

Sinclair, B. (2009). NPD: 2008 game sales reach $21 billion, Wii Play sells 5.28M. *Gamespot*. Retrieved May 2, 2009, from http://www.gamespot.com/news/6203257.html

Steuer, J. (1992). Defining virtual reality: Dimensions determining telepresence. *Journal of Communication, 42*(4), 73–94.

Chapter 2

Film

The Original Immersive Medium

Kimberly A. Neuendorf and Evan A. Lieberman

Introduction

> It is already possible by ingenious optical contrivances to throw ste-
> reoscopic photographs of people on screens in full view of an audi-
> ence. Add the talking phonograph to counterfeit their voices, and it
> would be difficult to carry the illusion of real presence much further.
> (The Talking Phonograph, 1877, p. 385)

> From the opening titles I was mesmerized. The bright blasts of delir-
> iously vibrant color, the gunshots, the savage intensity of the music,
> the burning sun, the overt sexuality ... the hallucinatory quality of
> the imagery has never weakened for me over the years. (Scorsese &
> Wilson, 1997, p. 14)

These quotes, separated as they are by more than a century—the century
of cinema, as it turns out—denote the centrality of the phenomenon of
presence to the evolution of the moving image through its entire history. The prescience of the first, by a *Scientific American* writer, was not
unique at that time, as documented by additional published reports of
a world-wide fascination with presence-inducing new media in the late
19th century. And the visceral, unbidden response noted by contemporary film director Martin Scorsese in the second quote clearly refers to
the vivid experience of immersive presence in a fictional and unlikely
world-on-film.

The two quotes bookend a stable trajectory of the pursuit of presence
in film since its inception. Because of its photographic, time-based representation, cinema was the original medium of presence. The history of
film as a medium is one of striving for an ever-greater level of presence
through technological innovation, changes in aesthetic form, and developments in narrative structures and performance styles. That the filmic
experience is based in a quest for presence has been acknowledged by
film scholars, filmmakers, critics, and audiences for over 100 years. This

chapter will outline that history, after an initial consideration of how the construct of presence may best be applied to film.

The basic definition of presence as the perceptual illusion of nonmediation (Lombard & Ditton, 1997) when applied to film begs the question—mediation between a receiver and *what*? There are several viable answers as to what the "presence referent" might be: (a) the "real"; (b) a new filmic reality, i.e., the diegesis; and (c) an alternative form of representation of the "real," one that may acknowledge the reality of spectatorship.

The first option fits most clearly the standard approaches to presence, and is most readily applicable to the viewing of documentaries and other reality-based film forms. The second option reminds us that the typical film experience is "transportation into a narrative world" (Green, 2004), a diegetic environment constructed by filmmakers. "When a movie is working, the viewer forgets everything else and becomes totally absorbed: there is now only the world of the movie" (McGinn, 2005, p. 139). This world of the movie, this diegesis, may be nearly, but not quite, representative of a physical reality, as in Alfred Hitchcock's mild distortion of San Francisco geography in *Vertigo* (1959; Kraft & Leventhal, 2002). Or, the diegesis may be highly and often purposefully "unreal" (Armour, 2009) or dreamlike (McGinn, 2005). The diegesis may even be seen as emulating the interior landscape of the mind itself. Ultimately, as psychologist and early film scholar Hugo Munsterberg (1916) noted, film is a medium of the mind, not of the world.

The third option allows for the possibility that film viewers may be transported to another, mid-level reality, that of the spectator in a theater or other presentation venue (e.g., seated before a theater's proscenium, viewing still photography in a gallery; Turvey, 2004). We might term this "theatrical presence." Theatrical presence acknowledges and reinforces the status of the audience member as spectator. It is this type of presence that is sought by television producers adding a laugh track to a sitcom in the hopes of emulating the experience of co-viewing with a live audience (Butcher & Whissell, 1984; Lieberman, Neuendorf, Denny, Skalski, & Wang, in press; Neuendorf with Fennel, 1988), or by movie director Robert Rodriguez adding an "audience reaction [audio] track" to the DVD releases of his films (e.g., *Sin City*, 2005; Gilchrist, 2005). Theatrical presence might also be stimulated by techniques of reflexivity (Feuer, 1993; Stam, 1992), as when performers break the "fourth wall" in direct address to the audience. Woody Allen's monologues to the audience in *Annie Hall* (1977) may remind the viewer that they are a film audience member, at this point joined by the filmmaker in a limbo territory between fiction and reality, perhaps engaged in a type of social presence with Allen. Another example is direct address by commentators on a DVD, in which spectators may join filmmakers in co-viewing the film.

Of the various types of presence studied to date by presence scholars, two seem particularly relevant to the film experience: Spatial presence or telepresence, and social presence or copresence (Zhao, 2003b). Both have been referenced as the principal types of presence by film scholars, film-makers, and other commentators over the last several decades (Klimmt & Vorderer, 2003). Telepresence was the avowed goal of many early film innovators; social presence has been a companion goal in many key cases. Both types will be referred to in sections below. A third type of presence, that of "self" presence (Lee, 2004), may come into play with regard to "theatrical presence." In those situations in which the viewer's own status as observer is clarified and reinforced by the film content, the viewer may gain an enhanced ability to "insert" him/herself into the mid-level reality (i.e., the place between diegesis and "reality").

As we shall see, film scholars, practitioners, and audiences have demonstrated a clear understanding of the role of presence in film's world-wide success as a medium. Presence scholars have been less likely to examine the case of film. In a rare application of the theoretic notions of presence to the film experience, Marsh (2003) builds on Boorstin's three ways of watching film and applies them to early film examples. First, the "voyeuristic" viewing experience entails the sense of space/place engendered by the very early "actuality" travel films by the Lumiere brothers, seemingly a very basic type of spatial presence. Second, "visceral" viewing is that which seeks a strong sensation of the spectacle, and may be exemplified by audience thrill reactions to early films identified by Gunning (1999) as the "cinema of attractions." This is foremost a seeking and finding of a high degree of telepresence. Third, "vicarious" viewing is motivated by a need to experience something through one or more characters, including an emotional empathy connection. This seems to correspond most closely to social presence; even the early narrative films of Edwin S. Porter and Cecil Hepworth would seem to appeal to this type of experience.

Ijsselsteijn (2003) identifies film as a vital component in media history that can give us an understanding of the role of presence in media evolution. He pinpoints French film scholar Andre Bazin as the harbinger, the first to draw attention to film inventors' goal of reproducing reality with "absolute accuracy and fidelity" (p. 19). Further, he documents hardware innovations of the pre-cinema and early cinema eras (e.g., magic lanterns, persistence of vision toys, the Lumieres' Cinematographe) and of the critical period of the 1950s (e.g., 3-D, Cinerama, Smell-O-Vision) that were clear appeals to the overt manifestation of presence.

Steuer (1995) has included film in his consideration of technological variables that influence presence (particularly, telepresence). He identifies the two independent dimensions of vividness and interactivity. While recent developments in the common mode of viewing films might bring a modicum of interactivity to the process—e.g., DVD playback with chapter stops—the main forte of film resides in its vividness. Steuer defines vividness as the representational richness of a mediated environment as defined by its formal features, the way in which information is presented to the senses (p. 11). It is this element of representational richness that has been the goal of film, and of the modes of representation that immediately preceded film.

The Broad Recognition of Film as the Original Immersive Medium

The entire history of Western art may be seen as bound up with a fundamental pursuit of presence. Painting (or drawing) and sculpture can be seen as the twin bases of visual representation, both predicated on a desire to retain traces of past events or people through their depiction in a plastic form less vulnerable to the ravages of time or fading memory. The historical development of these art forms has exhibited movement toward greater accuracy—note the physiological detail of Greek and Roman sculpture, and the Renaissance innovation of perspective.

With the development of photography in the late 1830s, representation again took a decisive step towards greater realism. What had always been, even in the most photorealistic paintings, an interpretation of the subject now became a literal reflection of the subject itself, the iconicity of the image enhanced by the directness of the process, by its mechanics to be sure, but even more so by the objectivity of the representation. The photographic image still lacked the dimension of time to truly replicate the dynamics of lived experience that would be necessary for full telepresence.

Before the emergence of cinema, the goal of a "presence effect" was the domain of toys and multi-media spectacles. The Thaumatrope, Phenakistoscope, and Zoetrope were among the best known of many such amusements that synthesized movement based on persistence of vision (or the phi-phenomenon) through which the mind sees a series of still images shown in rapid procession as smooth motion.

At the same time, immersive spectacles were popular. Magic lantern shows, which used light-projected painted images that could be dissolved into the barest simulation of motion accompanied by music, narration, and often sound effects and pyrotechnics, had been in existence since the late 17th century, but only during the 19th century did they develop into a significant entertainment form. The magic lantern show, along with other multi-media spectacles such as the cyclorama (an enormous, scrolling, narrative painting accompanied by narration, music, and effects) and Wagnerian opera, attempted to render spectators so sensorily stimulated that they would lose consciousness of their surroundings and be absorbed into the performance.

Ironically, the origins of movies are interwoven with the efforts of chronophotographers to stop motion rather than recreate it. Eadweard Muybridge and Etienne Jules Marey were two of the main proponents of the study of live motion via the high-speed exposure, photographic capture of the activities of animals and humans. The intent was, in essence, counter-presence—the notion was to slice cross-sections of time, with high awareness of the mediated nature of the process. Other scientists and businessmen capitalized on the series photographs of running horses and flying birds as published by Muybridge in the 1870s (1955, 1957), recreating motion by exhibiting the images in rapid succession (Skalski, Neuendorf, Lieberman, & Denny, 2008). It was these visionaries—Edison in America, and LePrince, Friese-Greene, the Lumieres in Europe, and others—who saw the potential of recreated motion to attract audiences to an experience of physical immersion, and, just a bit later, to a social connection of audience and performer.

In 1895 the moment finally arrived for full telepresence, as the Lumiere brothers projected several short films in the Salon Indien of the Grand Cafe in Paris, among them *Train Arriving at La Ciotat* (1895), which might be seen metaphorically as the vehicle that carried aboard it the future of representation. Though reports of audience members running from their seats in fear, believing that the train was truly headed for them, are almost certainly apocryphal (Loiperdinger, 2004), reaction to the film is well-documented.

Famed writer Maxim Gorky, viewing an early Lumiere presentation, observed, "Carriages coming from somewhere in the perspective of the picture are moving straight at you, into the darkness in which you sit" (1960, p. 407). Film pioneer Georges Melies remarked, "the train dashed towards us, as if about to leave the screen and land in the hall" (as quoted in Bottomore, 1999, p. 194), and the French newspaper *Le courrier du centre* (July 14, 1896) reported that "spectators draw back instinctively, fearing they'll be run over by the steel monster" (as quoted in Bottomore, 1999, p. 213).

Early on, there was much discussion of the motion picture's ability to preserve great performances such as opera, and overcome death by preserving our loved ones forever. On a very basic level, the motion picture apparatus of camera and projector became the first method by which we could sample, capture, store, and share space and time. Many early films based their essential structures and appeals on the capacity for spatial/transportation presence—films like the Lumieres' *Leaving Jerusalem by Railway* (1897), *The Georgetown Loop (Colorado)* (1903), and Pathe's *Moscow Clad in Snow* (Mundwiller, 1909), brought spectators across the globe images of distant lands and mechanized travel. It is interesting that the notion of transportation is underscored by the fact that in two of the above films the camera itself is mounted on a moving train, producing a heightened sense of visceral dynamism and realism. Early narrative films brought the addition of social presence generated by plot and characterization. Mary Heaton Vorse, writing in 1911, comments on the enthusiastic response by naive audiences confronted with the innovation of film, the "living picture book that has brought so much into the lives of the people who work" (2002, p. 51). At a movie theater in New York City, Vorse noted the vocal reaction of a woman seated behind her, who shouted warnings to film characters—"'Oh, boy, take care, take care! Those wild and awful people will get you!' ... to the woman it was reality at its highest ... it was happening for her now" (p. 51).

The industrial vision for film was always for this presence enhancing trajectory of innovation. Edison observed in 1910, "The future of the motion picture in the amusement line will be in the form of a combination between it and the phonograph," further predicting the addition of stereoscopic (i.e., 3-D) photography and color film (Who's Who in the Film Game, 1910, p. 64). Even earlier, a debate was started with the 1877 *Scientific American* article quoted at the beginning of this chapter, which first identified the goal of "real presence." In the next issue of *Nature* (January 24, 1878), British inventor Wordsworth Donisthorpe responded: "Ingenious as this suggested combination is, I believe I am in the position to cap it. By combining the phonograph with the Kinesigraph I will undertake not only to produce a talking picture of Mr. Gladstone ... but the life-size photograph itself shall move and gesticulate precisely as he did when making the speech, the words and gestures corresponding as in real life" (p. 242).

Early film theorists Rudolph Arnheim (1957) and Andre Bazin, writing in 1932 and 1946 respectively, both recognized a fundamental tendency of the motion picture to strive towards an ever greater verisimilitude of representation, hiding the marks of construction and engendering an ever deeper sense of belief in the viewer. Although the two theorists had polar opposite views about the effect of this teleological development on the aesthetics of the medium, both understood, like Edison and Donisthorpe before them, that the constituent factors of this collapsing distance between reality and image were color, synchronized sound, wide aspect ratios that engage peripheral vision, and 3-D.

Bazin provides the first in depth discussion of the relationship between cinema and presence in a section of his 1946 essay "Theater and Cinema" subtitled "The Concept of Presence" (1967): "Everything takes place in the time-space perimeter which is the definition of presence. The cinema offers us effectively only a measure of duration, reduced but not to zero, while the increase in the space factor reestablishes the equilibrium of the psychological equation" (p. 97). Bazin not only makes the first theoretic connection of cinema and presence but also offers one of the earliest significant analyses of telepresence as a distinct concept.

Other notable film scholars have explored nuances of the film experience that relate directly to presence. Siegfried Kracauer (1960) identifies film's "obligation" to record, reveal, and "redeem physical reality." Sergei Eisenstein (*The Battleship Potemkin*, 1925) proposes that the reception of film involves a synchronization of the senses, invoked through critical juxtapositions of images. "[T]he 'montage elements'—touch literally every sense—except perhaps that of taste, which is, however, present in implication" (1947, pp. 72–73).

For a number of reasons, including a perceived need to compete with television, the 1950s saw the introduction of a variety of hardware innovations that were aimed at drawing audiences back into theaters with promises of presence (Ijsselsteijn, 2003). New widescreen film formats such as Todd-AO and CinemaScope were employed to maximize telepresence. Writer/director Gerard Alessandrini notes, "films had become so huge and so clear ... and three-dimensional looking ... it's like looking at a big window ... Rather than coming at you, they sort of draw you in" (2006).

Thus, we see a recognition of the quest for presence throughout the development of the medium of film by a wide range of scholars, commentators, filmmakers, and technicians.

Although the experience of presence may best be thought of as a holistic phenomenon, a full understanding of its nuances requires a dissection of cinematic presence into its constituent elements. The factors that contribute to a sense of presence with film may be identified as falling into six categories: visual elements, sound, editing, narrative, performance, and exhibition. Certainly, these categories overlap, but may fruitfully be examined individually. It should be noted that our position is that the quest for presence has encompassed essentially all aspects of both film *form and substance* (Neuendorf, 2002; Zhao, 2003a), going well beyond the film production/exhibition apparati.

Exhibition

Perhaps the constituent element most central to the audience's perception of presence is the nature of film's exhibition. Even the first large-screen exhibition of film by the Lumieres (almost instantly replacing Edison's individual-view Kinetoscope) generated critical and audience response consistent with strong telepresence. Some historians contend that Thomas Edison was mistaken in his initial decision not to develop a system suitable for mass spectatorship, noting that he should have learned from the long success of the magic lantern system (Bohn & Stromgren with Johnson, 1975; Mast, 1971).

The critical role of the exhibition process was recognized by early exhibitors, as manifested in their manipulations of the film, including re-editing the film, adding sound effects, or presenting a live narrative commentary. An extreme case was Hale's Tours, the largest movie theater chain prior to 1906 (Gunning, 1990). The films were footage taken from moving vehicles, and the exhibition space was constructed to resemble the vehicle itself—a train car with a conductor who took tickets, with the projection supplemented by sound effects of rail clatter and hissing steam (p. 58).

The introduction of sound, color, and higher quality and larger gauge film stock all contributed to greater immersive potential, as will be outlined later. Additionally, the nature of the exhibition space, both technologically and architecturally, has changed over the past century in ways that directly affect the viewer's perception of the image. As early as 1931, the *Journal of the Society of Motion Picture Engineers* published specifications for the width of the screen with respect to the distance of the farthest seats (a minimum of one-sixth and a maximum of eight-tenths; Paul, 1996, p. 247). However, such recommendations were unevenly observed, especially given the dual purpose that most massive "movie palaces" served during the first half of the 20th century—most attempted to combine live theater with movie exhibition in a space that was ornately and exotically designed in ways that drew attention to the architecture (Allen, 2002), and screens often ended up a small portion of the proscenium space (e.g., Radio City Music Hall). Thus, many movie-goers were seated either too far away or at too oblique an angle to enjoy the full power of the projected film.

Then, with the 1952 debut of the short *This is Cinerama*, movie theater-goers were "suddenly plunged into one of the most visceral motion picture experiences ever created ... Cinerama put the audience in the front car of the roller coaster and surrounded them with eye-filling peripheral images which created an unprecedented illusion of depth" (Belton, 1992, p. 1). Onto a curved, triple-width screen were projected images from three projectors, accompanied by stereo and surround speakers. The film's introduction by newsreel commentator Lowell Thomas tags the film as the latest attempt by artists to "convey the sense of living motion" (as quoted in Belton, p. 1).

The introduction of widescreen technologies such as Cinerama and CinemaScope, according to Belton (2002), transformed the relationship between spectator and screen, redefining spectatorship as more participatory. In advertisements for Cinerama, explicit promises of spatial presence were made: "You won't be gazing at a movie screen—you'll find yourself swept right into the picture ... Everything that happens on the curved Cinerama screen is happening to you" (as quoted in Belton, 1992, pp. 188–189). Similarly, 1950s ads for CinemaScope (a single-projector, flat-screen widescreen system, with an aspect ratio of 2.66:1; introduced by Twentieth Century Fox in 1953) promised that audiences would be drawn into the physical world of the film as if they were attending a live theater production, with pictures that "depicted audiences together with the on-screen spectacle ... as if there were an actual copresence between screen and spectator" (p. 192). For 3-D movies of the same era, the advertising appeal was reversed. Instead of promises of entering the world of the film, potential audience members were told that the film space would invade their own—you could expect, for example, "a lion in your lap" or "a lover in your arms" (p. 190). Paul (1993, 2004) has labeled this phenomenon "'negative parallax,' or the emergence effect" (2004, p. 229), a feature that distinguishes 3-D from widescreen systems. Yet, Paul (1993, p. 335) also notes that both widescreen and 3-D technologies have "the common aim of breaking down our sense of the frame."

Evidence of greater presence resulting from these technologies is only anecdotal. One systematic study of a 3-D movie (*Spy Kids 3-D: Game Over*, Rodriguez, 2003) failed to confirm greater sensations of spatial presence than for the 2-D version (Bracken, Lombard, Neuendorf, Denny, & Quillin, 2004). Research on the effect of widescreen aspect ratios is only now underway (Neuendorf, Lieberman, Ying, & Lindmark, 2009). Some research on television screen size supports the notion that viewing on a larger screen results in a greater sense of physical movement, greater feelings of excitement and enjoyment, and more physiological arousal (Lombard, Reich, Grabe, Bracken, & Ditton, 2000).

The introduction of color, sound, and larger and wider screens, have all proved to be lasting innovations, cumulative additions to cinema's storehouse of technologies intended to produce presence. But in addition to 3-D, a number of other less-successful multisensory adjuncts have been attempted: Olfactory interfaces such as Odorama and Smell-O-Vision (Ijsselsteijn, 2003), and tactile add-ons such as Percepto were introduced and discontinued in the 1950s. A gimmick of Ballyhoo-meister William Castle, Percepto was the installation of vibrating devices in selected theater seats during the film *The Tingler* (1959)—persons who happened to be in these seats were given a surprise "shock" during moments in the film when the Tingler attacked, and the rest of the audience inevitably co-reacted.

Clearly, the contemporary extension of these post-war gimmicks is the 4-D movie. Defined as an entertainment presentation system that combines a 3-D film with synchronized physical effects in the theater, these films are currently found only in specialized venues such as amusement parks and museums. In shows such as *Shrek 4-D* (2003; found at Universal Studios parks), *Pirates 4-D* (1999; found at Sea World installations), *Honey, I Shrunk the Audience* (Kleiser, 1994), and *It's Tough to be a Bug* (1998; both found at Disney theme parks), the audience is treated to such effects as water sprays that emulate character sneezes and termite "acid spray," air jets that add to the illusion of fast motion, and a moving floor that simulates the effect of a giant dog threatening the theater (http://en.wikipedia.org/wiki/4-D_film). In 2007, the National Aquarium in Baltimore, Maryland, converted its auditorium into a "4D Immersion Theater" showing short 3-D films with the addition of sensory effects such as mist, scents, and wind (http://www.aqua.org/). And, on the Mall in Washington, DC, the Newseum opened in 2008 with a 4-D theater that features "environmental effects," including seats that move and air gusts (4D film at Newseum, 2008).

Visual Elements

The film stock itself it is an important factor in the ability of the image to accurately represent a reality. Film gauge, or the physical size of the film, was standardized very early in the history of the medium at 35mm, introduced by Edison and his assistant W.K.L. Dickson as early as 1893. There have been various attempts to move to a larger gauge film stock in order to provide a more immersive viewing experience and thereby compete with television, notably in Hollywood during the late 1950s and early 1960s. Indeed, the image produced by the 55mm, 65mm, and 70mm formats used for such films as *Oklahoma!* (Zinnemann, 1955), *Lawrence of Arabia* (Lean, 1962) and *2001: A Space Odyssey* (Kubrick, 1968) had double the resolution of 35mm and was promoted as "More than your eyes have ever seen" (Twentieth Century Fox Trade advertisement for their Cinemascope-55 format) and to more directly evoke the notion of presence, "You're in the show with Todd-AO" (advertisement for the 1955 world premier of *Oklahoma!*). Although a handful of films continue to be shot in large gauge formats, the primary contemporary venue for such films is IMAX theaters, which utilize the largest film image area of any film format in history. Acland (1998) writes that "The IMAX image astonishes with its vibrant colours and fine details ... it is easy to mistake the IMAX screen for a wonderful, varying window on to real and imagined worlds" (p. 430).

IMAX represents the pinnacle of cinematic presence due to its film gauge and corresponding reduced film grain. Film grain is defined as "the product of the human eye and brain working in combination when viewing clumps of small image particles, seen through the full thickness of the emulsion layer, often numerous layers. Thus, film grain is 'perceived' property rather than an actual physical 'particle'" (Vitale, 2007,

p. 6). Absent empirical testing on the matter, film grain has generally been considered an impediment to perceived realism due to its status as an artifact of the photographic process and not a quality intrinsic to normal human visual perception.

There is an irony that a convention of the low budget "art cinema" is the notion that grainy black-and-white imagery may be considered more "realistic" than the relatively grain-free and color imagery of commercial productions. This apparent contradiction is in fact the clash of two different aspects of cinematic realism—the authentic visual representation of the subject and the authentic dramatic presentation of the subject. While the former demands low-grain, color images, the latter is more dependent on naturalistic setting and lighting which requires a faster film stock. These faster stocks are generally shot on locations where it is impossible to employ the artificial lighting that is the norm in studio shooting. The fact that the faster film stocks are also more grainy is in part responsible for the convention of considering grain as a quality of cinematic realism.

However, as film stocks have generally become faster, allowing for shooting in more authentic conditions, the primary film manufacturers (Eastman Kodak and Fuji) have also developed techniques for limiting grain, so as to preserve the photographic realism of the image. Eastman Kodak introduced T-Grain stocks which, according to Kodak Motion Picture Publication H-1, "improves film speed without sacrificing fine grain" (Eastman Kodak Company, 1999, p. 24). Technological innovation in the moving image is motivated in this case by reconciling two opposing qualities of realism.

Perhaps the most presence-relevant aspect of film stock is color, a visual element foreseen by almost all the early pioneers of cinema but not perfected for widespread use until the 1930s. While the three-strip Technicolor process used in *The Wizard of Oz* and *Gone With the Wind* (both credited to Fleming, 1939) is not "realistic" in terms of its intense color saturation and extreme emphasis on primary hues, it was the first time in the history of the medium that relatively true color reproduction (including roughly equivalent reds, greens, and blues) was made possible. It is fitting then that the very expensive three-strip Technicolor process was used primarily for musicals and fantasy films and not for more realistic dramas. With the introduction of single-strip Eastmancolor in the early 1950s, noted for its more authentic, muted color palette, other genres begin to shoot in color as well. Fueled by audience demand and the need to compete with black-and-white television, within a decade virtually all major American film releases were in shot in color, and black-and-white moved from being thought of as the more "realistic" film stock to being the more stylized and artificial approach embraced by B-movies, experimental filmmakers, and the European "art cinema."

Interestingly, research has shown that audiences do not always find color representations more "realistic" nor more present than black-and-white. Sherman and Dominick, in a study of audience reactions to film colorization (1988) found that colorized films were no more likely to be evaluated as "real" than were the black-and-white versions. Denny (2004) has shown that film footage from World War II is judged to be more real and more present when it is presented in black-and-white than when it is shown in color. One possible explanation for this is that audiences associate World War II with black-and-white film since that is the nature of their previous exposure, and so the color seems less authentic. The Denny experiment reveals that there is an effect of history, culture, previous exposure, and expectation on the evocation of cinematic presence, and thus it is not a phenomenon strictly determined by technological qualities.

There have been similar advances in lens technology that also contribute to the aesthetic movement towards greater presence, particularly in terms of the image's capacity for a greater depth of field, defined by Bordwell and Thompson as "the measurements of the closest and farthest planes in front of the camera lens between which everything will be in sharp focus" (1993, p. 493). While numerous factors contribute to depth of field, the focal length of the lens is critical, with shorter lenses, referred to as wide angle because of their broader scope of view, having inherently greater depth of field. The resulting deep focus photography enables the director and cinematographer to compose their shots with action occurring on multiple spatial planes, a greater mobility of character and camera, and the potential for expressing dramatic relationships through differential and dynamic positioning of characters and objects in the frame. The use of wide angle lenses for these purposes was pioneered by cinematographer Gregg Toland (Lieberman & Hegarty, in press) in films including *Wuthering Heights* (1939) and *The Best Years of Our Lives* (1946), and even more notably in Orson Welles' *Citizen Kane* (1941). Toland's technique allowed the eye to freely explore the space by shifting from near objects to those further away, a freedom prohibited by the relatively shallow focus produced by longer lenses and traditional lighting. Andre Bazin saw this as "a revolution in the language of the screen [as] depth of focus brings the spectator into a relation with the image closer to that which he enjoys with reality" (1967, pp. 36–37). In this way we can see that there is an interaction between technology (of the lens in this case) and aesthetics (staging and composition in depth) that enhances the spectator's sense of immersion in the diegesis.

This correlation of science and art for the purposes of producing a deeper quality of spectator engagement can also be seen in the area of camera movement. From the mounting of cameras on trains in the early days of cinema to the development of camera dollies (c. 1914) and cranes

(c. 1929, for early Hollywood musicals), there has been a steady progression of methods for moving the camera and thus the perception of the spectator moving through space. The mobility of the camera has been among the most steady areas of new product development in the film industry with constant improvements in the dolly and the crane as well as exciting inventions for image stabilization like the Steadi-cam in the 1970s and the doggi-cam in the 1990s, all resulting in a higher degree of representational realism. For film theorist Munsterberg, writing in 1916 (Langdale, 2002), movement (along with depth) is among the mechanisms that causes the viewer's unconscious to become fused with the representations of the image, resulting in an immersive presence, while Panofsky writes (in 1934) that the spectator "is in permanent motion as his eye identifies itself with the lens of the camera, which permanently shifts in distance and direction" (1999, p. 296). In this way the motion of the image, of the camera, of the represented space becomes the movement of the viewer's consciousness, of emotion and thought, into the world of the film.

Similarly, we can see how production design has moved from theatrical painted backdrops to the often beautiful but rarely realistic sets of the studio period of production (in Hollywood and around the world) and finally to the increasingly realistic location shooting and finely detailed sets of contemporary cinema. Lighting has followed a similar trajectory evolving from a theatrical, front-lit approach to the elaborate glamour of the studio period to the increasingly naturalistic illumination of today's films. In every aspect of the image, the developmental pattern has been the same, with the ultimate goal being an enhanced belief in the representation and an intensified sense of presence.

Sound

By its very nature, sound may evoke a greater sense of presence than does the visual image. Extending queries by Soviet Montage filmmaker and scholar Vsevolod Pudovkin, Andrew (1976) muses, "Is sound more real than picture because it is the reproduction of an aural fact whereas an image is a representation in two dimensions of a [three-dimensional] visual fact?" (p. 9; also see Eisenstein, Pudovkin, & Alexandrov, 2004).

While nearly all "silent" films were accompanied by music, the critical moment for sound and film was the introduction of dialogue with 1927's *The Jazz Singer* (Crosland). Within three years, all the major American studios had converted to sound production (Rickitt, 2007). There now would be the potential for the addition of not only dialogue, but also sound effects, and music that might be either integral or supplemental (i.e., "mood" music).

Even in the silent era, film exhibition was often accompanied by sound effects created live. Since film's early sound era, almost every sound besides dialogue has been recorded separately and then mixed together in post-production. These sounds may come from a recorded sound effects library, be recorded by a sound technician from "real world" sounds, or be foleyed. Foleying is the addition of footsteps, doors closing, clothing rustling, and other (usually human-created) sounds to a segment of film by the physical performance of "Foley artists" in a "Foley room" equipped with various floor surfaces, doors, and props.

Music has been an expected feature of film-going since the inception of mass audience viewing. Although used in part to cover the sound of the film projector (Gorbman, 1987), live music also followed a tradition of melodramatic music cues in late 19th century theater (Darby & Du Bois, 1990). For silent films, the musical accompaniment ranged from a single musician on piano, organ, or violin in smaller venues, to full orchestral coverage in large, prestigious houses. While some silent films were wholly scored by a composer, most silent film music was generated by in-house musicians, often following cue sheets that indicated brief segments of music that would match the "mood" of a given scene (Prendergast, 1977).

With the introduction of sound film circa 1927, music could now be of two types: diegetic, music that emerges from within the film's storyline (e.g., a musical number performed by a character), or non-diegetic, the more typical musical score that is not part of the diegesis (i.e., music the characters do not hear). The former should enhance a sense of realism, while the latter is more similar to the mood music played in silent movie houses, and traces its roots directly to concert music (Palmer, 1990). While both are intended to draw the viewer in emotionally (Tobias, 2003/2004), there is no empirical research evidence to establish how or to what extent this works. There is the sense among film composers that they spend their lives writing music that no one is supposed to hear, yet the power of non-diegetic music to involve and to lead an audience's attentions is widely assumed.

The evolution of non-diegetic music to its current status is noteworthy. As Hollywood composer Max Steiner (*Bride of Frankenstein*, Whale, 1935) tells it, the Hollywood producers and directors of 1931 "began to add a little music here and there to support love scenes or silent sequences. But they felt it necessary to explain the music pictorially. For example, if they wanted music for a street scene, an organ grinder was shown" (Palmer, 1990, p. 17). Over time, audiences accepted the musical score as an integral component of the film viewing experience and the practice of grounding music with odd artifices ended. Many composers view the non-diegetic score as a mode of appending emotional weight to a film, giving the viewer "information that you wouldn't otherwise know" (composer David Raksin, quoted in Morgan, 2000, p. 2). Timm (1998) identifies the key functions of film music scoring, including several that seem presence-enhancing: To either intensify or relax the pace of the film, to reflect emotion, to create "unspoken" thoughts of a character or unseen implications of a situation, to literally parallel or underscore the action, and to create an atmosphere of time and place.

Over time, technological advances in sound recording formats have changed the quality and fidelity of the soundtrack, giving more power to the filmmaker to manipulate precisely what the audience hears. Noise reduction technologies, beginning with Dolby's system designed to reduce tape hiss (first used in film for *A Clockwork Orange* (Kubrick) in 1971; Belton, 1996), have increased fidelity. THX, developed at Lucas-films in 1982, is a quality assurance standard that is aimed at generating a reliable soundtrack—i.e., so that a film's soundtrack will sound the same regardless of exhibition venue. And, sound formats have moved from monaural to stereo to multitrack; there is some evidence of a corresponding increase in emotional response and sense of presence as a result of an increased number of tracks of sound (Vastfjall, 2003). The evolution of surround-sound systems (e.g., Dolby Surround, Dolby 5.1) adds the element of immersion within a 360-degree environment of sound.

The density of the soundtrack has generally increased over time, so that by the 1970s, the complex blend of dialogue, music, and numerous sound effects was delivered by a dedicated sound designer, an individual whose job it is to combine all auditory elements into a fully realized auditory experience (Ondaatje, 2002), and then parcel out this soundscape into, typically, six different loudspeakers in the theater. As Rickitt (2007) notes, "modern theatres have invested in state-of-the-art digital sound reproduction systems that can project a sound to any part of the screen or auditorium, creating a convincing three-dimensional soundscape that places the audience 'within' the action" (p. 340). However, it is possible that if this surrounding soundscape does not match the two-dimensional image, it might actually be a deterrent to a sensation of full immersion.

Editing

The very act of editing—that is, combining two or more bits of film—presents a problem in the maintenance of spatial and temporal continuity. Psychological research gives us some indication that viewers develop a "viewpoint-dependent mental representation" in a film's first shot that is disrupted when followed by non-matching images (Garsoffky, Schwan, & Hesse, 2002). Thus, we would assume, the generation and maintenance of spatial and temporal presence sensations are intricately linked to the editing process. While we might expect footage without editing to elicit a greater sense of either spatial or social presence, this "long take" style is so rare and unexpected (MacDougall, 1992/1993) that it actually calls attention to itself. The norms of film editing have been established over a century of film production. Early editing to maintain continuity intended simply to follow a narrative line without making the viewer aware of the cuts, as in Cecil Hepworth's *Rescued by Rover* (1905), in which the saving of a kidnapped baby by a collie is painstakingly documented in a series of static camera shots, with the dog running right to left. Each time the dog reaches screen left, the film cuts to another shot along his journey, with the dog entering screen right.

Building on this basic continuity cutting, throughout much of the golden age of the American Hollywood Studio System (the 1920s through the 1950s; Schatz, 1996), filmmakers further established a norm of editing that minimized viewer disruption, and therefore maximized a sense of presence. Marsh (2003) notes: "Central to the success of film and encapsulating transparency and continuity is the invisible style" (p. 540). This norm of "invisible editing" included maintaining a sense of spectator location by shooting from only one side of a line of action (the so-called 180-degree rule), using shot-reverse shot (after a shot of a character looking, the viewer is shown the subject of the look), the use of orientation cuts (in which the location of important elements in the frame is matched in adjacent shots; Ondaatje, 2002), and cutting on action (masking any small discontinuities by cutting while some motion is shown) (Thompson & Bordwell, 2003). Also important to this style is the use of the "master shot"—a relatively long shot that begins a sequence, establishing for the viewer the physical layout of the scene that will follow. All these techniques are designed to reduce distancing between the viewer and the diegesis.

Practicing editors take the perspective that the editor's work "should remain invisible to the viewers in order to affect them successfully on deeper levels" (Oldman, 1992, p. 221). As editor Evan Lottman notes, "Editing should never call attention to itself. The experience of seeing a movie should be an experience that is divorced from its technique. Anything that suddenly pulls you out of the totality of the experience, a beautiful shot, a gorgeous piece of photography, even a tour de force performance, can hurt the overall effect" (Oldman, p. 232).

Editing may be used to manufacture a believable space or geography, a spatial construction that may or may not correspond to a "real" space. In *The Birds* (1963), Alfred Hitchcock used exterior shots from three different real locations over a 10-mile area to construct one contiguous sequence of children chased by crows from their schoolhouse on a hill down to the wharf. This "creative geography" (Levaco, 1974) is believable but entirely fictional.

Continuity/invisible editing was the established norm for commercial cinema throughout much of the 20th century, but its easy accessibility was viewed by some as inartistic. Echoing Andre Bazin's "aesthetic paradox" (1999) that the "faithful reproduction of reality is not art," critic Walter Kerr (1975) contends that art necessarily involves the deletion of portions of reality—"No painter or poet or dramatist in his right mind ever attempts to reproduce the abundance of life *in toto*. . . Stripping down is the preparation for art" (p. 3). In cases of purposeful obfuscation, the filmmaker as artist may intentionally set up barriers to presence.

For example, the 1920s Soviet Montage group of filmmakers, whose experiments with aggressive forms of editing (inspired by French filmmaker Abel Gance) challenged the notion of continuity editing, substituting an aesthetic of collision and synthesis. Several examples of key Soviet Montage editing techniques are: Elliptical cutting (i.e., jump cutting), which involves the compression of time by leaving out segments of action; overlapping editing, which results in the extension of time by repeating parts of action in subsequent shots; non-diegetic inserts, which create a metaphorical connection between the narrative and a shot taken from outside the diegesis (as in the insertion of footage of a cow's slaughter into a sequence in which striking workers are massacred, in Eisenstein's *Strike*, 1925). In Soviet Montage, the mechanism of editing is highly apparent, and for the viewer to engage in a construction of the diegetic world the film represents requires a certain degree of concentration and effort. This effort theoretically should work against any sensation of presence—the medium is too apparent.

On the other hand, a very obtrusive style might evoke a sense of presence in unexpected ways. Eisenstein evinced a concerted attempt to use rather obtrusive techniques to generate cross-modal, or synesthetic, responses across the human senses (Eisenstein, 1947). And 1960s French New Wave filmmakers such as Jean-Luc Godard (e.g., *Breathless*, 1960) and Alain Resnais (*Last Year at Marienbad*, 1961) used "violations" of classical editing rules to direct attention to the form of the film itself (d'Ydewalle & Vanderbeeken, 1990). Limited experimental evidence indicates that violations of the 180-degree rule result in greater visual activity by observers (d'Ydewalle, Desmet, & Van Rensbergen, 1998). The cognitive engagement stimulated by obtrusive editing might result in greater involvement, which has been posited by some scholars as a factor critical to the experience of presence, or alternatively as an actual separate dimension of presence (Klimmt & Vorderer, 2003).

Ever-faster editing has become the norm in recent decades (Bordwell, 2002). There is some evidence that the pace of editing is related to audience response, both in terms of posing a challenge to cognitive processing and recall (Watt & Welch, 1983) and in escalating the emotional outcome of a viewing situation (e.g., making a happy film happier, and angry content even less pleasant; Heft & Blondal, 1987).

There is some experimental evidence, as indicated by reaction-time and eye-movement data, to support the notion that a recognizable narrative story line makes the viewer less aware of transitions from shot to shot (d'Ydewalle, Desmet, & Van Rensbergen, 1998; d'Ydewalle & Vanderbeeken, 1990). Thus, we ought to consider the narrative substance of film as well as its form.

Narrative

The element of narrative, defined most simply by Bordwell and Thompson as "a chain of events in cause-effect relationship occurring in time and space" (1993, p. 65), has been posited by Gunning (1990) as a dividing line in early film history separating the "cinema of attractions" period (c. 1895–1905), during which the very phenomenon of moving pictures was enough to capture the spectators' attention, and the subsequent production of films that told increasingly clear and complex stories. Audience demand for narrative became the driving force for the commercial development of the industry. The power of narrative to create immersion has been widely recognized, beginning with the novel. As Ryan writes, "The literary features that create a sense of participation in fictional worlds present many parallels with the factors leading to telepresence" (1999, p. 117). These qualities include depth of character and narrative universe that Ryan correlates with the spatial depth of an image, and "the omniscient, impersonal narrator" (p. 118) that allows for a freedom and mobility of representation. Green (2004), in experimental work, has found that those with prior knowledge or experience relevant to the themes of a story report greater "transportation into" the narrative world. In film no less than literature, the ultimate desire of many spectators is to be transported into a fictional world, to experience a degree of cognitive involvement in a story that allows for the temporary "forgetting" of the real, physical world.

Parallel Action   In cinema there have been a number of techniques developed for increasing narrative engagement. The earliest such technique was parallel action/editing, in which two lines of story material, such as a group of thieves escaping from a robbery and the posse of lawmen on their trail, are alternated, creating a question in the audience's mind of how the two will resolve. The indeterminacy of dramatic outcome, the dynamism of time and space, the evocation of a story world that extends beyond the frame, all are ways in which parallel action encourages immersion in the film's narrative. This basic method for constructing cinematic suspense, usually attributed to Edwin S. Porter in *The Great Train Robbery* (1903; Musser, 1991) though it appears as early as James Williamson's film *Fire!* (1901), exerted such a powerful effect on audiences that it helped transform the motion picture from a novelty into an industry.

Even greater spectator excitement was produced by D.W. Griffith's subsequent innovation of *triangulated* parallel action in films such as *The Lonely Villa* (1909) which added a third term to the equation, so that, in its most famous (and clichéd) example, the film would cut between the "damsel in distress," the villain or other threat like an oncoming train, and the hero rushing to the rescue. Griffith used this approach in a majority of the nearly 500 films he made between 1908 and 1912, leading not only to extraordinary commercial success but also to triangulated action becoming a fundamental convention of cinematic narrative. Following David Cook's analysis of Griffith's innovation of this technique (2004), triangulated parallel editing points to the idea that the way the story is told in cinematic terms, its enunciation in moving images and sound, is perhaps the most significant component in the creation of an immersive movie experience.

The construction of multiple lines of plot development is central to the workings of what might be the most addictive form of moving image narrative, the serial narrative or soap opera, in which the intertwining fates and problems of a large cast of characters are merged into a single story that becomes so real for many viewers that they are unable to easily distinguish between the fiction and reality. Allen (1991) accounts for the popularity of the soap opera in part because it "represents an 'over-coded' narrative form, in which characters and relationships are endowed with pluri-significative possibilities far exceeding that required by narrative function alone" (p. 521). The extensive story spaces of serial narratives help produce a sense of a larger diegetic world that goes beyond the scene, individual character, or episode to seem like a parallel reality, and that provides ample opportunity for the establishment of a level of familiarity that will engender greater presence (Green, 2004).

Narrative Complexity and Construction Increasing narrative complexity has, since the 1970s, been an important quality of the contemporary cinema. From the sprawling cast of characters in *The Godfather* (Coppola, 1972) and the multiple story lines characteristic of the work of Robert Altman (e.g., *Nashville*, 1975) to the fragmented time frames of *Pulp Fiction* (Tarantino, 1994) and *Memento* (Nolan, 2000), filmmakers have used narrative complexity as a mechanism for engaging audience attention. There is always the potential danger of complexity turning into confusion for the audience, which of course serves as an inhibiting factor to narrative immersion because of the way it calls attention to the construction of the story. Screenplay construction is oriented towards the creation of an engaging narrative, and such conventions as evenly spaced plot points that change the direction of the story in unexpected ways (Field, 1994), consistently rising action that presents escalating danger or threat to the protagonist, and a conclusive climax that resolves the story's major conflicts in a moment of peak excitement, are all designed expressly to create the most powerful appeal to the spectator. At the same time, these elements must never seem artificial or predictable despite their structural necessity, because as with excessive complexity, obviousness of construction also changes the focus of audience attention from the story to the structure. This hidden architecture of the narrative works along with an invisible narration that makes the story appear to be just unfolding before the eyes of the viewer and so produce a cinematic believability, a visual verisimilitude, in the terms of the Lumieres, an actuality.

Identification and POV Character identification and point-of-view are other aspects of narrative that contribute to the evocation of cinematic presence. Character identification might be thought of as a desire to connect psychologically and emotionally with the characters, or often just the main character, of a film because of positive traits, common problems, or intriguing situations, and to imagine oneself in similar situations (as supported by Zillmann's affective disposition theory; Zillmann, 1996; see also Klimmt & Vorderer, 2003). Point-of-view can be thought of in several ways including the attitude of the author(s) towards the issues of the film, the way a character sees the world in ideological terms, the actual gaze of a character (the showing of which is called a point-of-view shot), the perspective of the camera, and the physical and conceptual positioning of the audience. It is easy to understand how the point-of-view shot creates a heightened connection between spectator and film as the viewer looks literally through the eyes of a character in the drama. When Hitchcock consistently shows the audience what Jeffries (Jimmy Stewart) sees out his window in *Rear Window* (1954), he not only makes a visual connection between spectator and character but also motivates an acceptance of his way of seeing the dramatic situation as well as of his questionable ethics—he is after all spying on his neighbors. Though it works well in first-person-shooter video games, this type of audience positioning has its limitations, as the few experiments in making a film entirely from a character's point-of-view such as *Lady in the Lake* (Montgomery, 1947) have met with little success critically or commercially.

There have been numerous attempts on the part of psychoanalytic film theorists to explain the relationship between point-of-view and the phenomenon of cinematic absorption. The fetish-based models of Christian Metz (1982) and Laura Mulvey (1975) build on the psychoanalytic theories of Sigmund Freud and more centrally, Jacques Lacan, to suggest that, through an interplay of gazes (the viewer's at the screen, the camera's at the characters, and the characters' at each other), the image acts as a sort of mirror in which the spectator identifies with his own ego ideal, taking sadistic pleasure in the power dynamic of narrative (and often gendered) control. The concept of *Suture* (Oudart, 1969/1978; see also Dayan, 1974, and Silverman, 1983) represents a less psychosexual approach to the same issue of cinematic absorption. Suture works through positioning the spectator's consciousness within the narrative construct by the structure of the shots and edits, particularly the narrative/editing figure of shot-reverse shot. Dayan writes "when I occupy the place of the subject, the codes which led me to occupy this place become invisible to me. The signifiers of the presence of the subject disappear from my consciousness because they are signifiers of my presence" (p. 124). Browne (1976) offers a more rhetorical explanation of point-of-view that challenges Dayan's model by positing that, "identification asks us as spectators to be two places at once, where the camera is and 'with' the depicted person—thus its doubled structure of viewer/viewed. As a powerful emotional process it thus throws into question any account of the position of the spectator as centered at a single point or at the center of any simply optical system" (p. 157). There have been numerous other theoretical attempts to account for the connection between the spectator, point-of-view, and the powerful presence of the cinema, but all such models remain speculative, lacking empirical testing.

Realism and Spectacle   That cinema may evoke presence via a range of mechanisms is evident in the seeming paradox that both extreme realism and high spectacle can both lead to great immersion. The location shooting, naturalistic lighting, and authentic characters and situations pioneered in the Poetic Realist films of Jean Renoir (e.g., *La Chienne*, 1931) and developed into a conscious style by Italian Neorealists Roberto Rossellini (*Open City*, 1946), Vittorio De Sica (*Bicycle Thieves*, 1947), and Luchino Visconte (*Ossessione*, 1942) produce a level of believability that can transport the spectator into the film's narrative. On the other hand, the patently unreal, yet undeniably effective special effects in films like the *Star Wars* or *The Matrix* series can also absorb the viewer into their synthetic worlds. Spectacle works by overwhelming the senses, by pushing the aesthetic of astonishment so far that the spectator can hardly believe his eyes, becoming completely absorbed in the presentation while not necessarily accepting the reality of the representation.

Performance

Performance is an aspect of the cinematic construct that might not immediately be apparent as a factor in the evocation of cinematic presence, but it is in fact at the very center of the phenomenon. While a full consideration of the evolution of film acting styles that have variously contributed to and detracted from a sense of presence is beyond the scope of this chapter, some key concepts are worthy of mention. Notably, the Hollywood Studio "star system" has had important implications. Ellis (1982) details "the photo effect," which is dependent on the simultaneous presence and absence of a film's star. The fact that the star is both present in the theater in terms of likeness, movement, and voice, but at the same time is literally absent from the space of projection, creates a psychological state of both idealization and identification, so that the spectator connects with the representation of the star and in doing so becomes part of the diegesis. Further, the "knowledge" of the star produced by the information presented in subsidiary media circulation (e.g., newspapers, magazines, television talk shows) gives the spectator a sense of knowing the star as a person, though of course this knowledge is completely manufactured. It is the desire for stars that drives the popular cinema and the dimensions of the stars' personae that determine the nature of the stories told. It is this suspension, this middle ground between absence and presence that lies at the heart of the stars' appeal.

The maintenance of an imaginary "fourth wall," derived from the stage, assumes that the acknowledgement of an audience is a hindrance to the creation of a believable narrative. Thus, the norm in film from the earliest Lumiere actualities has been for performers to avoid looking at the camera. But as noted earlier, a type of "theatrical presence" may be created by the direct address to the spectator by the character on screen. So when Matthew Broderick in *Ferris Bueller's Day Off* (1986) violates the imaginary fourth wall, the effect is one that shifts the register so that the image is indeed a construct that addresses the spectator.

From the pantomime-based acting style that characterized the silent cinema to stage-derived acting techniques and highly stylized personae of actors like Humphrey Bogart, Joan Crawford, Cary Grant, and Greta Garbo, to the use of non-actor performers by the filmmakers of French Poetic Realism and Italian Neorealism, various attempts have been made to increase audience identification with the people who appear in films.

One notable attempt to assure the most authentic possible performance style was simply called "The Method." Developed by Konstantin Stanislavsky (2000) in the Soviet Union early in the 20th century, the Method was imported to the United States by Jacob and Stella Adler for use by their Group Theater in the 1940s. The Method required that the actor actually become the character, feel the emotions that the character in the drama would feel, and, in a sense, lose their own traits and characteristics. This technique asked the actor to know every aspect of his or her stage life, and also allowed for stuttered or mumbled lines, improvisational blocking, and other elements that added to the realism and believability of the performance. The success of Method acting on film by Marlon Brando and others led to an adoption of this more "present" acting style throughout the film industry.

The Current State of Film Exhibition

Despite technological advances in general theatrical exhibition, recent decades have seen a devolution of the theatrical co-viewing experience, with more than a third of Americans citing "rude and annoying people" as a top motivation for staying away from movie theaters (EW Online Poll, 2005). A majority report preferring to view movies at home, so long as they have a large screen TV and surround sound. As distractions in theatrical venues increase, contemporary audiences seek immersive experiences in the home. Krugman, Shamp, and Johnson (1991), in an early study of viewing movies in the home, found those with higher socioeconomic status (SES) treating the experience as more theatrical (with little food prep, talking, etc.), a seeming conscious attempt to emulate the immersive theatrical experience.

The reactions of the film industry to the devolution of theatrical viewing include the reintroduction of some "old gimmicks." Prompted by fears of falling box-office revenues, DreamWorks executive Jeffrey Katzenberg has proclaimed that all his new animated features will be in 3-D (Maney, 2008). He is joined by an assortment of studios and producers who are creating new films, and repurposing old (e.g., re-releases of the first two *Toy Story* movies) in 3-D, banking on the outfitting of thousands of theaters to accommodate the new/old technology. Once again, filmmakers and distributors are betting that audiences will be drawn to the most extreme efforts to produce sensations of immersive presence.

Concluding Remarks

A case can be made for the relevance of film as a topic for consideration in presence scholarship, given its enduring popularity and recent developments, including surround sound, digital projection, immersive cinema technologies such as OmniMAX and IMAX, and the special case of 4-D movies. Though film remains largely non-interactive in an interactive age, recent developments show how it, more than any other popular medium, is taking advantage of the range of vividness cues

(Steuer, 1995) likely to contribute to a sense of presence. Additionally, film has served since its inception and continues to serve as a model for other moving image media (e.g., videogaming, VR) in both its form and content (Skalski et al., 2008; Marsh, 2003), an example of what Bolter and Grusin (2000) call "remediation," the refashioning of new media from old.

A covering perspective of this chapter has been the notion that the audience's sense of presence is an historically (and likely culturally) determined phenomenon, an evolving, dynamic system. Thus, history itself impacts the nature of the audience's "presence reception." For example, early audiences might have felt the Lumieres' train as real, but within a few years *The Countryman and the Cinematograph* (Paul, 1901) self-referentially poked fun at an ignorant spectator who mistakes the cinematic image for reality. And, to the audiences of the 1930s the Hollywood cinema had an unprecedented force of presence, but now those same films are often rejected by contemporary viewers as the height of artifice.

The various techniques that draw attention to themselves, and thereby draw attention to the mediated nature of film, may be responded to differently by different audience cohorts. The dynamic complexity of the films of the Soviet Montage and the French New Wave might be challenging to the novice viewer, but may provide a sense of comfortable familiarity to aficionados. The current popularity of what Bordwell (2002) calls "intensified continuity," which includes fast cutting, bipolar extremes of lens lengths (i.e., a dense mixture of close-ups and long shots), extreme close shots in dialogue scenes, and free-ranging camera, as well as obtrusive sound design, is jolting and invasive to many, but may become the expected form for those growing up within this music video-related aesthetic tradition (Vernallis, 2001). The unrealistic size of the human form in close-up on a large-format movie screen may detract from a sense of social presence for current audiences (Bracken, Neuendorf, & Jeffres, 2003), but not necessarily those of the future, who will have grown up with wall-size home theater screens. Further, stop-motion animation guru Ray Harryhausen hints at a changing receptivity to heavy-handed visual effects when he notes that historically, "the main purpose of any film was to tell a story and transport viewers into a world of make-believe. But now it would seem that knowing how a film is made only makes people want to watch it even more" (Rickitt, 2007, p. 6). Whether knowledge about the methods of generating moving image content is an enhancer or detractor for the sensation of presence is yet another empirical question yet to be answered.

A fundamental problem that prohibits full validation of the claims and critiques of cinematic presence by filmmakers and scholars over the years is the nearly total lack of empirical research in the field of film studies (notable exceptions include Austin, 1989; Charters, 1933; and Dale, 1935). The study of cinema can benefit enormously from the influence of the social and behavioral sciences by moving into a more tangible, experimental direction that can attempt to answer the questions raised by our discussion in this chapter. Likewise, the community of presence researchers may profit from a consideration of the rich tradition of theorizing within film studies. Just as Klimmt and Vorderer (2003) have called upon presence scholars to expand their purview to include media psychology theories such as affective disposition theory and involvement theory, we also recommend a consideration of both theoretic notions and practical applications from the field of film for those studying the creation of and moderating impact of presence.

References

4D film at Newseum. (2008, February 8). *The New Zealand Herald*. Retrieved on July 3, 2008, from *LexisNexis Academic*.

Acland, C. (1998). IMAX technology and the tourist gaze. *Cultural Studies, 12*, 429–445.

Alessandrini, G. (Commentator). (2006; original film release 1958). On B. Adler (Producer) & J. Logan (Director), *South Pacific* [DVD]. Beverly Hills, CA: Twentieth Century Fox Home Entertainment.

Allen, R. C. (1991). A reader oriented poetics of the soap opera. In M. Landy (Ed.), *Imitations of life: A reader on film and television melodrama* (pp. 496–524). Detroit, MI: Wayne State University Press.

Allen, R. C. (2002). From exhibition to reception: Reflections on the audience in film history. In G. A. Waller (Ed.), *Moviegoing in America* (pp. 300–307). Malden, MA: Blackwell.

Andrew, J. D. (1976). *The major film theories*. London: Oxford University Press.

Armour, N. (2009). The machine art of Dziga Vertov and Busby Berkeley. *Images*. Retrieved August 25, 2009, from http://www.imagesjournal.com/issue05/features/berkeley-vertov.htm

Arnheim, R. (1957). *Film as art*. Berkeley: University of California Press.

Austin, B. A. (1989). *Immediate seating: A look at movie audiences*. Belmont, CA: Wadsworth.

Bazin, A. (1967). *What is cinema? Volume 1* (H. Gray, Trans.). Berkeley: University of California Press.

Bazin, A. (1999). The myth of total cinema. In L. Braudy & M. Cohen (Eds.), *Film theory and criticism: Introductory readings* (5th ed.; pp. 199–202). New York: Oxford University Press.

Belton, J. (1992). *Widescreen cinema*. Cambridge, MA: Harvard University Press.

Belton, J. (1996). New technologies. In G. Nowell-Smith (Ed.), *The Oxford history of world cinema* (pp. 483–490). Oxford. England: Oxford University Press.

Belton, J. (2002). Spectator and screen. In G. A. Waller (Ed.), *Moviegoing in America* (pp. 238–246). Malden, MA: Blackwell.

Bohn, T. W., & Stromgren, R. L., with Johnson, D. H. (1975). *Light and shadows: A history of motion pictures*. Port Washington, NY: Alfred Publishing.

Bolter, J. D., & Grusin, R. (2000). *Remediation: Understanding new media*. London: The MIT Press.

Bordwell, D. (2002). Intensified continuity: Visual style in contemporary American film. *Film Quarterly, 55*(3), 16–28.

Bordwell, D., & Thompson, K. (1993). *Film art: An introduction*. New York: McGraw-Hill.

Bottomore, S. (1999). The panicking audience? Early cinema and the "train effect." *Historical Journal of Film, Radio, and Television, 19*(2), 177–216.

Bracken, C. C., Lombard, M., Neuendorf, K. A., Denny, J., & Quillin, M. (2004, August). Do 3-D movies really reach out and grab you? The case of *Spy Kids 3-D. Proceedings of the Seventh Annual International Meeting of the Presence Workshop*, Valencia, Spain, 283–286.

Bracken, C. C., Neuendorf, K. A., & Jeffres, L. W. (2003, July). *Source credibility, presence, and screen size*. Paper presented to the Visual Communication Division of the Association for Education in Journalism and Mass Communication, Kansas City, MO.

Browne, N. (1976). The spectator in the text: The rhetoric of *Stagecoach. Film Quarterly, 34*(2), 26–38.

Butcher, J., & Whissell, C. (1984). Laughter as a function of audience size, sex of the audience, and segments of the short film Duck Soup. *Perceptual and Motor Skills, 59*(3), 949–950.

Charters, W. W. (1933). *Motion pictures and youth: A summary*. New York: Arno & the *New York Times*.

Cook, D. A. (2004). *A history of narrative film* (4th ed.). New York: W. W. Norton.

Dale, E. (1935). *The content of motion pictures*. New York: Macmillan.

Darby, W., & Du Bois, J. (1990). *American film music: Major composers, techniques, trends, 1915–1990*. Jefferson, NC: McFarland.

Dayan, D. (1974). The tutor-code of classical cinema. *Film Quarterly, 28*(1), 22–31.

Denny, J. (2004). *Color vs. black-and-white in filmed historical footage*. Masters thesis, Cleveland State University, Cleveland, OH.

Donisthorpe, W. (1878, January 24). Talking photographs. *Nature*, p. 242.

d'Ydewalle G., Desmet, G., & Van Rensbergen, J. (1998). Film perception: The processing of film cuts. In G. Underwood (Ed.), *Eye guidance in reading and scene perception* (pp. 357–367). Oxford, England: Elsevier

d'Ydewalle, G., & Vanderbeeken, M. (1990). Perceptual and cognitive processing of editing rules in film. In R. Groner, G. d'Ydewalle, & R. Parham (Eds.), *From eye to mind: Information acquisition in perception, search, and reading* (pp. 129–139). Oxford, England: North-Holland.

Eastman Kodak Company. (1999). *Kodak motion picture film publication h-1*, p. 24.

Eisenstein, S. (1947). *The film sense* (J. Leyda, Trans.). San Diego, CA: Harcourt Brace.

Eisenstein, S., Pudovkin, V., & Alexandrov, G. (2004). Statement on sound. In L. Braudy & M. Cohen (Eds.), *Film theory and criticism: Introductory readings* (6th ed.; pp. 370–372). New York: Oxford University Press.

Ellis, J. (1982). *Visible fictions*. London: Routledge & Kegan Paul.

EW Online Poll. (2005, May 13). *Entertainment Weekly*. Retrieved August 25, 2009, from http://www.ew.com/ew/article/0,,1058217,00.html

Feuer, J. (1993). *The Hollywood musical* (2nd ed.). Bloomington: Indiana University Press.

Field, S. (1994). *Four screenplays: Studies in the American screenplay*. New York: Dell.

Garsoffky, B., Schwan, S., & Hesse, F. W. (2002). Viewpoint dependency in the recognition of dynamic scenes. *Journal of Experimental Psychology: Learning, Memory, and Cognition, 28*, 1035–1050.

Gilchrist, T. (2005, August 10). *Robert Rodriguez interview: The Sin City director discusses a deluxe DVD and the forthcoming sequel*. Retrieved August 25, 2009, from http://dvd.ign.com/articles/641/641160p1.html

Gorbman, C. (1987). *Unheard melodies: Narrative film music*. Bloomington: Indiana University Press.

Gorky, M. (1960). (Trans. L. Swan). A review of the Lumiere programme at the Nizhni-Novgorod fair. In J. Leyda (Ed.), *Kino: a history of Russian and Soviet film* (pp. 407–409). London: Allen and Unwin.

Green, M. C. (2004). Transportation into narrative worlds: The role of prior knowledge and perceived realism. *Discourse Processes, 38*(2), 247–266.

Gunning, T. (1990). The cinema of attractions: Early film, its spectator and the avant-garde. In T. Elsaesser & A. Barker (Eds.), *Early cinema: Space, frame, narrative* (pp. 56–62). London: BFI.

Gunning, T. (1999). An aesthetic of astonishment: Early film and the (in)credulous spectator. In L. Braudy & M. Cohen (Eds.), *Film theory and criticism: Introductory readings* (5th ed.; pp. 818–832). New York: Oxford University Press.

Heft, H., & Blondal, R. (1987). The influence of cutting rate on the evaluation of affective content of film. *Empirical Studies of the Arts, 5*(1), 1–14.

Ijsselsteijn, W. (2003). Presence in the past: What can we learn from media history? In G. Riva, F. Davide, & W. A. Ijsselsteijn (Eds.), *Being there: Concepts, effects and measurement of user presence in synthetic environments* (pp. 18–40). Amsterdam, The Netherlands: Ios Press.

Kerr, W. (1975). *The silent clowns*. New York: Alfred A. Knopf.

Klimmt, C., & Vorderer, P. (2003). Media psychology "is not yet there": Introducing theories on media entertainment to the presence debate. *Presence, 12*, 346–359.

Kracauer, S. (1960). *Theory of film: The redemption of physical reality*. Princeton, NJ: Princeton University Press.

Kraft, J., & Leventhal, A. (2002). *Footsteps in the fog: Alfred Hitchcock's San Francisco*. Santa Monica, CA: Santa Monica Press.

Krugman, D. M., Shamp, S. A., & Johnson, K. F. (1991). Video movies at home: Are they viewed like film or like television? *Journalism Quarterly, 68*(1-2), 120–130.

Langdale, A. (Ed.). (2002). *Hugo Munsterberg on film: The photoplay: A psychological study and other writings*. New York: Routledge.

Lee, K. M. (2004). Presence, explicated. *Communication Theory, 14*(1), 27–50.

Levaco, R. (Ed.). (1974). *Kuleshov on film: Writings by Lev Kuleshov* (R. Levaco, Trans.). Berkeley: University of California Press.

Lieberman, E. A., & Hegarty, K. (in press). The cinematographer as *auteur*: Gabriel Figueroa, Gregg Toland and the paradigm of multiple authorship. *Journal of Film and Video.*

Lieberman, E. A., Neuendorf, K. A., Denny, J., Skalski, P. D., & Wang, J. (in press). The language of laughter: A quantitative/qualitative fusion examining television narrative and humor. *Journal of Broadcasting & Electronic Media.*

Loiperdinger, M. (2004). Lumiere's *Arrival of the Train*: Cinema's founding myth. *The Moving Image, 4*(1), 89–118.

Lombard, M., & Ditton, T. (1997). At the heart of it all: The concept of presence. *Journal of Computer Mediated Communication, 3*(2). Retrieved ugust 25, 2009, from http://www.blackwell-synergy.com/doi/abs/10.1111/j.1083-6101.1997.tb00072.x

Lombard, M., Reich, R. D., Grabe, M. E., Bracken, C. C., & Ditton, T. B. (2000). Presence and television: The role of screen size. *Human Communication Research, 26,* 75–98.

MacDougall, D. (1992/93). When less is less: The long take in documentary. *Film Quarterly, 46,* 36–46.

Maney, K. (2008, July). The 3-D dilemma. *Conde Nast Portfolio,* pp. 91–95.

Marsh, T. (2003). Presence as experience: Film informing ways of staying there. *Presence, 12,* 538–549.

Mast, G. (1971). *A short history of the movies*. Indianapolis: Pegasus.

McGinn, C. (2005). *The power of movies: How screen and mind interact*. New York: Vintage Books.

Metz, C. (1982). *The imaginary signifier: Psychoanalysis and the cinema* (C. Britton, A. Wiliams, B. Brewster, & A. Guzzetti, Trans.). Bloomington: Indiana University Press.

Morgan, D. (2000). *Knowing the score: Film composers talk about the art, craft, blood, sweat, and tears of writing for cinema*. New York: HarperCollins.

Mulvey, L. (1975). Visual pleasure in the narrative cinema. *Screen, 16*(3), 6–18.

Munsterberg, H. (1916). *The film: A psychological study*. New York: D. Appleton.

Musser, C. (1991). *Before the nickelodeon: Edwin S. Porter and the Edison Manufacturing Company*. Los Angeles: University of California Press.

Muybridge, E. (1955). *The human figure in motion*. New York: Dover.

Muybridge, E. (1957). *Animals in motion* (L. S. Brown, Ed). New York: Dover.

Neuendorf, K. A. (2002). *The content analysis guidebook*. Thousand Oaks, CA: Sage.

Neuendorf, K. A., Lieberman, E. A., Ying, L., & Lindmark, P. (2009, August). *Too wide to please? A comparison of audience responses to widescreen vs. pan and scan presentation*. Paper presented to the Visual Communication

Division of the Association for Education in Journalism and Mass Communication, Boston, MA.

Neuendorf, K. A., with Fennell, T. (1988). A social facilitation view of the generation of humor and mirth reactions: The effects of a "laugh track." *Central States Speech Journal, 39*, 37–48.

Oldman, G. (1992). *First cut: Conversations with film editors.* Berkeley: University of California Press.

Ondaatje, M. (2002). *The conversations: Walter Murch and the art of editing film.* New York: Alfred A. Knopf.

Oudart, J.-P. (1978). Cinema and suture. (K. Hanet, Trans.). *Screen, 18,* 35–47. (Reprinted from *Cahiers du Cinema, 211/212,* 1969).

Palmer, C. (1990). *The composer in Hollywood.* London: Marion Boyars.

Panofsky, E. (1999). Style and medium in the motion picture. In L. Braudy & M. Cohen (Eds.), *Film theory and criticism: Introductory readings* (5th ed.; pp. 279–292). New York: Oxford University Press.

Paul, W. (1993). The aesthetics of emergence. *Film History, 5,* 321–355.

Paul, W. (1996). Screening space: Architecture, technology, and the motion picture screen. In L. Goldstein & I. Konigsberg (Eds.), *The movies: Texts, receptions, exposures* (pp. 244–274). Ann Arbor: The University of Michigan Press.

Paul, W. (2004). Breaking the fourth wall: "Belascoism," modernism, and a 3-D *Kiss Me Kate. Film History, 16,* 229–242.

Prendergast, R. M. (1977). *Film music, a neglected art: A critical study of music in films.* New York: W. W. Norton.

Rickitt, R. (2007). *Special effects: The history and technique.* New York: Billboard Books.

Ryan, M.-L. (1999). Immersion vs. interactivity: Virtual reality and literary theory. *Substance: A Review of Theory and Literary Criticism, 28*(2), 110–136.

Schatz, T. (1996). *The genius of the system: Hollywood filmmaking in the studio era.* New York: Henry Holt.

Scorsese, M., & Wilson, M. H. (1997). *A personal journey with Martin Scorsese through American movies.* New York: Cappa Productions.

Sherman, B. L., & Dominick, J. R. (1988). Perceptions of colorization. *Journalism Quarterly, 65,* 976–980.

Silverman, K. (1983). *The subject of semiotics.* New York: Oxford University Press.

Skalski, P. D., Neuendorf, K. A., Lieberman, E. A., & Denny, J. (2008, May). *The parallel development of film and video game technologies: History and implications.* Paper presented to the Long History of New Media Preconference, sponsored by the *New Media and Society* journal and the Communication History Interest Group of the International Communication Association, Montreal, Canada.

Stam, R. (1992). *Reflexivity in film and literature: From Don Quixote to Jean-Luc Godard.* New York: Columbia University Press.

Stanislavsky, K. (2000). *An actor's handbook: An alphabetical arrangement of concise statements on aspects on acting* (E. R. Reynolds Hapgood, Ed. & Trans.). New York: Theatre Arts Books.

Steuer, J. (1995). Defining virtual reality: Dimensions determining telepresence. In F. Biocca & M. R. Levy (Eds.), *Communication in the age of virtual reality* (pp. 33–56). Hillsdale, NJ: Erlbaum.

The talking phonograph. (1877, December 22). *Scientific American*, 384–385.

Thompson, K., & Bordwell, D. (2003). *Film history: An introduction* (2nd ed.). New York: McGraw-Hill, Inc.

Timm, L. M. (1998). *The soul of cinema: An appreciation of film music*. Needham Heights, MA: Simon & Schuster.

Tobias, J. (2003/04). Cinema, scored: Toward a comparative methodology for music in media. *Film Quarterly, 57*(2), 26–36.

Turvey, G. (2004). Panoramas, parades and the picturesque: The aesthetics of British actuality films, 1895–1901. *Film History: An International Journal, 16*(1), 9–27.

Vastfjall, D. (2003). The subjective sense of presence, emotion recognition, and experienced emotions in auditory virtual environments. *CyberPsychology & Behavior, 6*(2), 181–188.

Vernallis, C. (2001). The kindest cut: Functions and meanings of music video editing. *Screen, 42*(1), 21–48.

Vitale, T. (2007). *Film grain, resolution, and fundamental film particles*. Retrieved August 25, 2009, from: http://aic.stanford.edu/sg/emg/library/pdf/vitale/2007-04-vitale-filmgrain_resolution.pdf

Vorse, M. H. (2002; orig. 1911). Some picture show audiences (1911). In G. A. Waller (Ed.), *Moviegoing in America* (pp. 50–53). Malden, MA: Blackwell.

Watt, J. H. Jr., & Welch, A. J. (1983). Effects of static and dynamic complexity on children's attention and recall of televised instruction. In J. Bryant & D. R. Anderson (Eds.), *Children's understanding of television: Research on attention and comprehension* (pp. 69–102). New York: Academic Press.

Who's who in the film game: Facts and fancies about a man you know or ought to know. (1910, August 1). *The Nickelodeon, IV*(3), 64.

Zhao, S. (2003a). "Being there" and the role of presence technology. In G. Riva, F. Davide, & W. A. Ijsselsteijn (Eds.), *Being there: Concepts, effects and measurement of user presence in synthetic environments* (pp. 137–146). Amsterdam, The Netherlands: Ios Press.

Zhao, S. (2003b). Toward a taxonomy of copresence. *Presence, 12*, 445–455.

Zillmann, D. (1996). The psychology of suspense in dramatic exposition. In P. Vorderer, H. J. Wulff, & M. Friedrichsen (Eds.), *Suspense: Conceptualizations, theoretical analyses, and empirical explorations* (pp. 199–231). Mahwah, NJ: Erlbaum.

Chapter 3

Telepresence and Television

Cheryl Campanella Bracken and Renée A. Botta

The average American home has more television sets than human inhabitants. According to Nielson Media Research, there are more than 2.73 television sets and only 2.55 humans in the average U.S. household (USA Today, 2006). These TV sets are also increasingly larger, with Sharp predicting the average television screen size being 60-inches by 2015 in the United States. This is supported by sales data on large screen TV sets—sales of 46-inch and larger TVs have increased 272% in 2007, and sales of 40–42-inch TVs have increased by 128% in the same time period.

Recently, Savitz (July, 8, 2008) reported that television viewing in the United States has actually increased in 2008 to 127 hours and 15 minutes per month (per person) along with an increase in use of Internet and mobile devices. Similar increases were found throughout Europe. Specifically, the United Kingdom is tied in the amount of television viewing with the United States (individuals watch 28 hours per week), Italy watches 23 per week and a similar amount of viewing is done by Australians (22 hours per week). Another source states that Turkey watches an average of 5 hours per day/per household (Couch Potatoes, 2007).

Even before television was a wide spread phenomenon, early advertisements portrayed television as an entry way to the world at large. In Britain, ads claiming that TV was "the magic carpet" allowing viewers to "'see by Wireless' any part of the world" were published as early as 1928. In the United States, an ad from 1931 promised viewers would be amazed to see what they could currently only hear on radio with television's ability to "bring pictures into your home" (TVHistory, n.d.). These types of claims continued throughout the following decades. Even as television became ubiquitous, the proclamations continued with each new awe-inspiring technological development. Recently, the introduction of high definition television has made claims to audiences that HDTV will deliver images that jump out [of the screen] at you, it should be noted that most of the technological developments of television have moved the medium increasingly towards being more immersive or capable of grabbing viewer's attention and keeping it. This trend is true for larger screens, surround sound, improved image quality, and higher numbers of pixels. Indeed many of these technologies are grouped together for home theater packages and companies promise viewers a sense of being in the action (telepresence experiences). For example, "We want your next concert at home to be even better than being there; when the boulder is rolling after Indiana Jones it should be coming right thru your home" (Theatrical Concepts, 2008). Chalke (2007) argues that the desire for these "telepresence" experiences is not new to the early 21st century but existed even prior to the introduction of television. As early as 1911 an advertisement selling the "Homograph Projector" promised "moving pictures" for the purpose of recreating the feeling of the cinema experience at home (see chapter 2, this volume, for a full discussion of film and telepresence). So, while the desire for such experiences may not be new, the affordability of these communication technologies has made them very popular in viewers' homes.

Further, the prominence of many of these communication technologies coincided with the introduction of telepresence within the field of Computer Science. Early telepresence research started as way to examine the experiences of participants in virtual environments in the 1980s. The term "telepresence" is credited to Marvin Minsky (1980) and was incorporated into the research on virtual reality in the late 1980s and early 1990s. The term first appears in the Communication literature in 1992, when Steuer explicated virtual reality. According to Steuer, telepresence is "the experience of presence in an environment by the means of a communication medium" (p. 83). He noted that two properties of media contribute to telepresence: vividness (realness or media richness) and interactivity, features which continue to be of interest to telepresence researchers.

It should be noted that even early in telepresence research different fields were using terms differently. For example, Cruz-Neira, Sandin, DeFanti, Kenyon, & Hart (1992) in their introduction of the Cave Automatic Virtual Reality (CAVE)[1] discuss immersion as "the degree of visual simulation a virtual reality interface provides for the viewer—the degree of the suspension of disbelief" (p. 67) or as a natural result of using immersive technologies. Communication scholars discuss both these same terms but especially "suspension of disbelief" as being a personal characteristic associated with the media user or viewer themselves.

The migration of the concept to television developed much later with the first published article on telepresence and television in 2000 (Lombard, Reich, Grabe, Bracken, & Ditton, 2000). However there are earlier studies that examined the concept of telepresence under various names. Many studies of the "direct responses" to television examined viewers' responses to the medium (i.e., Calvert, Huston, Watkins, & Wright, 1982; Flavell & Flavell, 1990).

While most research on media users' experiences of telepresence is focused on virtual reality environments, some researchers have been able to demonstrate that television viewing can also induce sensations of telepresence in viewers (Freeman, Avons, Davidoff, & Pearson, 1997; Lombard et al., 2000). Some examples of research on television and telepresence include the extent to which form variables such as screen size (Lombard et al., 2000), image quality (Bracken, 2005), and sound quality and dimensionality (Lessiter & Freeman, 2001) impact the extent to which television viewers experience presence. Additionally, previous research suggests that content types can also make a difference in the extent to which audiences experience a sense of presence (Dillon, Keogh, Freeman, Davidoff, 2001; Lombard & Ditton, 1997). However, it is still unclear if both form and content are necessary, or if one aspect of television viewing contributes more to the likelihood viewers experience a sense of telepresence. This chapter discusses our current knowledge relating to telepresence and television and then presents an experiment that explores the role of TV content and form in evoking sensations of telepresence in viewers.

Telepresence

The concept of telepresence is variously defined as a sense of "being there" during a mediated experience, and more generally as "an illusion of nonmediation" (Lombard & Ditton, 1997). While there are numerous definitions of telepresence, most attempt to define the experience in highly immersive virtual reality systems. There are several widely used definitions that have been applied within Communication. First, Kim and Biocca (1997) defined telepresence as having two subdimensions: arrival (i.e., being there in the mediated environment) and departure (i.e., the feeling of not being in the unmediated environment). Lee (2004) defines telepresence as "a psychological state in which virtual objects are experienced as actual objects in either sensory or nonsensory ways" (p. 37) and identifies three types of telepresence. They are physical, social, and self presence. However, Lombard and Ditton (1997) have identified six subdimensions of telepresence but only four of them are relevant to television, and those include: perceived realism, spatial presence or transportation, immersion, and social richness. *Perceived realism* refers to the plausibility of the media content. *Immersion* involves being perceptually and psychologically "submerged" in a mediated environment (Lombard & Ditton, 1997; Biocca & Delaney, 1995). *Spatial presence* refers to the sense of "being there" in the space of the media environment (Wirth et al., 2007). *Social realism* refers to the extent to which media/artificial environment is comparable to the real world; this is sometimes identified as behavioral realism (Freeman, 2004). The definition created based on contributions from many telepresence researchers is offered by International Society for Presence Research (ISPR) and expands the Lombard and Ditton definition. ISPR states that presence is "a psychological state of subjective perception in which even though part or all of an individual's current experience is generated by and/or filtered through human-made technology, part or of all of the individual's perception fails to accurately acknowledge the role of the technology in the experience" (ISPR, 2000).

Recently, Bracken, Pettey, Rubenking, & Guha (2008) have modified the ISPR definition of telepresence to be more applicable to popular media:

> Telepresence requires the use of technology and results in a psychological state in which media users voluntarily suspend the experience of mediation in order to feel a sense of connection with the mediated content they are using (e.g., a part of the action, connected to characters, involved in the story line). This state is often influenced by the expectation of the technology, the media content, and characteristics of the media user. A sense of telepresence is felt by media users when the technology becomes transparent in the interaction. (p. 4)

Thus, telepresence is an interaction among the user, the content and the technology. The remainder of this chapter looks more specifically at this interaction, examining how content and form differences of television (the technology) impacts television viewers' experiences of telepresence.

Television and Telepresence

In the discipline of Communication, interest in the idea of "being there" (Reeves, 1991) while watching television served as an entry way into the larger concept of telepresence. There are several noteworthy studies that explored this concept prior to the use of the term telepresence (Detenber & Reeves, 1996; Reeves, Detenber, & Steuer, 1993; Reeves, Lombard, & Melwani, 1992; Lombard, 1995), with each finding that participants responded as if the television was providing a window to the real world and that larger screens enhance the dependent variable examined. For example, Reeves et al. (1992) found that when participants viewed faces on larger screens they paid more attention to the images, while Lombard (1995) found that valance was impacted by screen size, with attractive faces being rated significantly more attractive on the larger screens. The idea that telepresence could be experienced with television grew from these earlier findings. In a series of studies, Freeman, Avons, IJsselsteijn, and de Ridder (1999) concluded that television was able to induce sensations of telepresence and that the concept was useful for studying less immersive technologies such as television. It is now widely accepted among scholars that television viewers also experience a sense of presence. Indeed, studies have found that viewers respond to objects and people on the screen as if they were real (Bracken, 2005; Grabe, Lombard, Reich, Bracken, & Ditton, 1999; Freeman et al., 1998).

Television Form

Researchers in the area of entertainment and telepresence have studied some of the variables that have been linked to encouraging telepresence sensations—these include both form (i.e., how the information is delivered and how the information is displayed to the audience) and content (i.e., what the audience actually sees or does) variables.

Previous research has found that manipulating form variables alters the amount of presence experienced by viewers. Two general categories of form variables were previously identified: User controlled and producer controlled (Lombard & Ditton, 1997) aspects of television presentation. Examples of user controlled variables are television screen size, sound quality (home theater), and image quality. Findings related to user controlled variables demonstrate that larger screen size (or field of view; Bracken & Atkin, 2004; IJsselsteijn, de Ridder, Freeman, Avons & Bouwhuis, 2001), improved sound quality (Lessiter, Freeman, & Davidoff, 2001), and improved image quality (Botta & Bracken, 2002; Bracken, 2005, 2006, 2007; Bracken & Horowitz, 2006) increase the likelihood that the media user will experience a sense of telepresence.

Screen Size   The most commonly studied form variable is screen size. One of the earliest experiments of screen size[2] tested the impact of screen size (8-inch, 12-inch, 15-inch, and 23-inch) on participants' ability to recognize text (Lewin, 1972). The results indicated that participants' recognition was better for those who sat closer and saw the text on larger screens. This is just one of a number of studies that investigated television screen size in the early 1970s. Most of these studies, however, were primarily focused on the impact of the television screen size for uses other than entertainment. Examples include consumer responses to viewing text on the different sized television screens (O'Donnell, 1971), instructional/learning outcomes (Murphy, 1970), and evaluation of the meaning of the images (Bollman, 1971). After this series of television screen size studies there was a long period—until the early 1990s—without much investigation.

The results of the studies from the 1990s suggest that larger image sizes increase television viewers' sensations of telepresence. This hypothesis has been supported by a number of studies. Moreover, Grabe et al. (1999) state in a review of screen studies that "there is substantial evidence for the idea that larger screens promote perceived realism of media content and perceptions of presence" (p. 5). One reason offered for larger images being able to evoke higher levels of telepresence is because larger images (or screens) fill a greater percentage of viewers' field of vision (Reeves & Nass, 1996), thus invoking a greater sense of being there.

While there are numerous screen size studies that have examined the role of image size on various media effects (see Detenber & Reeves, 1996; Reeves, Lang, Kim, & Tatar, 1999), there are very few that have focused upon screen size and presence. Some examples of screen size studies include the early work on image size and viewing distances (Hatada, Sakata, & Kushaka, 1980[3]; Lund, 1993). Other early work includes an experiment that examined the interaction of screen size (20-, 42-, or 70-inch) and the type of content viewed. The participants reported feeling more fatigue and dizziness when watching fast moving scenes (horse racing) on the larger screens (Ohtani & Mitshuhashi, 1973). More recently, screen size studies focused on whether differences in screen size affect attention (Detenber & Reeves, 1996; Reeves, Detenber, & Steuer, 1993; Reeves et al., 1999), memory (Kim & Biocca, 1997), and arousal (Lombard, Grabe, et al., 1996, Lombard, Reich, et al, 2000; Reeves et al., 1999). Lombard et al (2000) also found that participants reported higher levels of enjoyment, and a sense of telepresence (immersion) when viewing a larger screen.

The size of images seen on television screens also impacts viewers' perceptions of what is seen on the screen. Lombard (1995) found that participants who viewed people on large versus small screens evaluated the people seen on larger screens more positively, while Bracken, Neuendorf, & Jeffres (2003) reported that viewers who watched presidential debates on a larger screen felt the candidates were less credible than reported by viewers of the same candidates on a smaller screen.

Image Quality   Even less empirical research has been conducted on image quality, in part due to the difficulty of obtaining or creating stimuli prior to the digital conversion in Australia, the United States, and Europe. Nevertheless, the results of these studies are fairly consistent with viewers reporting favorable responses to higher image quality content. In an early examination of higher image quality content, Neuman (1990) found viewers preferred larger images with any image resolution. However, for 35-inch and 180-inch television displays, the participants rated the image quality as better and had a more positive overall reaction when watching the larger images. A more recent investigation found that the level of telepresence (immersion, social realism, and spatial presence) experienced by viewers while watching high definition television (HDTV) was higher than when participants viewed NTSC images (Bracken, 2005).

In other studies of high definition content (Bracken, 2006, 2007), participants consistently rated the high definition content as more enjoyable and also reported higher levels of immersion, realism, and in the 2007 study also spatial/physical presence. The experience of telepresence is not only impacted by the image quality of the stimulus but experiencing telepresence impacts other media effects (see chapter 8, this volume, for a fuller discussion).

Content

Lombard and Ditton (1997) identified another area of television that may impact telepresence—content. However, the empirical investigation of television content as an independent variable is scant. Researchers who posit a difference based on content tend to focus in and study only one type of content rather than to test differences between content types. Television content can differ in a number of ways. Traditionally, scholars have divided television content into genres such as situation comedy, drama, action-adventure, game show, etc. According to Mittell (2001), "genre is the primary way to classify television's vast array of textual options" (p. 3). Although cultural studies, film and literary scholars focus more broadly on differences derived from historical, cultural and interpretive contexts of the content, effects scholars tend to differentiate genres based on formal features of the programs such as laugh and music tracks, camera angles, settings, plot structures, themes, etc. Although scholars may not all agree on how to categorize television content, many agree that research often requires such a taxonomy. According to Chandler (2000), "Defining genres may be problematic, but even if theorists were to abandon the concept, in everyday life people would continue to categorize texts" (p. 3). The implication for effects scholars is that different genres impact audiences in diverse ways. A situation comedy is meant to elicit laughter, whereas an action-adventure show is vicariously thrilling. Thus, categorizing content will allow scholars to better examine how different content affects telepresence. It is beyond the scope of this chapter to examine or argue for a strict delineation of genres. Rather, our point is that content differences do indeed exist and have been found to produce varying viewing effects. In a study of the cognitive impact of genre, Hawkins et al. (2005) conducted an experiment examining the amount of attention paid to each content type (with three genres represented[4]) via measuring length of looking and found that different content types elicited different lengths of attention. Moreover, as posited by uses and gratifications theory and supported by extant literature, television viewers make decisions about what to watch based on differing gratifications they expect to receive from different content. Thus, we propose that telepresence scholars need to begin to extrapolate content differences and how they impact viewers' experiences of telepresence.

Telepresence and Content

Content has been identified as a contributor to viewers' sensations of presence (IJsselsteijn et al., 2000; Lombard & Ditton, 1997). Television content is less interactive than previous media content used to explore sensations of presence (virtual reality, MUDs, video games). To date, most studies exploring television and presence have employed visual stimuli that seemed likely to evoke a sense of presence (i.e., content that contains quick cuts or point-of-view movement) with the goal of demonstrating television could evoke a sense of presence. The variety of content available to television viewers has yet to be investigated to see which (if not all) television content types can provide viewers with sensations of presence. However, previous research suggests that television audiences will experience different levels of presence when viewing different types of content. This assertion has some support from Freeman et al. (1999), who found that interest levels in a particular program influenced the level of telepresence reported by the participants and that interest was impervious to the form of the presentation.

In another experiment which attempted to demonstrate a correlation between viewers' physiological responses and self-reported sensations of presence, Dillon, Keogh, Freeman, and Davidoff (2001) employed two different content types: (a) a relaxing boat ride and (b) a rally car race. They found that the relaxing boat sequence evoked more of a sense of presence than the rally sequence, suggesting that content need not be action packed to evoke presence. Moreover, the results found by Dillon et al. (2001) suggest that there is an interaction between content and form. Additionally, Reeves et al. (1999), who manipulated screen size (to assess its impact on arousal) and content (varying levels of valence), suggest that the interaction between form and content merits further investigation.

Synthesis

Therefore, while there is not a large body of literatures examining television and telepresence, the results are fairly consistent: larger screens led to higher perceptions of realism (and higher levels of telepresence). There is limited literature on television content and telepresence, but again there is a fairly consistent set of results that telepresence is impacted by content with differing content eliciting different levels of telepresence experienced by television viewers. Since there are few studies that have examined television and telepresence directly, the remainder of this chapter details an experiment that manipulated television form and content and the impact of these variables on telepresence. Based on the earlier discussion that larger screens have led to higher sensations of telepresence being reported, the following hypotheses examining the impact of screen size on telepresence are posited: It is expected that participants who watch television on the large screen will report higher levels of telepresence (*immersion, spatial presence,* and *perceptual realism*) than viewers who watch television images on the smaller screen (Hypothesis 1). Further, it is anticipated that participants who watch television images in HDTV will report higher levels of telepresence (*immersion, spatial presence,* and *perceptual realism*) than viewers who watch images in NTSC (Hypothesis 2). Lastly, participants who watch television images in HDTV on the larger screen will report higher levels of telepresence than participants who watch HDTV images on the small screen, NTSC images on the large screen, or NTSC images on the small screen (Hypothesis 3).

As little and contradictory evidence exist regarding the influence of content on telepresence, the following research questions are put forth: First, we wondered if there : Is a difference in the level of reported sensations of presence based on different types of content (action adventure versus serial drama)? (Research Question 1). Second, to see if there is a difference between the level of reported sensations of presence for the interaction of form and the various content types? (Research Question 2).

The Experiment

An experiment was conducted with image quality, screen size, and content as the independent variables.[5] Participants were randomly assigned to watch HDTV or NTSC television images (image quality) on either a large (65-inch) or small (32-inch) HD compatible television set (screen size) with one of two content types (action-adventure or drama). HDTV was used because high definition television provides both larger screen sizes and improved image quality. Specifically, the participants watched *Terminator 2* (Cameron, 1991) in the action adventure condition and *The Young and the Restless* (Bell & Bell, 1973) in the drama condition. These particular programs were chosen due to the restrictive programming available in HDTV at the time this study was conducted. Further, these particular types of content represent the range of programming the viewers are likely to watch. This study uses a between subjects design to examine the influence of form (image quality and screen size) versus content.

Participants[6] were recruited from an introductory communication class and offered extra credit from their instructor. At least a week prior to the experiment, participants completed a questionnaire to collect information on viewing habits, size of television most often watched, and their general sensations of presence. The participants were randomly assigned to one condition (explained below) in a television viewing experiment, which participants were told was being conducted to analyze viewers' responses to the television viewing experience. Each participant watched a 25-minute segment from either *Terminator 2* or *The Young and the Restless*. The program was viewed in either HD or NTSC and on either a large (65 inch wide screen/ 165 cm) or small (32 inch/81 cm) television screen. They watched alone in a comfortable chair in a naturalistic setting with low lighting. After viewing the television images, the participants completed a paper-and-pencil questionnaire measuring several dimensions of presence: immersion, engagement, perceptual realism, social richness, social presence, social realism, and spatial presence, along with items that are part of another study.

For this study, we have chosen two distinctly different types of content (an action-adventure film and a dramatic daytime soap opera) that we believe should result in significant differences in experiences of presence. Action-adventure content is event-driven and draws the viewer in physiologically, whereas soap opera content is relationship-driven and draws the viewer in emotionally.

The first was a segment from the film *Terminator 2*. The segment seen by the participants begins with the terminator entering the pool room of a bar, includes a chase scene with point-of-view camera angles (i.e., the viewer sees the action from the point-of-view of the character), and concludes with a large explosion. *The Young & the Restless* segment is also 25 minutes in length and starts with two characters arguing on the telephone; each segment has some type of interpersonal conflict. The segment concludes with two characters in a heated face-to-face argument.

The researchers were able to obtain copies of these programs in both High-definition and NTSC. The NTSC copy was dubbed directly from the HD copy and was an exact replication with the only difference being the image quality.

The participants were randomly assigned to one of the two content conditions (*Terminator 2, The Young & the Restless*), and then to one of the four television conditions (large HD, large NTSC, small HD, or small NTSC). Each participant was lead to the appropriate room (there were separate rooms for the large and small televisions). Each room contained a comfortable chair, a table, lamp, and the television. The rooms were set-up to resemble a living room. The instructions were read to each participant who was told they were going to watch a program for

25 minutes and then answer a questionnaire. The entire procedure took about 45-minutes.

Measures

Content was manipulated with one group randomly assigned to view *Terminator 2* and the other group randomly assigned to view *The Young & the Restless*. The image quality of the content was manipulated with participants randomly assigned to watch their assigned segment in either high-definition or NTSC. There were two televisions: The large screen television was a rear-projection 65-inch with a 43-degree field-of-view. The small screen was a 32-inch television with a 20-degree field-of-view.

The dependent measures were a variety of presence dimensions which were measured via a paper-and-pencil questionnaire. The amount of presence experienced by the participants was measured using a multidimensional presence scale developed by Lombard and Ditton (2001) and previously used in several telepresence studies (Bracken, 2005, 2006; Bracken & Atkin, 2004; Botta & Bracken, 2002). The individual items were submitted to exploratory factor analysis (Park, Dailey, & Lemus, 2002), using varimax rotation. Three unique factors were revealed: immersion,[7] spatial (physical) presence,[8] and perceptual realism.[9]

Results

Separate two-way analyses of variance with image quality and screen size as independent variables were conducted for content (*Terminator 2* and *The Young and the Restless*) for Hypotheses 1 and 2.

Hypothesis 1, which predicted that participants would report higher levels of telepresence (immersion, spatial presence, and social richness)

Table 3.1 Analysis of Variance Table: Image Quality and Screen Size on Immersion for *Terminator 2*

Source of Variation	Sum of Squares	df	Mean Square	F	Eta2
Main Effects					
Image Quality	11.08	1	11.08	3.61*	.02
Screen Size	.08	1	.08	.87	.00
2-Way Interactions					
Image Quality x Screen Size	.001	1	.001	.001	.00

Note: + p < .10; *p <.05; **p < .01; ***p < .001

Table 3.2 Analysis of Variance Table: Image Quality and Screen Size on Perceptual Realism for Terminator 2

Source of Variation	Sum of Squares	df	Mean Square	F	Eta2
Main Effects					
Image Quality	5.99	1	5.99	4.50*	.002
Screen Size	.31	1	.31	.24	.00
2-Way Interactions					
Image Quality x Screen Size	.05	1	.05	.03	.001

Note: + p < .10; *p < .05; **p < .01; ***p < .001

when watching images on larger screens, was not supported. So, for this study screen size did not play a significant role (see Table 3.1).

Hypothesis 2 inquired about the impact of image quality on sensations of telepresence. This hypothesis was not supported. However, when the content types were analyzed separately some of the subdimensions were impacted by image quality (see Tables 3.2 and 3.3).

Specifically, higher levels of immersion (F $(1, 158)$ = 3.62, p = .05) were reported by participants who watched Terminator 2 in HD (M = 5.01; SD = 1.86) than by participants who watched it in NTSC (M = 4.48; SD = 1.61) (see Table 3.1). Perceptual realism was higher when participants watched Terminator 2 in HD (M = 2.38; SD = 1.16) than in NTSC (M = 1.99; SD = 1.10) (see Table 3.2). The differences were not significant for spatial presence or for any of the presence dimensions when participants viewed The Young and the Restless.

Hypothesis 3, which predicted participants who watch television images in HDTV on the larger screen will report higher levels of telepresence than participants who watch HDTV images on the small screen, NTSC images on the large screen, or NTSC images on the small screen, was supported (see Figures 3.1 and 3.2). The results demonstrate that image quality is more important than screen size at least for Terminator 2.

Based on these results, with significant telepresence responses only to Terminator 2, content was tested in an analysis of variance with image quality, screen size, content, and gender as the independent variables. The dependent variables were the three presence dimensions: immersion, spatial presence, and perceptual realism. The results presented in Table 3.1 indicate that the participants reported higher levels of telepresence when viewing Terminator 2 than The Young & the Restless for the immersion and spatial presence dimensions but the reverse was true for perceptual realism. These results demonstrate that content impacts

Table 3.3 Analysis of Variance Table: Image Quality, Screen Size, and Content

Source of Variation	Sum of Squares	df	Mean Square	F	Eta2
Immersion					
Main Effects					
Image Quality	.30	1	.30	.17	.001
Screen Size	1.52	1	1.52	.84	.003
Content	127.26	1	127.26	70.38***	.20
2-Way Interactions					
Image Quality x Screen Size	1.43	1	1.43	.79	.003
Screen Size x Content	.17	1	.17	.10	.00
Image Quality x Content	6.49	1	6.49	3.59*	.012
3-Way Interactions					
Image Quality x Screen Size x Content	.55	1	.55	.30	.001
Spatial Presence					
Main Effects					
Image Quality	1.00	1	1.00	.80	.003
Screen Size	.26	1	.26	.21	.001
Content	13.65	1	13.65	10.83***	.04
2-Way Interactions					
Image Quality x Screen Size	.35	1	.35	.28	.001
Screen Size x Content	2.47	1	2.47	1.96	.007
Image Quality x Content	1.25	1	1.25	.10	.003
3-Way Interactions					
Image Quality x Screen Size x Content	.10	1	.10	.08	.001
Perceptual Realism					
Main Effects					
Image Quality	.09	1	.09	.06	.001
Screen Size	.31	1	.31	.23	.001
Content	9.39	1	9.39	6.87**	.02
2-Way Interactions					
Image Quality x Screen Size	1.84	1	1.84	1.34	.005
Screen Size x Content	.04	1	.04	.03	.001
Image Quality x Content	9.11	1	9.11	6.66**	.02
3-Way Interactions					
Image Quality x Screen Size x Content	2.69	1	2.69	1.97	.007

Note: $+ p < .10$; $*p < .05$; $**p < .01$; $***p < .001$

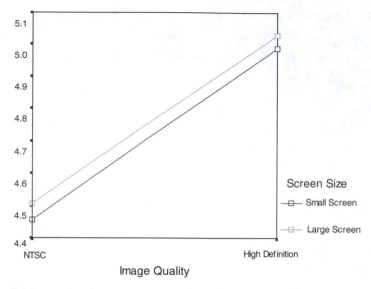

Figure 3.1 Interaction between image quality and screen size for immersion with *Terminator 2*.

viewer's perceptions of telepresence. Specifically, there are significant main effects for all three telepresence dimensions. Participants reported higher levels of immersion after viewing *Terminator 2* (*M* = 4.59; *SD* = 1.43) than *The Young & the Restless* (*M* = 3.26; *SD* = 1.23). Spatial pres-

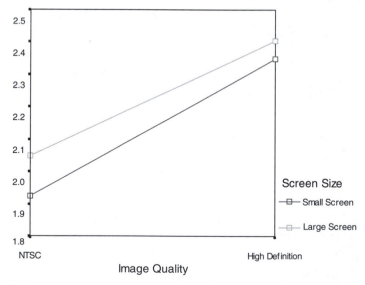

Figure 3.2 Interaction between image quality and screen size for perceptual realism with *Terminator 2*.

ence sensations were higher when participants viewed *Terminator 2* (*M* = 2.08; *SD* = 1.27) than *The Young & the Restless* (*M* = 1.67; *SD* = .91). However, the reverse was significant for perceptual realism with participants reporting higher levels of perceptual realism with *The Young & the Restless* (*M* = 2.56; *SD* = 1.20) than when they viewed *Terminator 2* (*M* = 2.18; *SD* = 1.16).

The authors also tested the interaction between form and content. For all telepresence dimensions, the 3-way interactions between image quality, screen size, and content are not significant. However, the results indicate that for two of the three telepresence dimensions there is a significant 2-way interaction between image quality and content. Specifically, for the immersion dimension, participants reported higher levels of immersion for the HD *Termintor 2* than the NTSC version, but the NTSC version of *The Young & the Restless* was more immersive than the HD version (see Figure 3.3).

Interestingly, perceptual realism has a different interaction. Participants reported higher levels of perceptual realism for *The Young & the Restless* than *Terminator 2* in NTSC, but all the participants rated both content types as equally as realistic when viewed in HD (see Figure 3.4).

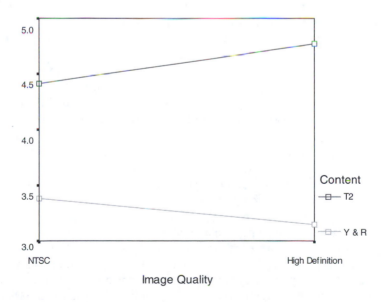

Figure 3.3 Interaction between image quality and content for immersion.

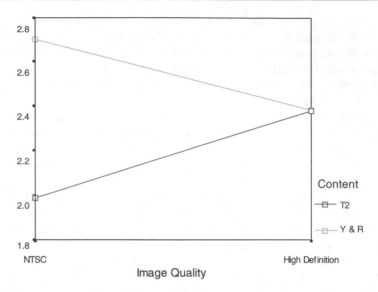

Figure 3.4 Interaction between image quality and content for perceptual realism.

Discussion

The results of this study illustrate the role of content as a contributing factor to viewers' experiences of telepresence when viewing television. The results support previous research that viewing television can induce sensations of telepresence in audiences (Freeman et al., 1997, 1999; Lombard et al., 2000). While previous studies have found differences in how audiences rate the dimensions of telepresence (Botta & Bracken, 2002; Bracken, 2005; Bracken & Pettey, 2007), this study uncovered overwhelming differences between how viewers responded to different content, thus supporting the claims that different interest levels in the content has a strong impact on sensations of telepresence (Freeman et al., 1999) and suggesting telepresence researchers need to select stimulus content carefully. Further, these results indicate that additional research is necessary to expand our understanding of the impact of content on telepresence. While content dominates the results, form variables, namely image quality, also impacted the level of telepresence experienced by participants. Specifically, higher image quality led to participants reporting higher levels of telepresence, at least for *Terminator 2*. The fact that image quality increased sensations of presence for *Terminator 2* but not for *The Young & the Restless* suggests content not only matters on its own in producing different types and amounts of presence experienced but that content also makes a difference for whether some form variables will increase sensations of presence. More research is necessary to determine whether other action adventure and dramatic content will similarly interact with image quality.

The results of this study bring us one step closer to understanding the impact of popular media and telepresence. Not only do the results support previous research that television audiences experience telepresence sensations while viewing TV (Bracken, 2006; Lombard et al. 2000), but they also allow telepresence researchers to have an understanding of how content influences viewers' media experiences. Specifically, Freeman et al. (1999) found that interest in the content overrode the form variables of stereoscopic images and screen size suggesting a possible link between telepresence and selective exposure where audiences choose content that is consistent with their views and values (Sears & Freedman, 1967). Further, these results suggest that Hawkins' et al. (2002, 2005) findings that content preferences influence both the attention paid and the types of looking by audiences should be further investigated in relation to telepresence. Taken together, these earlier findings suggest that allowing participants to select the genre they watch may be more likely to result in higher sensations of telepresence rather than being required to watch a particular genre, suggesting that when participants are "forced" to watch something they would not have chosen, then telepresence sensations are diminished for some participants.

This is a potential explanation for the lack of telepresence results with *The Young & the Restless*, as daytime soap operas are not widely popular and participants reported liking *Terminator 2* more than *The Young & the Restless*. It follows that study designs requiring research participants to watch pre-selected content may reduce the level of telepresence experienced by television viewers as suggested by Pettey, Bracken, Rubenking, Buncher, and Gress (in press). In other words, content that might ordinarily induce telepresence in some television viewers could result in avoidance or rejection of the content and result in lower levels of telepresence.

Another contribution of the current study is the significant interactions between image quality and content in which high definition brought about increased telepresence for *Terminator 2* but not *The Young & the Restless*. This is an important contribution to research on telepresence because it exposes the flaw in the assertion that it is the technology only that creates a sense of telepresence in media users and supports the definition put forth by Pettey et al (in press). The interaction effects suggest that media and telepresence scholars need to conduct additional empirical studies to ascertain how audiences respond to different genres.

Our supposition that content differences would elicit different experiences of presence was supported. Thus, we propose that telepresence scholars need to continue to extrapolate content differences and how they impact viewers' experiences of telepresence. Future research should examine the ways in which structural features unique to particular content produce different forms of telepresence. In this study, we found a number of differences between our two content types that need to be further explored. For example, our participants experienced less telepresence while viewing the soap opera, which contained a lot of close-up shots. Future research should examine the extent to which close-up shots versus point of view shots impact presence experiences. Additionally, the role of other structural features that are linked to genres (i.e., pace) should also be studied to examine their impact on telepresence.

There were differences in the structural features between the two content types. Specifically, *Terminator 2* was faster paced and contained point-of-view (POV) movement, while *The Young & the Restless* was slower paced and contained more close-up shots. These close ups might have been overwhelming for the participants, which was previously suggested by Reeves and Nass (1996) and Bracken, Neuendorf, and Jeffres (2003). For example, genres that include a lot of close-ups, such as soap operas like *The Young & the Restless*, may induce telepresence when examined on their own, but when combined with high definition television on a large screen the close-up shot may overwhelm the viewer and result in a need to back off or turn away rather than immerse themselves in the viewing experience. This is borne out by the data, with viewers who watched *The Young & the Restless* in NTSC reporting higher levels of telepresence than those participants viewing the soap opera in high definition. For the participants who watched the soap opera in NTSC the program was more immersive and perceived as more real than the high definition condition. This seems to suggest that telepresence scholars should not assume that the form of a technology (e.g., image quality) is the only factor in affecting experiences of telepresence.

These results have implications for advertisers, politicians, and production companies. With the average size of television sets increasing more than 10 inches in the last decade (Average TV, 2008), there are more large screen television sets than ever. The results of this study suggest that larger screens do not always lead to higher levels of telepresence, contrary to studies that have isolated screen size.

Lombard et al. (1997) argue that screen size is distinct from image size studies because the later is achieved through camera techniques such as shot scale or type. This is important to note because in some television genres including soap operas there are frequent extreme close-up shots of characters faces resulting in large image size being displayed on large screens. While this is partially a form issue, the fact remains that it is confounded by genre.

While the content types were selected for the extreme differences in presentation, *Terminator 2* was made for larger screens and does not have the extreme close-ups often seen on television. Further, the content type (i.e., action) may be seen as having a gender bias. However, the authors examined participant preferences through exploratory analyses and did not find any significant gender differences for the telepresence dimensions. However, many participants reported having seen *Terminator 2* prior to the experiment. It has been suggested by Freeman et al. (1999) that prior experience with content can influence the level of telepresence experienced and reported. The film was selected in part because of the limited selection of films available in high definition at the time the study was conducted.

In conclusion, this chapter discussed the history of television and telepresence, and explored the interaction of form and content. The results of an experiment demonstrated that content is an important factor in television viewers' sensations of telepresence and suggest the content of stimuli employed in studies needs to be considered when planning telepresence studies. Form variables of image quality and screen size continue to be important in telepresence research, but difference subdimensions of telepresence have unique interaction patterns. The future of viewing presents media users with far more screen size options than ever before and suggests a continuing line of screen size research ... even if the screens are no longer connected to televisions.

Notes

1. A CAVE is a room-sized cube with projection screens for walls and floor. Users wear glasses allowing them to see 3-D graphics. The users' movements are tracked and incorporated into the virtual environment providing a highly immersive media experience.
2. Lombard, Ditton, Grabe, & Reich (1997) argue that screen size is distinct from image size studies because the later is achieved through camera techniques such as shot scale or type.
3. While this study did not focus on the concept of presence, the results provided evidence that increasing the visual angle (larger screen size and closer viewing distances) lead to an increase in subjective evaluation of the sensation of reality.
4. The genres included in the final analyses were situation comedy, drama, news, and entertainment magazines.
5. 2 (image quality) × 2 (screen size) × 2 (content) factorial design was employed for this study
6. There were an total of 292 participants, 121 males (42%) and 171 females (58%), whose average age was 24 (range 18–62 years old) and whose ethnic backgrounds were 64.0% European American, 23.3% African or Caribbean American, 3.1% Asian American, 2.4% Latin American or Hispanic, and 7.2% who reported themselves as other.
7. Participants responded from not at all (1) to very much (7) for nine statements based on a scale developed to measure the extent to which television

viewers reported feeling immersed in the television environment. Example statements include: "How involving was the media experience," and "To what extent did you feel mentally immersed." The Cronbach's alpha for the additive index was .94.

8. Participants responded from not at all (1) to very much (7) for eight statements based on a scale developed to measure the extent to which television viewers reported a sense of being there in the television environment. Example statements include: "I had a sense of being in the scenes displayed," and "I felt as though I was participating in the TV environment." The Cronbach's alpha for the additive index was .92.

9. Participants responded from not at all (1) to very much (7) for seven statements intended to measure the extent to which television viewers feel a sense of realism when viewing television. The six statements included such questions as: "The scenes depicted could really occur in real life," and "The content seemed believable." The Cronbach's alpha for the additive index was .81.

References

Austin, E. W., & Dong, Q. (1995). Source versus content effects on judgments of news believability. *Journalism Quarterly, 71,* 973–983.

Average TV Size in the UK Rises Dramatically. (2008, November 20). Retrieved December 17, 2008, from http://hdtvorg.co.uk/news/articles/2007112001. htm

Bell, L. P. & Bell, W. J. (1973). *Young & the Restless.* [Television series]. Los Angeles: Columbia Broadcasting Company.

Biocca, F., & Delaney, B. (1995). Immersive virtual reality technology. In F. Biocca & M. R. Levy (Eds.), *Communication in the age of virtual reality* (pp. 57–124). Mahwah, NJ: Erlbaum.

Bollman, C. G. (1971). The effect of large-screen, multi-image display on evaluation of meaning. *Dissertation Abstracts International, 31,* 5924-A.

Botta, R. A., & Bracken, C. C. (2002, May). *Muscle bound: Men, muscularity, and social comparisons.* Presented to Mass Communication division of the annual conference of the National Communication Association, New Orleans, LA.

Bracken, C. C. (2004). Social presence and children: Praise, intrinsic motivation, and learning with computers. *Journal of Communication, 51*(1), 22–37.

Bracken, C. C. (2005). Presence and image quality: The case of high definition television. *Media Psychology, 7*(2), 191–205.

Bracken, C. C. (2006). Perceived source credibility of local television news: The impact of television form and presence. *Journal of Broadcasting & Electronic Media, 50*(4), 723–741.

Bracken, C. C. (2007, April). *"That was a great ad": The impact of high definition television commercials on audiences' attitudes toward brands.* Paper presented to the Second Annual Persuasive conference, Stanford, CA.

Bracken, C. C., & Atkins, D. (2004). A survey of presence evoking technology in our living room. *Visual Communication Quarterly, 11*(1–2), 23–27.

Bracken, C. C. & Horowitz, E. M. (2006, April). *Can we be too immersed? The impact of presence and image size on audience reactions to televised presidential debates.* Paper presented to the Research Division of the annual meeting of the Broadcast Education Association, Las Vegas, NV

Bracken, C. C., Neuendorf, K. A., & Jeffres, L. W. (2003, August). *Screen size, source credibility, and presence: Audience reactions to televised presidential debates.* Paper presented to the annual meeting of the Association of Journalism and Mass Communication Educators, Kansas City, MO.

Bracken, C. C., & Pettey, G. (2007). It is REALLY a smaller (and smaller) world: Presence and small screens. *Proceedings of the Tenth Annual International Meeting of the Presence Workshop, Barcelona, Spain,* pp. 293–290.

Bracken, C. C., Pettey, G., Guha, T., & Rubenking, B. E. (2008, May). *Sounding out presence: The impact of screen size, pace and sound.* Presented to the Information Systems Division at the annual conference of the International Communication Association, Montreal, Canada.

Cameron, J. (1991). *Terminator 2.* [Motion picture]. United States: Lions Gate.

Calvert, S. L., Huston, A. C., Watkins, B. A., & Wright, J. C. (1982). The relation between selective attention to television forms and children's comprehension of content. *Child Development, 53,* 601–610.

Chandler, D. (2000). An introduction to genre theory. Retrieved December 4, 2008, from http://www.aber.ac.uk/media/Documents/intgenre/chandler_genre_theory.pdf

Chalke, S. (2007). Early home cinema: The origins of alternative spectatorship. *Convergence: The International Journal of Research into New Media Technologies, 13*(3), 223–230.

Couch Potatoes. (2007, July 19). *The Economist.* Retrieved November 5, 2008, from http://www.economist.com/research/articlesBySubject/displaystory.cfm?subjectid=7933596&story_id=9527126

Cruz-Neira, C., Sandin, D., DeFanti, T., Kenyon, R., & Hart, J. (1992). The Cave: Audio visual experience automatic virtual environment. *Communications of the ACM, 35*(6), 65–72.

Detenber, B. H., & Reeves, B. (1996). A bio-informational theory of emotion: Motion and image size effects on viewers. *Journal of Communication, 46*(3), 66–84.

Dillon C., Keogh, E., Freeman, J., & Davidoff, J. (2001). Presence: Is your heart in it? *Proceedings of the Fourth Annual International Workshop on Presence.* Retrieved from http://nimbus.temple.edu/~mlombard/P2001/dillon.htm

Flavell, J., & Flavell, E. (1990). Do young children think of television images as pictures or real objects? *Journal of Broadcasting & Electronic Media, 34*(4), 399–419.

Freeman, J., Avons, S. E., Davidoff, J., & Pearson, D. E. (1997). Effects of Stereo and Motion manipulations on measured Presence in Stereoscopic Displays. *Perception, 26* (suppl.), 42.

Freeman, J., Avons, S. E., IJsselsteijn, W., & de Ridder, H. (1999). Measuring presence through television — TAPESTRIES review. *Proceedings of the Second Annual International Workshop on Presence.* Colchester, UK.

Freeman, J. Avons, S. E., Pearson, D., Harrison, D., & Lodge, N. (1998). Behavioral realism as a metric of presence. *Proceedings of the First Annual International Workshop on Presence.* Ipswich, UK. Retrieved from http:// www.temple.edu/ispr/prev_conferences/proceedings/98-99-2000/1998/ Freeman%20et%20al.pdf/ Retrieved from http://www.temple.edu/ispr/ prev_conferences/proceedings/98-99-2000/1999/Freeman%20et%20al.pdf

Grabe, M. E., Lombard, M., Reich, R. D., Bracken, C. C., & Ditton, T. B. (1999). Screen size and viewer responses to television: Research findings. *Visual Communication Quarterly, 6*(2), 4–9.

Hatada, T., Sakata, H., & Kusaka, H. (1980). Psychological analysis of the sensation of reality induced by a visual wide field display. *SMPTE Journal, 89,* 560–569.

Hawkins, R., Pingree, S., Hitchon, J., Gorham, B., Kannaovakun, P., Gilligan, E., et al. (2001). Predicting selection and activity in television genre viewing. *Media Psychology, 3*(3), 237–263.

Hawkins, R. P., Pingree, S., Hitchon, J. B., Gilligan, E., Kahlor, L., Gorham, et al. (2002). What holds attention to television? Strategic inertia of look at content boundaries. *Communication Research, 29,* 3–30.

Hawkins, R. P., Pingree, S., Hitchon, J. B., Radler, B., Gorham, B. W., Kahlor, L., Gilligan, E., Serlin, R. C., Schmidt, T., Kannaovakun, P., Kolbeins, G. H. (2005). What produces television attention and attention styles? Genre, situation, and individual differences as predictors. *Human Communication Research, 31*(1), 162–187.

IJsselsteijn, W. A., de Ridder, H., Freeman, J., & Avons, S. E. (2000). Presence: Concept, determinants, and measurement. *Proceedings of the SPIE, Human Vision and Electronic Imaging V, 39,* 59–76.

IJsselsteijn, W. A., de Ridder, H., Freeman, J., Avons, S. E., & Bouwhuis, D. (2001). Effects of stereoscopic presentation, image motion, and screen size on subjective and objective corroborative measures of presence. *Presence: Teleoperators and virtual enviorments, 10*(3), 289–311.

International Society for Presence Research. (2000). *The Concept of Presence: Explication Statement.* Retrieved August 26, 2009, from http://ispr.info/

Kim, T., & Biocca, F. (1997). Telepresence via television: Two dimensions of tele-presence may have different connections to memory and persuasion. *Journal of Computer-Mediated Communication, 3*(2). Retrieved from http://www. ascusc.org/jcmc/vol3/issue2/kim.html

Lee, K. M. (2004). Presence, Explicated. *Communication Theory 14*(1), 27–50.

Lessiter, J., Freeman, J., & Davidoff, J. (2001). Really hearing? The effects of audio quality on presence. *Proceedings of the Fourth Annual International Workshop on Presence.* Retrieved from http://nimbus.temple. edu/~mlombard/P2001/lessiter.htm

Lewin, E. P. (1972). *Some effects of television screen size and viewer distance on recognition of short sentences.* Unpublished Master's thesis, Temple University, Philadelphia, Pennsylvania.

Lombard, M. (1995). Direct responses to people on the screen: Television and personal space. *Communication Research, 22*(3), 288–324.

Lombard, M., & Ditton, T. B. (1997). At the heart of it all: The concept of presence. *Journal of Computer-Mediated Communication, 13*(3). Retrieved from http://www.ascusc.org/jcmc/vol3/issue2/lombard.html

Lombard, M., & Ditton, T. B. (2001, May). *Measuring presence: A literature-based approach to the development of a standardized paper and pencil instrument.* Presented to the Presence 2001: The Third International Workshop on Presence, Philadelphia.

Lombard, M., Ditton, T. B., Grabe, M. E., & Reich, R. D. (1997). The role of screen size in viewer responses to television fare. *Communication Reports, 10*(1), 95–106.

Lombard, M., Grabe, M. E., Reich, R. D., Bracken, C. C., & Ditton, T. B. (1996, August). *Screen size and viewer responses to television: A review of research.* Presented to the Theory and Methodology division at the annual conference of the Association for Education in Journalism and Mass Communication, Anaheim, CA.

Lombard, M., Reich, R. D., Grabe, M. E., Bracken, C. C., & Ditton, T. B. (2000). Presence and television: The role of screen size. *Human Communication Research, 26*(1), 75–98.

Lund, A. M. (1993). The influence of video image size and resolution on viewing-distance preferences. *SMPTE Journal, 102,* 406–415.

Minsky, M. (1980, June). Telepresence. *Omni,* 45–51.

Mittell, J. (2001). A cultural approach to television genre theory. *Cinema Journal, 40*(3), 3–24.

Murphy, H. J. (1970). The effects of types of reinforcement, color prompting, and image size upon programmed instruction with deaf learners. *Dissertation Abstracts International, 31,* 2742-A.

Neuman, W. R. (1990). *Beyond HDTV: Exploring subjective responses to very high definition television* (Research report). Cambridge: Massachusetts Institute of Technology, Media Lab.

O'Donnell, L. B. (1971). Determinations of optimal angels and distances for viewing alphanumeric characteristics and geometric patterns on a television receiver. *Dissertation Abstracts International, 31,* 5943-A.

Ohtani, T., & Mitsuhashi, T. (1973). Picture quality of a high definition television system. *TEBS,* 3–4.

Park, H. S., Dailey, R., & Lemus, D. (2002). The use of exploratory factor analysis and principal components analysis in Communication research. *Human Communication Research, 28,* 562–577.

Pettey, G., Bracken, C. C., Rubenking, B., Buncher, M, & Gress, E. (in press). Telepresence, soundscapes and technological expectation: Putting the Observer into the equation. *Virtual Reality.*

Reeves, B. R. (1991). *"Being there:" Television as symbolic versus natural experience.* Unpublished manuscript. Stanford University, Institute for Communication Research, Stanford, CA.

Reeves, B. R., Lombard, M. L., & Melwani, G. (1992, May). *Faces on the screen: Pictures or natural experience?* Paper presented at the conference of the International Communication Association, Miami, FL.

Reeves, B., Detenber, B., & Steuer, J. (1993, May). *New televisions: The effects of big pictures and big sound on viewer responses to the screen.* Paper presented to the Information Systems Division at the annual meeting of the International Communication Association, Washington, DC.

Reeves, B., Lang, A., Kim, E. Y., & Tatar, D. (1999). The effects of screen size and message content on attention and arousal. *Media Psychology, 1,* 49–68.

Reeves, B., & Nass, C. (1996). *The media equation: How people treat computers, television, and new media like real people and places.* Cambridge, UK: Cambridge University Press.

Santo, B. (July, 8, 2008). Nielsen: Average TV viewing going up. Retrieved November 11, 2008, from http://www.cedmagazine.com/Nielsen-Average-TV-viewing-up.aspx

Savitz, E. (2008, July 8). Americans watching more TV than ever, Neilsen says. *Barrons.* Retrieved August, 26, 2009, from http://blogs.barrons.com/techtraderdaily/2008/07/08/americans-watching-more-tv-than-ever-neilsen-says/

Sears, D., & Freedman, J. (1967). Selective exposure to information: a critical review. *Public Opinion Quarterly, 31*(2), 194–213.

Snyder, J. (1996, May). *Structural features in film: Can psychological research inform film theory?* Paper presented to the Second Annual Mid-Atlantic Graduate Communication Conference. Philadelphia.

Steuer, J. (1992). Defining virtual reality: Dimensions determining telepresence. *Journal of Communication, 42*(4), 73–94.

Theatrical Concepts. (2008). Theatrical Concepts: The ulimate solution. Retrieved December 3, 2008, from http://www.theatricalconcepts.com/

TVHistory (n.d.) Retrieved November 5, 2008, from http://www.tvhistory.tv/western-.jpg

USA Today. (2006. September, 21). *Average home has more TVs than people.* Retrieved October 6, 2008, from: http://www.usatoday.com/life/television/news/2006-09-21-homes-tv_x.htm

Wirth, W., Hartmann, T., Böcking, S., Vorderer, P., Klimmt, C., Schramm, H., et al. (2007). A process model of the formation of spatial presence eExperiences. *Media Psychology, 9*(3), 493–525.

Chapter 4

Computers and Telepresence

A Ghost in the Machine?

David Westerman and Paul D. Skalski

What is "real"? How do you define "real"?

The above quote is spoken by the character Morpheus (Laurence Fishburne) in the modern classic sci-fi film *The Matrix*. In this film, Morpheus helps a computer hacker named Neo (Keanu Reeves) discover a frightening truth—that human beings are actually slaves of intelligent machines in the future and that all of "reality" as we know it is actually a computer simulation called "the Matrix." Morpheus, Neo and other humans spend the rest of the *Matrix* series battling back against their machine captors, both in and out of the Matrix.

To many people, the idea of feeling present in a computer environment may conjure up scenes like something in the *Matrix*. While computers have not reached that level yet (unless we are all part of the matrix unknowingly now), computers are a medium ripe with potential for creating feelings of presence. This chapter will describe the ways in which computers can lead to presence in two main domains of study: Human-Computer Interaction (HCI) and Computer-Mediated Communication (CMC). It will review the extant literature on presence in both fields and will discuss how presence applies to many computer applications used widely today. The chapter will argue that computers have potential to help create feelings of different types of presence, and it will also give some reasons why computers are good for creating presence (both technological and personological). It will begin first with a definition of what presence is.

What is Presence?

Although other chapters in this volume give more complete definitions of presence, we feel it is important to quickly define it again for our own purposes. The concept of presence is generally defined as a sense of "being there" caused by media technologies (Reeves, 1991) or a "perceptual illusion of nonmediation" (Lombard & Ditton, 1997), though

Tamborini and Skalski (2006) downplay the illusory nature of the experience. The International Society for Presence Research (2000) further defines presence as "a psychological state or subjective perception in which even though part or all of an individual's current experience is generated by and/or filtered through human-made technology, part or all of the individual's perception fails to accurately acknowledge the role of the technology in the experience." Thus presence is communication in a mediated environment with some varying feeling of non-mediation. This perception of nonmediation occurs when the individual does not perceive the communication as being mediated and/or responds as if the medium were absent.

It is important to note that presence, as conceptualized herein, is a psychological state that exists as a continuum. Although it can be enhanced by features of the presentation, such as image size (Lombard, Reich, Grabe, Bracken, & Ditton, 2000) or image quality (Bracken, 2005; chapter 3, this volume), presence is not something inherent within a given medium. Instead, people are thought to be more or less present at a given time, and presence is a psychological state. As noted by Bracken "presence is a property of a person, and because it results from an interaction among form and content characteristics of a medium and characteristics of the media user, it can and does vary across individuals and across time for the same individual" (p. 193).

Many scholars have noted distinctions between varying kinds of presence (i.e., Lee, 2004a; Tamborini & Skalski, 2006). Generally, these distinctions break presence down into three different categories: physical presence, social presence, and self-presence. According to Lee (2004a) physical presence is "a psychological state in which virtual physical objects are experienced as actual physical objects" (p. 44). Important to the current chapter is that this also applies to experiencing virtual environments as actual physical environments. Social presence can generally be defined as "a psychological state in which virtual social actors are experienced as actual social actors" (Lee, 2004a, p. 45). It can also be thought of as the stimulation of ones intelligence by a technological actor or the realization of intelligence in a virtual actor (Biocca, 1997) without noticing the technological means (Lee, 2004a). Self-presence is defined as "a psychological state in which virtual selves are experienced as the actual self" (Lee, 2004a, p. 46). This can even lead to an awareness of oneself as existing within a virtual environment (Biocca, 1997).

All three of these types of presence, as defined here, imply that presence occurs when people experience something virtual (an environment, a person, or themselves) as if it was something non-virtual. The remainder of this chapter will focus on explaining on how computers can accomplish this for all three types of presence. It will first consider the notion of HCI, and focus on the CASA (Computers Are Social Actors) literature (e.g., Reeves & Nass, 1996) as an example of the great power that computers can have for eliciting feelings of social presence. It will then discuss CMC literature that demonstrates how computers (and the Internet) can help achieve all three types of presence.

HCI and Presence: The Media Equation

Human-computer interaction was rare in the early days of computing technology. By the 1960s, International Business Machines (IBM) dominated the business computer industry and controlled virtually all aspects of their client's computing operations, leaving few opportunities for ordinary people to use the bulky, imposing machines (Zittrain, 2008). Yet the promise (and perils) of human-computer interaction manifested itself in several popular science fiction works and characters of the era, ranging from the calmly sinister Hal 9000 in *2001: A Space Odyssey* (1968) to the adorably helpful R2-D2 in *Star Wars* (1977). These and other fictional representations of HCI likely helped prepare people for what was to come. In the 1980s, personal computers (PCs) began to diffuse widely, and in the 1990s the Internet emerged as computing's "killer app" (Dasgupta, 2002), paving the way for mass adoption of HCI technologies. Although HCI is still not at the level of the more imaginative science fiction works of the past, it currently exists in many popular forms, including daily use of desktop, notebook, and mobile computing devices, communication with online social agent applications, and even personal companionship with robots. People are interacting with computers now more than ever before.

This section reviews scholarship on HCI and presence, specifically social presence. A considerable body of evidence has accumulated suggesting that people will respond to computers in social ways. Although this chapter primarily uses human computer interaction to refer to the phenomenon and line of research, branches of it have been referred to alternatively as scholarship on CAS and "The Media Equation," the latter of which begins this discussion.

The Media Equation: Computers = Real People

In their seminal book *The Media Equation* (1996), Byron Reeves and Clifford Nass demonstrate how people's interactions with computers and other media are virtually identical to real social relationships. The "media equation" they advance in the book is that "media equal real life" (p. 5). As evidence for this idea, Reeves and Nass conducted a series of studies that re-created a broad range of social experiences, only with media talking the place of people. Their strategy was to (a) pick a social science finding about how people respond to each other, (b) find the place in the report where the social rule was summarized and substitute "media" for "person," (c) do the same with how the rule was tested, (d) run a replication experiment, and (e) draw implications, both theoretical and practical. Specific goals of their work included improving the design of media and advancing HCI and social scientific theories.

A total of 35 studies are reported in *The Media Equation*, and together they provide very convincing support for the premise that "media equal real life." In one experiment on politeness effects of computers, for example (Nass, Moon, & Carney, 1999), participants were asked to use a computer to learn about topics and then evaluate the machine's performance. Half of the people were asked to do the evaluation on the same computer, while the rest were asked to do it on a different computer. Results showed that participants who did the rating on the same computer they learned from gave significantly more positive answers than those who did the evaluation on a different computer, demonstrating that human politeness rules extend to computers. People were more polite to the computer they used, seemingly out of a need to not hurt its feelings, even though computers obviously have no real emotions. This outcome was identical when, in a second experiment, the social nature of the computer was accentuated by having the computers communicate through voice instead of text. Reeves and Nass concluded that even simple computer cues like text communication can create the "social presence" of a human.

Other studies summarized in *The Media Equation* offer further evidence for the basic prediction of the book (i.e., "media = real life") and suggest many fascinating things about HCI, including the following:

- *Computer manners matter:* When people were flattered by a computer after performing a task, they believed they did better on the task and liked the computer more than participants who were not flattered (Fogg & Nass, 1997).
- *(Computer) personality goes a long way:* People perceived computers that used dominant or submissive text as having more dominant or submissive personalities. They also preferred computers that had personalities similar to their own (Nass, Moon, Fogg, Reeves, & Dryer, 1995).
- *That's human-computer teamwork:* People teamed with a computer for a collaborative task felt more similar to the computer, thought better of it, cooperated with it more, and agreed with it more (Nass, Fogg, & Moon, 1996).
- *Gender stereotypes even extend to computers:* When male voiced computers evaluated people, they were taken more seriously and liked more than female ones. Female voiced computers were also

perceived as less knowledgeable about technical matters but more knowledgeable about love and relationships (Nass, Moon, & Green, 1997).

To help validate the computer-based research in *The Media Equation*, a final study reported in the book tested whether people who received information from a computer thought they were interacting with the computer or the programmer. Results showed that people considered the computer, and not the programmer, to be the source of information. Clear differences were also found between those who were *asked* to think about the programmer and those who were not—interestingly, participants who were *not* asked think about the programmer felt significantly *more* positive toward the computer. Reeves and Nass (1996) conclude that the easiest and most natural response for people is to orient toward the most proximate social actor in an interaction, even if the actor is a machine. Overall, the authors convincingly show in *The Media Equation* that the social and natural rules people expect computers to follow come from the world of interpersonal interaction.

Why do people respond to computers this way? Reeves and Nass (1996) believe that these reactions are a function of evolution. For almost all 200,000 years of human history, only people exhibited rich social behaviors, and our brains have therefore become hard-wired to treat anything that *seems* real as a person, including mediated presentations. As Reeves and Nass succinctly put it, "modern media engage old brains" (p. 12). With effort, people can think their way out of these primitive reactions, but people more often *don't* scrutinize their actions or environment and instead rely on automatic responses like the ones observed in the Media Equation studies. This perspective on HCI has been since elaborated upon by Lee (2004b), who uses principles of evolutionary psychology to further explain presence and Media Equation responses. According to Lee, human survival has long depended on the automatic application of innate causal reasoning modules for the physical and social worlds. These include rapidly developed "folk physics" modules about that physical world that prevent infants from walking off cliffs, for example, as well as "folk psychology" (or "theory of mind") mechanisms about the social world that help infants quickly understand the minds of other people and later identify both helpful others and enemies. This "folk psychology" extends to computers as well, and Lee argues that the Media Equation findings "demonstrate how human beings keep using their Stone Age causal reasoning modules...when they interact with Space Age media and simulation technologies" (p. 499). As a result, he says people feel social presence even while interacting with nonhuman social actors like computers.

HCI and Social Presence Research

Unlike Lee, Reeves and Nass do not explicitly discuss the concept of social presence in *The Media Equation*, but they do use the phrase "social presence" in several places. When they refer to how computers communicate and interact like humans, for example, they say "as long as there are some behaviors that suggest a social presence, people will respond accordingly" (p. 22). They also state, while explaining the politeness research, that "we wondered what would happen if the social presence were more explicit" (p. 25). This treatment of social presence is different than how the concept is understood today, given recent advances in conceptualizing the concept as a multi-dimensional psychological state (e.g., Biocca, Harms, & Burgoon, 2003). But Reeves and Nass clearly had something similar in mind in *The Media Equation*, and a handful of studies since have tried to measure and test the idea that computers create a sense of social presence affecting exposure outcomes.

In the first major published study to explicitly address this phenomenon, Lee and Nass (2005) examined how social responses to technology influence social presence. They conducted two experiments in which participants were exposed to computer-generated voices manifesting different personalities within an e-commerce setting. They then measured social presence using a four-item index created to tap the co-presence and psychological involvement dimensions of the concept (Biocca, Harms, & Burgoon, 2003). Findings from both experiments supported the prediction that users would feel more social presence when the computer voices they heard manifested similar personalities to their own. Aside from having implications for the design of HCI technologies, this work provides empirical evidence for the assumption that social presence underlies and plays an important role in Media Equation processes.

More recent studies offer additional support and extend social presence effects into other HCI contexts, including human-robot interaction (Lee, Park, & Song, 2005), virtual social agent effects (Skalski & Tamborini, 2007), and the use of emoticons for e-learning (Tung & Deng, 2007). All of these studies measured social presence and demonstrate that it can be both an effect of media technologies (i.e., robots, interactive agents, emoticons) as well as an influence on outcomes of media exposure (i.e., social responses, information processing and attitude/behavior change, and motivation for learning, respectively). Although the measures of social presence varied from study to study, making direct comparisons difficult, this type of work nevertheless situates social presence within HCI research as an important mediating/moderating variable in several contexts.

Related HCI Research

Other studies in this area point to additional considerations. These make reference to the concept of social presence or Media Equation/CASA research without directly measuring social presence. This research has concentrated mostly on HCI applications for education. David, Lu, and Cai (2002), for example, found that adding social cues to a computer quiz versus having no cues adversely affected judgments. When a computer help agent named Phil (with a photo of a White male) blamed participants for poor performance, fairness ratings dropped significantly among female participants. This finding suggests that more social cues does not necessarily equal better with HCI, which is supported by the commercial failure of visible social agents such as the Microsoft Office "Clippy" character (Merritt, 2008). In another study looking at social agent effects, Lee et al. (2007) found that they can have positive effects in computer-based learning environments when they manifest cooperative and caring personalities. These agents were textual in nature instead of visual, however. Overall, results of studies on agent effectiveness seem to indicate that text or voice is sufficient for creating positive social responses from computers, and that the effects may be enhanced by instilling the technologies with positive personality traits.

Although the vast majority of HCI research to date has examined adult responses to computing technology, some studies have used children as participants, with consistent results. Bracken and Lombard (2004) ran an experiment in which 8- to 10-year-olds received either praise or neutral feedback from a computer and found that children have social responses to computers affecting learning, specifically recall and recognition. Turkle (2005) found that when children interact with computers, they refer less to physical qualities over time and instead focus on psychological qualities, such as the ever present statement that "the computer must be cheating" when, for example, they are unable to defeat the computer-controlled opponent in a football game. The aforementioned Tung and Deng (2007) study also used children as participants (sixth graders) and found that dynamic emoticons in an e-learning environment had positive effects on social presence and motivation to learn. This study explicitly establishes that children feel social presence and also suggests that they may be more receptive to agents and other virtual social representations, which would make sense given their greater acceptance of animated/virtual characters in general.

The Future of HCI and Social Presence

The research reviewed in this section only skims the surface of a much larger palate of possibilities for scientific inquiry into HCI and social presence. From a research standpoint, many unanswered questions remain. Findings thus far from Media Equation and CASA studies demonstrate that variables such as personality, use of language, voice, and interactivity can influence people's social responses to computers (Lee & Nass, 2005). However, these are part of a much more complicated interaction between technology users, technology effects, and technologies themselves.

In terms of user variables, the subjective experience of social presence seems key and needs to be accounted for in future HCI research. This will allow researchers to generalize beyond specific technology variables when explaining HCI and its effects. For example, instead of attributing a positive computer-based learning outcome to a specific type of interactivity, it can be attributed to social presence that happens in predictable ways as a result of exposure to different forms of interactivity or other technological variables. Social presence has already been shown in a few HCI studies to mediate technology effects (e.g., Lee et al., 2005; Skalski & Tamborini, 2007). Contemporary social presence research is still in its infancy, however, and as mentioned, research thus far has tended to use different measures of the concept. This calls attention to the value of developing a standardized social presence measure, which can facilitate comparison across a variety of HCI technologies and effects. In addition to social presence, other individual difference and user variables, such as gender and personality characteristics (Reeves & Nass, 1996), may also play a part in social responses to computer technologies and also demand attention.

In terms of effects, the research highlighted in this section has focused on social responses to computers and educational outcomes of HCI. These are important areas, and the social responses work begun by Reeves and Nass (1996) in particular highlights fundamental aspects of HCI. Social responses to computers, along with the experience of social presence, underlie potential outcomes of HCI in educational contexts and beyond. Skalski and Tamborini (2007), for example, showed how interactive social agent technology may be used to create more positive attitudes and behavioral intentions toward a health issue. Other research has looked at the ability of presence to affect consumer persuasion (see chapter 6, this volume). It is not difficult today to imagine the use of HCI technologies for these and other outcomes, including companionship and personal assistance. In fact, many of these applications of computer technologies are with us today.

This section began by describing some imaginary manifestations of HCI like Hal 9000 and R2-D2, and on the technology side, these fantastic representations are closer than ever to becoming a reality. The Lee et al. (2005) study cited earlier, for example, examined the long-term effects of interaction with a robotic dog, the Sony Aibo. Findings revealed clear linkages between social presence with the robot and positive social responses toward it. These types of responses should become even more pronounced in the future as robots increase in sophistication, and we may not be far from having our own R2-D2s. However, some see the downside of super advanced robots in society, inspired no doubt and the dystopian vision of HAL 9000 and science fiction creations such as the Terminator, and one Internet millionaire, Ben Way, has even started a firm called Weapons Against Robots (WAR) to develop anti-robot technologies for the future defense of humanity (Flynn, 2008). This may just be a publicity stunt, but it nevertheless points to the negative social presence that robots and other HCI applications have the potential to engender.

For now, the future of human-computer interaction seems bright. This section highlighted how humans have social responses to computer technologies and how these reactions produce generally favorable outcomes. Regular and widespread interaction with robots may be years away, but social interaction with computer technologies has become a ubiquity of modern life. GPS navigation systems, automated online help agents, virtual pets, video game characters, and personal computers themselves are a few of many potential sources of HCI today. These technologies and the social presence they create will be an increasingly fascinating and important area of inquiry in coming years.

CMC and Presence: Why the Internet?

As suggested above, computers have great potential to elicit social presence. The seemingly social, intelligent nature of a computer allows it to elicit feelings in users as if they responding to an actual intelligence. However, one major computer application that also allows people to feel more present is the Internet. As a large and amorphous channel, the Internet allows users to do a variety of things. The nature of the Internet allows for the potential for all three types of presence to occur. The main characteristic of the Internet that specifically increases the possibility for presence is the highly interactive nature of the medium.

Many different definitions of interactivity exist, but two definitions of highlight the differences in these definitions. Steuer (1992) defined interactivity as "the extent to which users can participate in modifying the form and content of a mediated environment in real time" (p. 84). This definition is more of a mass-communication definition, and brings to mind technologies such as video games, interactive TV, and virtual reality. The second definition of interactivity considered here is "an expression of the extent that in a given series of communication exchanges, any third (or later) transmission (or message) is related to the degree to which previous exchanges referred to even earlier transmissions"

(Rafaeli, 1988, p. 111). This definition is more in line with interpersonal communication, and brings to mind talking to other people (no matter the channel). Because the Internet combines aspects of both mass and interpersonal communication, both types of interactivity are possible using computers in this way. Thus, both of these types of interactivity highlight the increased potential of presence that computers can offer. The next sections will highlights some ways that computers, because of various Internet applications, can help foster feelings of physical, social, and self-presence.

Physical Presence

Marshall McLuhan (1962) believed that big changes were brought upon society by the proliferation of electronic media. He believed that electronic media were changing culture, and thus society at large, from individualism to a unified collective identity. As he later wrote, "As electrically contracted, the globe is no more than a village" (1964, p. 5).

Although he never explicitly discussed computers in his writings (Press, 1995), today the term "global village" is most often associated with the Internet. Interestingly, this is a traditional geographic metaphor used to describe something created electronically. However, this is by no means the only geographical metaphor utilized with computers and the Internet. Graham (1998) compiles many others, such as a "web*site*," "the information super*highway*," and "electronic *communities*," and also the old Microsoft tagline "*Where* do you want to go today?"

The use of these geographic metaphors suggests a conceptualization of the Internet as a "place." The term "cyberspace," originally popularized in Gibson's (1984) *Neuromancer* (although originally coined in an earlier (1982) Gibson story called *Burning Chrome*), again implies that what exists through the Internet is a thought of a place. As Sterling also pointed out:

> Cyberspace is the "place" where a telephone conversation appears to occur. Not inside your actual phone, the plastic device on your desk. Not inside the other person's phone, in some other city. *The place between* the phones…. Since the 1960s, the world of the telephone has cross-bred itself with computers and television, and though there is still no substance to cyberspace, nothing you can handle, it has a strange kind of physicality now. It makes good sense today to talk of cyberspace as a place all its own. (1992, p. xi)

The use of geographic metaphors for computers and the Internet and conceptualizing cyberspace as a place suggests that people are experiencing these virtual environments as actual environments, and thus, experiencing a high level of physical presence. How do these virtual worlds accomplish this? First, it is important to note what these worlds generally look like. According to the Dave Chappelle sketch (Brennan & Chappelle, 2004), "What if the Internet was a real place," it would look like a place of dubious character. However, as Ketchum (1998) noted, online spaces often bear great resemblance to similar spaces in the physical world (so the "shady" nature of the Internet jokingly brought up by Chappelle may just be a reflection of our own shadiness).

One example of this is Second Life. Second Life is an online virtual world started in 2003 by Linden Labs that is completely created by its users, known as Residents (What is Second Life, n.d.). The world is presented in 3-D, and provides a place where people can virtually interact (through their avatar) with a virtual continent, full of businesses, entertainment, and other avatars. Second Life was designed to mimic the Metaverse, a concept created in Neal Stephenson's novel *Snow Crash* (Maney, 2007). Second Life has its own economy, universities have started holding classes there, and politicians have even set up campaign houses there.

The fact that these places look like actual places should help accomplish a sense of physical presence by increasing the chance of activating *mental models*, or cognitive representations of entities, situations, and events in real and imagined worlds (Roskos-Ewoldsen, Roskos-Ewoldsen, & Dillman-Carpentier, 2002). People have pre-existing images of places and other entities from their real-world experiences and these should facilitate their sense of presence in response to computer simulations (see chapter 5, this volume, for a more detailed discussion of this topic).

This suggests that computers, because of user's ability to create their own content, can aid in the creation of environments that, although exist only virtually, can be experienced as actual environments [interestingly, there is a relatively recent branch of geography called cyber-geography, with one major goal of "mapping" cyberspace (see http://www.aboutus.org/CyberGeography.org) As Negroponte (1995) said, "If I could really look out the electronic window of my living room in Boston and see the Alps, hear the cowbells, and smell the (digital) manure in summer, in a way I am very much in Switzerland" (p. 165). Although popular virtual reality systems have yet to be developed that can create this, by the same token, if I look out the electronic window of my computer screen, and see the world of Second Life, and feel as if I am in that world and respond to it as if what I see is actually happening, then I am very much in Second Life, and feelings of physical presence should be high.

As mentioned above, some of the virtual objects that people can interact with in Second Life are other avatars. This virtual interaction is a large part of this virtual community, and suggests that computers and the Internet also allow the potential for feelings of social presence.

CMC and Social Presence

Some early scholars of CMC suggested that interaction using computers was only possible as impersonal, task oriented communication. According to early formulations of social presence, intimate social interaction would not be possible using the Internet (or at least would be very difficult). Social Presence Theory (SPT; Short, Williams, & Christie, 1976) suggests that the degree of interpersonal interaction is a function of the number of cues systems present in a given communication channel. Channels with fewer systems available will allow for less social presence with an interaction partner, which results in less interaction. The interaction that does exist in this situation would be more task-oriented as a result.

However, current thought on people's interaction using computers makes it obvious that people can, and do, engage in intimate interpersonal interaction online, including relationship formation and maintenance (e.g., Chan & Cheng, 2004; Mesch & Talmud, 2006; Merkle & Richardson, 2000; Parks & Floyd, 1996; Parks & Roberts, 1998). Some scholars even suggest that sometimes conditions exist in interaction through computers that lead to even greater levels of socialness than would exist in face-to-face interactions (dubbed hyperpersonal communication, Walther, 1996). How is this possible? It would seem that for people to establish relationships using computers, they would need to feel some levels of social presence when interacting with others using this channel.

We know people use channels with few cue systems for interpersonal interaction. In fact, interpersonal interaction is often cited as the biggest reason for Internet use. Stafford, Kline, and Dimmick (1999) reported that 61% of all e-mail usage was personal in nature. In line with this, scholars have also found that people report feeling social presence using such systems as e-mail (Tu, 2002) and IM (Harms & Biocca, 2004) which contains a very limited number of cue systems.

First, as noted in the beginning of the chapter, social presence is conceived as a psychological feeling. As Nowak and Biocca (2003) suggest, social presence may have started as a technological concept, but it moved into a focus on people, as discussed in other recent work on the topic (e.g., Biocca, Harms, & Burgoon, 2003; Zhao, 2003). One approach that may help explain how a system with limited cues can induce feelings of social presence is Social Information Processing Theory (SIPT; Walther, 1992).

Social Information Processing Theory

Social Information Processing Theory (Walther, 1992) assumes that communicators make attempts to achieve communication goals in online settings as much as in offline settings. When the lack of cues available in an online setting presents obstacles to accomplishing their goals, users adapt their behaviors to the cues that are available. Thus, given enough time, people can utilize these circumventions to accomplish goals online just as well as they do face-to-face. SIPT focuses on the ways people overcome limitation of a technology instead of only focusing on the limitations of the technology (as SPT would do).

One metaphor that helps explain SIPT is to think of social information about a person like water in a glass. Online communication is like "sipping" from that glass of water, whereas offline interaction is like "gulping" from the same glass (Griffin, 2006). Both methods can result in an empty glass, but "sipping" takes a longer time, just like interacting with someone online can result in achieving the same goals as interacting offline, but online takes longer to accomplish those goals..

A body of research exists suggesting that SIPT is a useful framework to study CMC in a variety of settings (i.e., Gibbs, Ellison, & Heino, 2006; Hobman, Bordia, Irmer, & Chang, 2002; Pena & Hancock, 2006; Tidwell & Walther, 2002; Utz, 2000; Walther & Bunz, 2005; Walther & Burgoon, 1992; Walther, Loh, & Granka, 2005; Walther & Tidwell, 1995). One part of research in SIPT examines what circumventions people use to overcome limitations of CMC and to accomplish their goals. These circumventions include the use of emoticons (Walther & D'Addario, 2001), chronemics (Walther & Tidwell, 1995) and using more and deeper questions and questions in an online interaction (Tidwell & Walther, 2002). In fact, things that can be considered circumventions such as emoticons (Na Ubon & Kimble, 2003), avatars (Nowak & Biocca, 2003), and location awareness systems (Licoppe & Inada, 2008) have been found to increase feelings of social presence as well.

A more recent potential addition to SIPT that has undertones of social presence ideas comes from recent work on electronic propinquity (Walther & Bazarova, 2008). As originally defined, electronic propinquity was "electronic presence" (Korzenny, 1978, p. 7) and can be thought of as "the psychological feeling of nearness that communicators experience using different communication channels" (Walther & Bazarova, 2008, p. 624). In this regard, electronic propinquity sounds very much like social presence. Consistent with the theory of electronic propinquity (Korzenny, 1978), Walther and Bazarova found that differences did not exist in reported electronic propinquity for users of a variety of channels when that channel was the only option. However, when options were available, text-only chat (a low bandwidth option) led to less electronic propinquity. Communication skills were the rationale offered for this finding, as those participants with higher skills were better able to achieve electronic propinquity, even in conditions of lower bandwidth and increased task difficulty. Walther and Bazarova conclude that skills are an important inclusion for SIPT, and indeed they (along with channel options) seem important for feelings of social presence using computer technologies to interact with other people.

Computers may also be a prime place for experiencing social presence because, as Donath and boyd (2004) suggest "People are accustomed to thinking of the online world as a social space" (p. 71). Many of the most commonly used Internet applications, such as e-mail, IM, and social networking sites, are designed to foster interaction between two people. If, through the use of these technologies, people have become accustomed to thinking of this world as a social place and have developed the medium-specific skills (another relevant construct for the Theory of Electronic Propinquity (TEP); Korzenny, 1978) necessary to use these channels, it is possible that they have also become more accustomed to activating mental models when using these technologies. For example, when the first author interacts with his good friends over IM, he often visualizes them as he reads their messages, and sometimes hears their voices speaking the words as he reads them. In this way, he is experiencing the virtual actor (avatars and text on a screen) as the actual person behind those online representations and feels more socially present then. Furthermore, if people have an already established notion of how to respond to something in the actual world, and they see something that looks and seems like that in the virtual world, they are more likely to respond to it as they would in the actual world. In line with this, Yee, Bailenson, Urbanek, Chang, and Merget (2007) found that non-verbal norms that existed in offline society also existed among avatars in Second Life, suggesting that people are experiencing these virtual environments as they would actual environments, and thus feeling a sense of social presence.

Some recent systems have been developed to induce feelings of presence as well. These systems, falling generally under the category of teleconferencing systems, are designed to make users feel as if they are in the same meeting or class room, even if they are thousands of miles apart. As Gates (1999) said, "We need software that makes it possible to hold a meeting with distributed participants—a meeting with interactivity and feeling, such that, in the future, people will prefer being telepresent." This goal of making people feel as if they are together can be seen in Cisco's tagline in an ad for its TelePresence system: "Welcome to a network where being here is being there. Welcome to the human network." And it is the ability to connect humans that they are playing upon in their ad depicting a relief worker chatting with his family at home on other side of the globe. One study of these systems found that increasing the information the system provided (audio, audio-video, and avatar), compared to text only, increased the feelings of social presence (Bente, Ruggenberg, Kramer, & Eschenburg, 2008).

Social Presence in Educational Settings

Another area of study that demonstrates the ability of computers to enhance social presence is the educational realm. Social presence has been argued to be a necessary component to improving education, both in face-to-face and computer-mediated settings (Gunawardena, 1995). Low social presence is seen as decreasing interaction (Garramone, Harris, & Anderson, 1986) and increasing frustration while lowering affective learning (Hample & Dallinger, 1995).

Research on computers, social presence, and education falls into two major types: First, some studies examine what increases social presence in e-learning environments. Second, some research has looked at how social presence affects certain learning outcomes in e-learning environments.

Causes

Several studies examining the causes of social presence have focused on what channels increase it (very much in line with Social Presence Theory thinking). Results of these studies have been inconclusive. Tu (2002) found that e-mail and real-time discussion induced greater feelings of social presence in students than bulletin boards. Dirkin, Mishra, and Altermatt (2005) found that students reported higher levels of social presence in either a text-only or fully animated social agent condition compared to voice only or static image with voice conditions. Interestingly, it seems that students either wanted all or nothing in this study. Horner, Plass, and Blake (2008) compared lecture that contained video or not. They found that the inclusion of video had no impact on reported social presence. Overall, this research is not consistent with SPT predictions, as the inclusion of greater numbers of cue systems was not enough to increase social presence, and sometimes fewer cue systems led to increased social presence.

Other studies examining what increases social presence in educational setting has looked at ways that people create social presence within computer technologies. Very much in line with Social Information Processing Theory (Walther, 1992), Na Ubon and Kimble (2004) found that social presence accrues over time in online learning communities. Other research has looked at mechanisms people utilize (these can be thought of as circumventions in SIPT thought). Na Ubon and Kimble (2003) suggest that people use emoticons and capitalizations to express emotions and also used phatic, and these things have potential to lead to increased social presence. Tung and Deng (2007) found that children interacting with a dynamic avatar felt greater social presence than those interacting with a static one. Finally, Defino and Manca (2007) found that people may use more figurative language to increase social presence. All of these are suggestions of how people may overcome the limitations of the channel and accomplish their goals (in this case, the goal of establishing a feeling of social presence).

Outcomes

Finally, research on social presence and e-learning has looked at outcome measures associated with education from increased social presence. Generally speaking, increased social presence has been found to be associated with increases in other positive educational outcomes. Increased social presence has been found to be associated with increased satisfaction for online learning (Lin, Lin, & Laffey, 2008) and course satisfaction and instrumentality (Johnson, Hornik, & Salas, 2008). Dirkin, Mishra, and Altermatt (2005) found that students in a text-only condition (which was one of the highest in social presence) had more positive interpretations of the class. Tung and Deng (2007) found that the use of dynamic emoticons, which led to higher social presence than static emoticons, also increased children's intrinsic motivations.

Overall, this research helps demonstrate the importance and the ability of social presence to exist using computers. It suggests that there are ways to overcome limitations of the channel, and that when people find them, they feel more socially present. This increase in social presence also leads to increases in other outcomes, such as positive learning outcomes.

Much of the social interaction that takes place over the Internet does so with systems that allow users to create some sort of online representation or profile for themselves. The use of a virtual self in these interactions draws attention top the possibility that people can experience feelings of self-presence.

CMC and Self-Presence

Computers offer unparalleled potential among popular media for the experience of self-presence. Applications such as online social networks like facebook.com allow users to create a sense of social presence with a variety of "friends," but they also allow users to put a version of their self into the medium. In fact, some scholars argue that the online self people can create in such worlds may be more of a "true" self than the physical self is (Bargh, McKenna, & Fitzsimmons, 2002).

One of the hallmarks of the Internet, and thus computers, is that they allows for a great amount of potential for self-generated content (Kelly, 2005), much more so than other popular media such as television and even video games. Indeed, much of this user-generated content is comprised of users creating profiles of themselves. Creating a profile of oneself online is a main part of social networking sites (Donath & boyd, 2004) such as facebook.com and myspace.com. These sites allow users to create a profile of themselves and thus a "self presence" in the virtual world.

No published articles were found explicitly looking at self-presence and the Internet/computers. This is not surprising, as self-presence has been identified as the least explored type of presence overall (Tamborini & Skalski, 2006). However, there is some literature that speaks to the power of the Internet to promote feelings of self-presence, i.e., experiencing one's virtual self as one's actual self. It is interesting to note that this definition of self-presence is very similar to clinical identification, defined as "the process in which one individual takes on the behaviors, values, or goals of another" (Cramer, 2001, p. 667). In the case of self-presence, it may be that the other that one is taking on the experience of is one's virtual self.

Sherry Turkle (1984) has long maintained that the Internet can be used to allow people to play through different identities. Using Multi-User Dungeons (MUD; not an incredibly popular medium today, but one that can seen as a forerunner to today's MMORPG's), she demonstrated how her patients could create online identities and work on psychological issues they had through those identities. For example, Turkle (1994) tells the story of Peter, a shy person who had issues meeting women at his college. However, in a MUD, he was able to create a character named Achilles, a heroic warrior who was able to meet and talk to the most desired female character in the virtual world. In this way, Peter is experiencing his virtual self and his actual self, even if only during the time he spent playing the game (up to 40 hours a week). However, rather than just being an exercise that only elicits effects online, people also transfer this identity play into their actual self. In this way, her patients used their virtual selves as themselves and experienced their virtual selves as themselves (because the avatars were themselves).

Jeremy Bailenson and his colleagues have also contributed a line of research that suggests that people can and do treat their virtual selves as their actual selves. Presenting this research under the title of "Self Presence" (Bailenson, 2008), he and his team have consistently demonstrated that people do respond to their virtual selves as their actual selves. They label one example of this the "Proteus Effect" (Yee & Bailenson, 2007). The main idea of the "Proteus Effect" is that people will behave in a stereotypic manner expected of their virtual representation. Yee and Bailenson (2007) have demonstrated this effect with both attractiveness and height. A similar effect was found using elderly avatars (Yee & Bailenson, 2006), which was found to reduce negative stereotyping of elderly. Another study found that males (used the most words) and females (used the fewest words) behaved in a more stereotypic manner when they were given opposite sex avatars in a World of Warcraft game environment (Grundnig, Petri, Polzer, Strafling, & Kramer, 2008). These studies show that people take on characteristics of their virtual self, and, even if only momentarily, treat their virtual selves as themselves, suggesting that they are engaging in self-presence.

Overall, this literature suggests that people put themselves online. It also suggests that the representations that people choose for themselves (or are chosen for them) have the potential to be experienced as the actual self (and in some cases may be a part of the actual self manifested online). More research is necessary to examine both how computers can help foster a sense of self-presence, and how the experience of self-presence impacts those experiencing it.

The Future of Presence and Computers

This chapter has addressed ways in which computers, and some of their most common uses, can help foster a sense of presence. Due to some of their characteristics and uses, computers may actually be the most presence-inducing technology, especially for social and self-presence. However, there are scholars that believe that computers may only be scratching the surface of their potential today. In the future predicted by some of these scholars, technologies brought about by computer expansion will lead to the creation of what will become the ultimate presence inducing technology.

Key among these scholars is Ray Kurzweil. His key ideas, from 1999 are as follows: First, computing power is growing at an exponential rate. Because of this exponential growth, he predicts that by 2020, a $1,000 computer will match the computing speed and capacity of the human brain. As this computing power increases, and computers eventually exceed human capabilities, we will look to increasingly meld ourselves to our technology. As Kurzweil puts it, "*We will be software, not hardware*" (p. 129). In today's ideas, this can be thought of as a push to leave our physical bodies behind, and instead to download our intelligence into the Internet. This will be possible, according to Kurzweil, because as brain mapping becomes more sophisticated, and more knowledge is gained about what electrical impulses do what, the human brain will effectively be reduced to an electric map, which can be replicated by exponentially more powerful computer technology of the future. As Morpheus also says in the movie *The Matrix,* "If real is what you can feel, smell, taste and see, then 'real' is simply electrical signals interpreted by your brain creating a matrix type world." Kurzweil's (2005) term for this "matrix type world" is the Singularity (which he now says is "near"). If the Singularity does come to pass as Kurzweil predicts, this will be the ultimate demonstration of the presence power of computers, as it will allow humans to become entirely present, leaving their physical bodies behind and becoming a ghost in the machine.

References

Bailenson, J. (2008, May). *Self presence*. Paper presented to the International Communication Association Conference, Montreal, Canada.

Bargh, J. A., McKenna, K. Y. A., & Fitzsimmons, G. M. (2002). Can you see the real me?: Activation and expression of the "True Self" on the Internet. *Journal of Social Issues, 58,* 33–48.

Bente, G., Ruggenberg, S., Kramer, N. C., & Eschenburg, F. (2008). Avatar-mediated networking: Increasing social presence and interpersonal trust in net-based collaborations. *Human Communication Research, 34,* 287–318.

Biocca, F. (1997). The cyborg's dilemma: Progressive embodiment in virtual environments. *Journal of Computer Mediated Communication, 3*(2). Retrieved June 2, 2008, from http://jcmc.indiana.edu/vol3/issue2/biocca2.html

Biocca, F., Harms, C., & Burgoon, J. K. (2003). Toward a more robust theory and measure of social presence: Review and suggested criteria. *Presence: Teleoperators and Virtual Environments, 12*(5), 456–480.

Bracken, C. C. (2005). Presence and image quality: The case of high definition television. *Media Psychology, 7,* 191–205.

Bracken, C. C., & Lombard, M. (2004). Social presence and children: Praise, intrinsic motivation, and learning with computers. *Journal of Communication, 54,* 22–37.

Brennan, N., & Chappelle, D. (Writers), & Cundieff, R. (Director). (2004). Chappelle's show, episode 2.6 [Television series episode]. In N. Brennan & D. Chappelle (Executive producers), *Chappelle's Show.* USA: Comedy Central.

Chan, D. K. S., & Cheng, G. H. L. (2004). A comparison of offline and online friendship qualities at different stages of relationship development. *Journal of Social and Personal Relationships, 21,* 305–320.

Cramer, P. (2001). Identification and its relation to identity development. *Journal of Personality, 69,* 667–688.

Dasgupta, C. (2002). Killer applications. Retrieved October 12, 2008, from http://cactus.eas.asu.edu/partha/Columns/2002/07-01-killer-app.htm

David, P., Lu, T., & Cai, L. (2002, October). *Computers as social actors: Testing the fairness of man and machine*. Proceedings of the Fifth Annual International Presence Workshop. Porto, Portugal: Universidade Fernando Pessoa.

Defino, M., & Manca, S. (2007). The expression of social presence through the use of figurative language in a web-based learning environment. *Computers in Human Behavior, 23,* 2190–2211.

Dirkin, K. H., Mishra, P., & Altermatt, E. (2005). All or nothing: Levels of sociability of a pedagogical software agent and its impact on student perceptions and learning. *Journal of Educational Multimedia and Hypermedia, 14,* 113–127.

Donath, J., & boyd, d. (2004). Public displays of connection. *BT Technology Journal, 22,* 71–82.

Flynn, C. (2008). Weapons against robots: The time to prepare is now. *Botropolis*. Retrieved October 20, 2008, from http://botropolis.com/tag/weapons-against-robots/

Fogg, B. J., & Nass, C. (1997). Silicon sycophants: The effects of computers that flatter. *International Journal of Human-Computer Studies, 46*, 551–561.

Garramone, G. M., Harris, A. C., & Anderson, R. (1986). Uses of political computer bulletin boards. *Journal of Broadcasting & Electronic Media, 30*, 325–339.

Gates, B. (1999). The future of software. *TechTalk*. MIT News Office, Cambridge, MA. Retrieved October 27, 2008, from http://web.mit.edu/newsoffice/1999/gates2-0414.html

Gibbs, J. L., Ellison, N. B., & Heino, R. D. (2006). Self-presentation in online personals: The role of anticipated future interaction, self-disclosure, and perceived success in Internet dating. *Communication Research, 33*, 136–151.

Gibson, W. (1984). *Neuromancer*. New York: Ace Books.

Graham, S. (1998). The end of geography or the explosion of place: Conceptualizing space, place, and information technology. *Progress in Human Geography, 22*, 165–185.

Griffin, E. (2006). *A first look at communication theory*. Boston: McGraw-Hill.

Grundnig, S., Petri, T., Polzer, C., Strafling, N., & Kramer, N. (2008). Proteus in World of Warcraft? The effects of being represented by a gender-typical avatar on behavior and self-concept. In A. Spagnolli & L. Gamberini (Eds.), *Proceedings of the Eleventh Annual International Presence Workshop* (pp. 148–149). Padova, Italy: University of Padua.

Gunawardena, C. N. (1995). Social presence theory and implications for interaction and collaborative learning in computer conferences. *International Journal of Educational Telecommunications, 1*, 147–166.

Hample, D., & Dallinger, J. M. (1995). A Lewinian perspective on taking conflict personally: Revision, refinement, and validation of the instrument. *Communication Quarterly, 43*, 297–319.

Harms, C., & Biocca, F. (2004, October). *Internal consistency and reliability of the networked minds measure of social presence*. Paper presented at the Seventh Annual International Presence Workshop. Valencia, Spain: Universidad Politecnica De Valencia Editorial.

Hobman, E. V., Bordia, R., Irmer, B., & Chang, A. (2002). The expression of conflict in computer-mediated and face-to-face groups. *Small Group Research, 33*, 439–465.

Horner, B. D., Plass, J. L., & Blake, L. (2008). The effects of video on cognitive load and social presence in multimedia learning. *Computers in Human Behavior, 24*, 786–797.

International Society for Presence Research. (2000). *The concept of presence: Explication statement*. Retrieved June 16, 2008, from http://ispr.info/

Johnson, R. D., Hornik, S., & Salas, E. (2008). An empirical examination of factors contributing to the creation of successful e-learning environments. *International Journal of Human-Computer Studies, 66*, 356–369.

Kelly, K. (2005). We are the web. *Wired, 13*. Retrieved June 19, 2008, from http://www.wired.com/wired/archive/13.08/tech.html

Ketchum, R. M. (1998). Towards geographies of cyberspace. *Progress in Human Geography, 22,* 385–406.

Korzenny, F. (1978). A theory of electronic propinquity: Mediated communications in organizations. *Coimmunication Research, 5,* 3–24.

Kubrick, S. (Producer & Director). (1968). *2001: A space odyssey* [Motion picture]. USA: MGM.

Kurtz, G. (Producer), & Lucas, G. (Director). (1977). *Star wars* [Motion picture]. USA: Lucasfilm.

Kurzweil, R. (1999). *The age of spiritual machines: When computers exceed human intelligence.* New York: Penguin Books.

Kurzweil, R. (2005). *The singularity is near: When human transcend biology.* New York: Viking.

Lee, K. M. (2004a). Presence, explicated. *Communication Theory, 14,* 27–50.

Lee, K. M. (2004b). Why presence occurs: Evolutionary psychology, media equation, and presence. *Presence: Teleoperators and Virtual Environments, 13,* 494–505.

Lee, K. M., & Nass, C. (2005). Social-psychological origins of feelings of presence: Creating social presence with machine-generated voices. *Media Psychology, 7,* 31–45.

Lee, J-E. R., Nass, C., Brave, S. B., Morishima, Y., Nakajima, H., & Yamada, R. (2007). The case for caring colearners: The effects of a computer-mediated colearner agent on trust and learning. *Journal of Communication, 57*(2), 183–204.

Lee, K. M., Park, N., & Song, H. (2005). Can a robot be perceived as a developing creature?: Effects of a robot's long-term cognitive developments on its social presence and people's social responses toward it. *Human Communication Research, 31,* 538–563.

Licoppe, C., & Inada, Y. (2008). The social and cultural implications of 'Co-Presence at a Distance' in an augmented location aware collective environment (the Mogi case). In A. Spagnolli & L. Gamberini (Eds.), *Proceedings of the Eleventh Annual International Presence Workshop* (pp. 137–145). Padova, Italy: University of Padua.

Lin, Y.-M., Lin, G.-Y., & Laffey. J. M. (2008). Building a social and motivational framework for understanding satisfaction in online learning. *Journal of Educational Computing Research, 38,* 1–27.

Lombard, M., & Ditton, T. (1997). At the heart of it all: The concept of presence. *Journal of Computer-Mediated Communication. 3*(2). Retrieved June 3, 2008, from http://jcmc.indiana.edu/vol3/issue2/lombard.html

Lombard, M., Reich, R. D., Grabe, M. E., Bracken, C. C., & Ditton, T. B. (2000). Presence and television: The role of screen size. *Human Communication Research, 26,* 75–98.

Maney, K. (2007, February 5). The king of alter egos is surprisingly humble guy. *USA Today.* Retrieved June 19, 2008, from http://www.usatoday.com/printedition/money/20070205/secondlife_cover.art.htm

McLuhan, M. (1962). *The Gutenberg galaxy: The making of typographic man.* Toronto: University of Toronto Press.

McLuhan, M. (1964). *Understanding media: The extensions of man.* New York: McGraw-Hill.

Merkle, E. R., & Richardson, R. A. (2000). Digital dating and virtual relating: Conceptualizing computer mediated romantic relationships. *Family Relations, 49,* 187–192.

Merritt, T. (2008). Top 10 worst products. *CNET.* Retrieved October 20, 2008, from http://www.cnet.com/1990-11136_1-6313439-1.html?tag=cnetfd.ld

Mesch, G., & Talmud, I. (2006). The quality of online and offline relationships: The roles of multiplexity and duration of social relationships. *The Information Society, 22,* 137–148.

Na Ubon, A., & Kimble, C. (2003, July). Supporting the creation of social presence in online learning communities using asynchronous text-based CMC. Proceedings of the 3rd International Conference on Technology in Teaching and Learning in Higher Education, Heidelberg, Germany (pp. 295–300). Retrieved June 12, 2008, from http://www.chris-kimble.com/Publications/Documents/Ubon_2003.pdf

Na Ubon, A., & Kimble, C. (2004, July). *Exploring social presence in asynchronous text-based online learning communities.* Paper presented at the Proceedings of the 5th International Conference on Information Communication Technologies in Education. Retrieved June 12, 2008 from http://www.chris-kimble.com/Publications/Documents/Ubon_2004.pdf

Nass, C., Fogg, B. J., & Moon, Y. (1996). Can computers be teammates? *International Journal of Human-Computer Studies, 45*(6), 669–678.

Nass, C., Moon, Y., & Carney, P. (1999). Are respondents polite to computers? Social desirability and direct responses to computers. *Journal of Applied Social Psychology, 29*(5), 1093–1110.

Nass, C., Moon, Y., Fogg, B. J., Reeves, B., & Dryer, D. C. (1995). Can computer personalities be human personalities? *International Journal of Human-Computer Studies, 43,* 223–239.

Nass, C., Moon, Y., & Green, N. (1997). Are computers gender-neutral? Gender stereotypic responses to computers. *Journal of Applied Social Psychology, 27,* 864–876.

Negroponte, N. (1995). *Being digital.* New York: Vintage Books.

Nowak, K. L., & Biocca, F. (2003). The effect of the agency and anthropomorphism on users' sense of telepresence, copresence, and social presence in virtual environments. *Presence: Teleoperators and Virtual Environments, 12,* 481–494.

Parks, M. R., & Floyd, K. (1996). Making friends in cyberspace. *Journal of Commuication, 46,* 80–97.

Parks, M. R., & Roberts, L. D. (1998). Making MOOsic: The development of personal relationships on-line and a comparison to their off-line counterparts. *Journal of Social and Personal Relationships, 15,* 517–537.

Pena, J., & Hancock, J. T. (2006). An analysis of socioemotional and task communication in online multiplayer video games. *Communication Research, 33,* 92–109.

Press, L. (1995). McLuhan meets the Net. *Communications of the ACM, 38,* 15–20.

Rafaeli, S. (1988). Interactivity: From new media to communication. In R. P. Hawkins, J. M. Wiemann, & S. Pingree (Eds.), *Sage annual review of communication research: Advancing communication science: Merging mass and interpersonal processes, 16* (pp. 110–134). Beverly Hills: Sage.

Reeves, B. R. (1991). *"Being there": Television as symbolic versus natural experience*. Unpublished manuscript. Stanford University, Institute for Communication Research, Stanford, CA.

Reeves, B., & Nass, C. (1996). *The media equation.* New York: Cambridge University Press.

Roskos-Ewoldsen, D. R., Roskos-Ewoldsen, B., & Dillman-Carpentier, F. R. (2002). Media priming: A synthesis. In J. B. Bryant & D. Zillmann (Eds.), *Media effects: Advances in theory and research* (2nd ed., pp. 97–120). Mahwah, NJ: Erlbaum.

Short, J. A., Williams, E., & Christie, B. (1976). *The social psychology of telecommunications.* New York: Wiley.

Skalski, P., & Tamborini, R. (2007). The role of social presence in interactive agent-based persuasion. *Media Psychology, 10*(3), 385–413.

Stafford, L., Kline, S. L., & Dimmick, J. (1999). Home e-mail: Relational maintenance and gratification opportunities. *Journal of Broadcasting & Electronic Media, 43,* 659–669.

Sterling, B. (1992). *The hacker crackdown: Law and disorder on the electronic frontier.* New York: Spectra Books.

Steuer, J. (1992). Defining virtual reality: Dimensions determining telepresence. *Journal of Communication, 42*(4), 73–93.

Tamborini, R., & Skalski, P. (2006). The role of presence in the experience of electronic games. In P. Vorderer & J. Bryant (Eds.), *Playing video games: Motives, responses, and consequences* (pp. 225–249). Mahwah, NJ: Erlbaum.

Tidwell, L. C., & Walther, J. B. (2002). Computer-mediated communication effects on disclosure, impressions, and interpersonal evaluations: Getting to know one another a bit at a time. *Human Communication Research, 28,* 317–348.

Tu, C.-H. (2002). The impacts of text-based CMC on online social presence. *The Journal of Interactive Online Learning, 1,* 1–24.

Tung, F.-W., & Deng, Y.-S. (2007). Increasing social presence of social actors in e-learning environments: Effects of dynamic and static emoticons on children. *Displays, 28,* 174–180.

Turkle, S. (1984). *The second self: Computers and the human spirit.* New York: Simon and Schuster.

Turkle, S. (1994). Constructions and reconstructions of self in virtual reality: Playing in the MUDs. *Mind, Culture, and Activity, 1,* 158–167. Retrieved June 19, 2008, from http://web.mit.edu/people/sturkle/pdfsforstwebpage/ST_Construc%20and%20reconstruc%20of%20self.pdf

Turkle, S. (2005). Computers games as evocative objects: From projective screens to relational artifacts. In J. Raessens & J. Goldstein (Eds.), *Handbook of computer game studies* (pp. 267–279). London: MIT Press.

Utz, S. (2000). Social information processing in MUD's: The development of friendships in virtual worlds. *Journal of Online Behavior, 1*. Retrieved June 6, 2004, from http://www.behavior.net/JOB/v1n1/utz.html.

Walther, J. B. (1992). Interpersonal effects in computer-mediated interaction: A relational perspective. *Communication Research, 19*, 52–90.

Walther, J. B. (1996). Computer-mediated communication: Impersonal, interpersonal, and hyperpersonal interaction. *Communication Research, 23*, 3–43.

Walther, J. B., & Bazarova, N. N. (2008). Validation and application of electronic propinquity theory to computer-mediated communication in groups. *Communication Research, 35*, 622–645.

Walther, J. B., & Bunz, U. (2005). The rules of virtual groups: Trust, liking and performance in computer-mediated communication. *Journal of Communication, 55*, 828–846.

Walther, J. B., & Burgoon, J. K. (1992). Relational communication in computer-mediated interaction. *Human Communication Research, 19*, 50–88.

Walther, J. B., & D'Addario, K. P. (2001). The impacts of emoticons on message interpretation in computer-mediated communication. *Social Science Computer Review, 19*, 323–345.

Walther, J. B., Loh, T., & Granka, L. (2005). Let me count the ways: The interchange of verbal and nonverbal cues in computer-mediated communication and face-to-face affinity. *Journal of Language and Social Psychology, 24*, 36–65.

Walther, J. B., & Tidwell, L. C. (1995). Nonverbal cues in computer-mediated communication, and the effect of chronemics on relational communication. *Journal of Organizational Computing, 5*, 355–378.

What is Second Life? (n.d.). Retrieved June 17, 2008, from http://secondlife.com/whatis/

Yee, N., & Bailenson, J. N. (2006, August 24–26). Walk a mile in digital shoes: The impact of embodied perspective-taking on the reduction of negative stereotyping in immersive virtual environments. *Proceedings of PRESENCE 2006: The 9th Annual International Workshop on Presence*, Cleveland, OH.

Yee, N., & Bailenson, J. N. (2007). The Proteus effect: Self transformations in virtual reality. *Human Communication Research, 33*, 271–290.

Yee, N., Bailenson, J. N., Urbanek, M., Chang, F., & Merget, D. (2007). The unbearable likeness of being digital: The persistence of nonverbal social norms in online virtual environments. *Cyberpsychology and Behavior, 10*, 115–121.

Zhao, S. (2003). Toward a taxonomy of copresence. *Presence, 12*(5), 445–455.

Zittrain, J. (2008). *The future of the Internet and how to stop it*. New Haven, CT: Yale University Press.

Chapter 5

Presence in Video Games

Ron Tamborini and Nicholas D. Bowman

The experience of presence during game play has become an increasingly central component of video game research. Ongoing developments in video game technology have continued the long-standing practice of making games more vivid and interactive, two factors thought to invoke feelings of presence (Steuer, 1992). Advances in graphic and sound quality, the widespread use of first-person viewpoints, and the inclusion of haptic feedback systems have increased the vividness of these virtual environments, while the expanded use of a variety of different control devices—including the more recent use of naturally mapped game controllers—has increased the interactivity of video games. In sum, as video games have continued to become more vivid and interactive, the experience of presence has become a critical component of understanding how they are used (Klimmt & Vorderer, 2003; Tamborini et al., 2004).

We begin this chapter by defining the concept of presence as it applies to video game experience, and discussing how developments of game technology are related to three specific dimensions: spatial presence, social presence and self presence. Although video game technology has obvious implications for both social presence and self presence, this chapter will focus specifically on unique aspects of video game technology related to spatial presence, such as the ability of users to control game environments and the need for them to participate actively in order to attain this control. From this discussion, we will examine the role of natural mapping and mental models in the experience of spatial presence, as well as the short-term and long-term implications of experiencing spatial presence in video games.

What Does It Mean to Feel Present in Video Games?

In simple and somewhat limited terms, the essence of presence is often described as the perception of non-mediation (Lombard & Ditton, 1997).[1] Presence can be understood as a psychological state in which a user's subjective experience in a mediated environment is shaped by technological features of the environment in ways that are not readily apparent to the user. Although definitions of presence are still muddled by different uses of the term in different areas of study, there appears to be general agreement that the construct is multi-dimensional in nature (e.g., Biocca, 1997; Heeter, 1992; Lee, 2004). For purposes of our discussion, we consider presence in video games along three dimensions prominent in this literature: *spatial presence, social presence,* and *self presence.*[2]

Spatial presence (and related terms such as physical presence) is best understood as the sense of being physically located in a virtual environment (Ijsselsteijn, de Ridder, Freeman, & Avons, 2000) or interacting with virtual objects as though they have actual, physical properties (Lee, 2004). For video game players, spatial presence is understood as the extent to which one feels as if they are inside the game world, a feeling that Steuer (1992) describes as being *involved* and *immersed* in the virtual environment. Tamborini (2000) argues that a video game's influence on cognitions and behaviors is determined in part by the game's ability to enhance feelings of involvement and immersion, and that these feelings are enhanced by technological features associated with vividness and interactivity inherent in most video games.

Social presence refers to how users in a virtual environment experiences virtual social actors as though they are actual social actors (Lee, 2004). Though social presence might seem like a simple concept, many definitions of the construct have been advanced. Biocca, Harms, and Burgoon (2003) distinguish dimensions of social presence common across several definitions as copresence, psychological involvement, and behavioral engagement. Each of these dimensions highlights the complex sensation of social presence that can be experienced in response to video games. Copresence involves sensory awareness of an embodied other, whereas psychological involvement is a sense of access to intelligence and behavioral engagement focuses on behavioral interaction or synchronization. When considering characters in video games, most games include a bevy of distinguishable visible others (copresence) who appear as intelligent beings (psychological involvement) and are capable of engaging in interaction (behavioral engagement). Perhaps the central focus of research on social presence in gaming deals with massively multiplayer online games (MMOGs), which feature thousands of avatars representative of any number of non co-located social others, each of whom can be interacted with individually or as a whole, thereby creating a sense of "being with."

Self presence has been defined as a state in which users experience their virtual self as if it were their actual self (Lee, 2004), perhaps even leading to an awareness of themselves as social beings inside a virtual environment (Biocca, 1997). Although a relatively new concept, self presence is something that has been greatly enhanced by recent video game technologies. A simple example of this is the use of the first-person point of view, which allows the player to experience the virtual environment through the eyes of the game character. Other games go beyond using this intimate perspective, allowing players to see themselves in the actual game environment. For example, Nintendo's Wii game system allows characters to create a cartoon avatar called a Mii, a caricaturistic representation of the self. Other games, such as the war simulator *Rainbow Six*, allow players to place high-resolution photos of their face onto game characters. Newer game technologies have taken this a step further, generating whole body representations of players inside the virtual environments. The most notable example of this type of technology is the Sony EyeToy, a small camera that captures real-time images of players and puts these images into games.

Video Games: Technology Tailor-Made for Spatial Presence

Some would argue that features of technology inherent in modern video games are ideal for stimulating all forms of presence. This is easy to see when we consider how the first person perspective of some shooter games seems to naturally stimulate self presence, or how the ability of avatars and artificial agents can evoke feelings of social presence in MMOGs. However, the characteristic of video games that most conspicuously distinguishes their ability to promote presence from the ability of other entertainment technology is their capacity for interactivity. As noted above, interactivity—along with vividness—is recognized as a key determinant of spatial presence. Yet while the capacity for heightened vividness is often found in other media (as mentioned earlier), the level of interactivity afforded by video games is rare in these other entertainment forms. Thus, it can be argued that the interactive nature of video games is one of their most distinguishing features, a feature central both to its presence producing capacity and many outcomes from game play (Lombard & Ditton, 1997; Steuer, 1992).

Interactive Game Technology and Spatial Presence

Interactivity has been defined alternatively in terms of subjective perception (Lee, Park, & Jin, 2006), in terms of technology (e.g., Biocca, 1997), or in terms of setting (e.g., Rafaeli, 1988). Though each of these might be important to understanding various dimensions of presence in video games, interactive features of game technology are particularly relevant to spatial presence. Salen and Zimmerman (2004) define interactivity in video game play as the extent to which players make use of design choices and procedures, such as using a joystick to maneuver a game character. In this sense, interaction is the result of the player's knowledge of the game design rules (i.e., how the system will respond) and decisions to behave in a manner that uses those rules to control the game environment. Understood this way, interactivity in video game play occurs between the player and the system. System design allows the player interactive control, which is the ability to influence the form and content of the environment (Steuer, 1992). This type of control is considered a prerequisite of spatial presence by some (e.g., Zahorik & Jenison, 1998).

The interactive control afforded by video game controllers has progressed considerably over time, from single-button joysticks of the late 1970s to the multi-button, multi-function gamepads of the most recent game systems (Skalski, 2004). The latest generation of video game systems—which includes the Wii, Sony's PlayStation 3, and Microsoft's Xbox 360—has ushered in revolutionary forms of game controls that are naturally mapped; that is, they allow players to control game action through realistic body movements (Steuer, 1992). Tamborini and colleagues (Tamborini et al., 2004; Tamborini & Skalski, 2006) argue that natural mapping is a key component of video game induced presence due to its ability to provide more complete mental models, or what has been thought of as cognitive representations of situations in real or imagined worlds (Roskos-Ewoldsen, Roskos-Ewoldsen, & Dillman Carpentier, 2002). Moreover, natural mapping and the strengthened mental models that result from this are considered key determinants of outcomes experienced from video game play.

Natural Mapping and Spatial Presence in Video Games

Natural mapping is understood as "the ability of a system to map its controls to changes in the mediated environment in a natural and predictable manner" (Steuer, 1992, p. 47). In video gaming, natural mapping is commonly thought of as how closely actions represented in the game environment match the natural actions used to bring about change in a real environment. Biocca (1992) explains that, since our human perceptual systems are optimized for real life interaction, adapting virtual controls to movements of the human body should bring about heightened levels of presence.

Skalski, Tamborini, Lange, and Shelton (2007) present a typology of a natural mapping that represents a hierarchy of presence inducing capacity from low to high labeled as *directional, kinesic,* and *realistic-tangible natural mapping.* Directional mapping denotes natural mapping in its most basic form and represents situations in which there is a simple correspondence between the directions provided for using a control device to control interaction and the results on a screen. In a video game, the simplest form of directional mapping is the ubiquitous directional pad, in which the inputs up, down, left, and right correspond to movements in these directions in the mediated environment. Kinesic mapping allows the user to control a game environment with the same body movements used in real-life, but does not provide a realistic, tangible controller. Perhaps the best example of this is seen in video games such as Sony's *Air Guitar*, where players "strum" the air to control the game without an actual tangible game controller. Realistic-tangible mapping is simply kinesic mapping that makes use of an actual controller. With this type of mapping, players use the game controller just as they would a similar device in in real life. For example, a realistic-tangible mapped version of *Air Guitar* would have players holding an actual guitar controller, strumming notes with different control inputs on the controller; games such as *Rock Band* and *Guitar Hero* are popular examples of this sort of natural mapping.

The idea of using naturally mapped video game technology to induce a sense of presence is not new. For example, Namco's popular PolePosition arcade game was one of the first racing simulations that allowed players to use a steering wheel and gearshift to control their virtual race car as though they were speeding along a real-world racetrack. Indeed, since their inception racing games and other simulator-type games—such as flight simulators—have incorporated natural mapping interfaces that are both realistic and tangible. However, modern video game designers have developed naturally mapped game interfaces beyond flight and driving simulations by extending natuarally mapped technology to other types of video games, such as sports and action-adventure games, which require more active and physical activities.

One of the more popular applications of these newer naturally mapped controls is the Wii, which has sold over 21 million units worldwide as of March 2008 (Nintendo, 2008), more than any other seventh-generation game console. The Wii's most distinguishing characteristic is its proprietary motion-sensor remote, the Wiimote, that replaces the standard gamepad controller as the primary input device for the system. Using a combination of accelerometers and an infrared laser system, the controller is able to translate a wide variety of user motions into game controls, allowing for a heightened level of interactivty and resultant presence. Applications of this control system have been quite varied. The most popular games on the Wii system appear to be the sports simulators, such as *Wii Sports* (which includes baseball, bowling, boxing, golf, and tennis games). Yet a variety of games with varying levels of natural mapping have also been very well-received by the gaming community, such as those that feature shooting, fishing, cooking, carnival games, and even surgical procedures. Other realistic-tangible naturally mapped video games that have enjoyed similar market success include the already mentioned *Guitar Hero* and *Dance Dance Revolution*, both part of a growing segment of rhythm video games that require players to play musical instruments or dance on a pressure-sensitive floor mat to the beat of different songs. These games make use of a variety of player inputs, which in turn increases the gamer's sense of spatial presence in the game environment.

Relatively little is known about the psychology behind the appeal of naturally mapped video games. Despite the fact they are often relatively simplistic and graphically inferior to other games, some naturally mapped video games such as those listed above have enjoyed immense market success. At the same time, others have done very poorly. Van Lent (2008) argues that although graphics and processing power have been generally accepted as the hallmarks of a great video game or game system, "nothing matters as much as creating fun-to-play games" (pp. 103). A recent analysis of game ratings for the three seventh-generation video game consoles—Xbox 360, Wii, Playstation 3—shows that although all three systems have a comparable number of games rated in the 90th percentile (3% of games for the Xbox 360 and Wii, 2% of games for the Playstation 3), nearly twice as many games for the Wii—almost 40% of all games on the system—have been rated below the 50th percentile (Game Informer, 2008). Generally, games that were developed for other systems and later ported to the Wii have not done nearly as well as games that were designed specifically to take advantage of the Wii's motion-sensor technology. In part, this is likely because the ported games are not really designed to take advantage of the many different user inputs provided by the Wiimote. Indeed, the clunky controls and poor natural mapping that often result from these ported games likely serve as a hindrance to "being there." This suggests—albeit anecdotally—that there is more that explains the attraction to these games than just jumping around and playing. We argue that one contributor to the success of naturally mapped video games is a game's ability to provide more complete mental models and the resultant spatial presence.

Spatial Presence and Mental Models

While video game technology's capacity for natural mapping and the feelings of interactivity this can produce might be the features that seem to distinguish gaming's presence-inducing capacity from traditional entertainment media, other presence-inducing features of video games should not be overlooked. Advances in game technology produce more rich sensory environments that have added to the vividness of games. Most new game technologies not only possess increased graphic and sound resolution but also stimulate additional sensory channels, such as the use of force-feedback controllers to recreate haptic sensations of physical touch. Notably, all of these game technology features provide the user with a more complete cognitive representation of the game environment. In essence, these technologies provide players with a more complete mental model of the virtual world. Indeed, we see the provision of more complete mental models as key to understanding not only the experience of presence during video game play, but outcomes from these presence inducing experiences.

Mental models are cognitive constructions that describe an individual's understanding of a content domain in some particular aspect of the world (Sowa, 1984). They are like small-scale models of reality that the mind creates for use in attempts to explain how the world works, to predict events, and to decide how to act (Craik, 1943). These representations are thought to form when knowledge of the world combines with past experiences to guide future actions (vanDijk, 1998). Roskos-Ewoldsen et al. (2002) observe that mental models can be developed for both real or imagined objects (such as mediated experiences with objects) and defines mental models as cognitive representations of real or imagined situations, entities found in those situations, and relationships between those entities.

A great deal of research examines how the inherently incomplete nature of mental models can produce errors in human judgment (cf. Gigerenzer, Hoffrage, & Kleinbolting, 1991), yet it would seem imprudent to think that mental models are generally dysfunctional. Instead, we might expect that mental models are functional to the extent that their structure corresponds to the structure of what they are meant to represent. Consider again the Sony EyeToy. In many regards the technology's ability to place the user's mirror image into the game environment and allow player actions to control game characters and objects offers considerable structural correspondence between the player's actual and virtual worlds. Yet as Demming (2004) notes, the lack of isomorphism in some aspects can make it difficult for players to form a mental model that allows them to effectively manipulate their own image. For example, although characters in certain EyeToy games are programmed to respond in a 3-D manner, the game represents the player as a 2-D entity. Though the players are located in a 3-D space, they must behave as if they were a 2-D character. In addition, the lack of tangible feedback through handheld controls or haptic sensors attached to the player's body prevents users from connecting tactile interaction with the feedback on the screen (Diniz-Sanches, 2004). As such, players are unable to effectively use their body movements to control objects and events in the game. Demming (2004) suggests that although EyeToy is immediately popular due to its interactive novelty, problems with forming useful mental models interfere with its ability to elicit high levels of spatial presence.

By contrast, we should expect mental models to be more useful to the extent that the salient aspects of their structural and functional features accurately corresponds to the structure and function of the objects, entities, situations, or relationships they are intended to represent. In these situations, mental models are more likely to be used to engender thoughts, inferences, and feelings that govern behaviors in the virtual and real environment (Johnson-Laird, Girotto, & Legrenzi, 1998). For example, we might expect the success of virtual reality training simulations to be a function of the training simulation's fidelity to the corresponding real world activity. Rheingold (1991) uses the example of training fighter pilots using high-end virtual reality simulations, and Gearan (1996) discusses the U.S. Marines' use of a modified version of the first-person shooter game *Doom II*, appropriately called *Marine Doom*, which was designed to train U.S. Marines to coordinate their efforts to destroy enemy bunkers and rescue hostages from foreign embassy. Similarly, recent studies have suggested that playing video games improves the hand-eye coordination of surgeons (Rosser et al., 2007; Waxberg, Schwaitzberg, & Cao, 2005). These types of successful virtual reality experiences model the essential structural and functional features of actual practices well enough so that users can learn the behaviors necessary to perform these tasks in real life.

Both Tamborini (2000) and Skalski (2004) draw parallels between newer video games and training simulators, maintaining that attributes of presence-inducing technology found in video games help generate more complete and accessible mental models than other media. They argue that the presence induced by these games combined with other attributes commonly found in them is likely to strengthen the mental model's impact on subsequent user thoughts and actions. For example, the reward structures of video games are often designed to cultivate the type of repeated play that promotes the development and use of enacted mental models (Braun & Giroux, 1989; Dill & Dill, 1998). Moreover, the fact that video games require users to take an active role in decisions to perform in-game behaviors should not be overlooked. Tamborini (2000) argues that decision making is one of the most salient functional features of any behavioral mental model. Video games provide models of decision making processes that are not represented in television and other entertainment media where the user's role is passive. Thus, not only do video games have the capacity to provide more complete mental models than other media experiences, but the repeated enactment of these mental models during the course of game play should strengthen the learning of decisional cues linked to associated behaviors.

Natural Mapping in Games and the Formation
of More Complete Mental Models

Mental models are understood to be formed when knowledge of real life combines with past experience (vanDijk, 1998). As such, it would make sense that video games providing users with naturally mapped control schemes would influence the formation of mental models in ways that other non-naturally mapped games do not. The logic here is that naturally mapped video games incorporate control schemes with an extremely high fidelity to real life actions, whereas the traditional video game controller incorporates control schemes that have no real life analog. Put another way, naturally mapped control schemes use real life knowledge, whereas traditional game controllers require the user to learn an entirely new knowledge system. By tapping into real life knowledge, naturally mapped video games allow the user to rely on and adapt existing mental models, rather than requiring the creation of an entirely new mental model based on the manipulation of a toggle or key pad with no tangible relationship to corresponding on-screen behaviors. Understanding the relationships between entities within the mediated environment should be a key component of a mental model's efficacy (Roskos-Ewoldsen et al., 2002). In video games—and, for that matter, any virtual reality environment—the relationship between the control inputs and the corresponding on-screen actions is a mental model that must be formed. The ease with which this occurs is likely to be determined by the existence of user models that can be easily adapted to accommodate the new model to be formed. In turn, this ease is likely to determine the magnitude of the model's use and consequence.

Consider the experience of playing a video game version of tennis. If a player had only a cursory knowledge of tennis and relatively little experience playing video games, the additional step of learning how to manipulate a traditional game controller to make the tennis game work (i.e., learning which controls move the avatar, which controls are used to hit the ball, etc.) might be rather daunting. By contrast, with a naturally mapped video game, even novice tennis players could apply their basic level of knowledge about how tennis is played and begin playing the tennis video game with few obstacles. Players who understand how to swing a tennis racket to hit a tennis ball over a net and into the center of the court have an existing mental model with most of the salient structural and functional features needed to play the tennis video game. Their past experiences with tennis coupled with the naturally mapped controller in their hand—in this case, a virtual tennis racket—tells them to swing their racket controller to hit the ball, just as they would in real life. Even a person whose experience with tennis came from watching the game on television might have a functional mental model containing the basic principles of the game telling them to swing their arm to hit the ball over the net, to swing it harder if the ball does not go far enough, and to swing softer if it goes to far. Conversely, if the same game were being played with a traditional game controller, knowing the principle of "swing my arm" does little to inform the player about which combination of button pushes will cause the on-screen character to perform the desired action. The novice player must develop a somewhat complex mental model before being able to play the video game with any acumen. For the novice, natural mapping should facilitate successful play by allowing users to easily adapt existing mental models to the game environment.

Outcomes for Presence in Video Games

The levels of natural mapping and interactive control available to video game players have continued to rise with developments in gaming technology, and this has greatly increased the capability for video games to induce heightened levels of presence. In turn, the arresting nature of these technological advances has drawn attention to questions about how greater levels of presence might influence outcomes from video game play. Though traditional media entertainment theory can begin to inform us in this regard (Klimmt & Vorderer, 2003), new theorizing is needed to account for the unique features of this interactive entertainment technology that have gone unexamined in prior research (Vorderer, 2000). How does presence-inducing technology influence the selection of different game titles, the time people spend with games, and the manner in which video games are played? How does this technology alter the experience of playing video games, and how does this change the social and psychological impact of video game play on individuals?

Natural mapping, interactive control, and other unique attributes of the presence-inducing technology found in video games can be expected to affect both the short-term and long-term consequences of play. With regard to transient influences, we expect that feeling of presence from video games may alter experiences of enjoyment, the use of video games for mood management, and the priming of thoughts and behaviors. With regard to more long-lasting influences, we expect that presence resulting from video game play may influence the development of new mental models, as well as routines and habitual response.

The Transient Influences of Video Game-Induced Presence

Enjoyment   Most research examining video-game experiences in general and presence related outcomes in particular has looked at the short-term effects of game play on things such as enjoyment, mood, and priming, with the study of enjoyment typifying the majority of this research (cf. chapter 7, this volume). Tamborini, Bowman, Eden, Grizzard, and Organ (2008) define enjoyment as the satisfaction of needs related to different motivations, noting that different attributes of video game technology make games well suited for experiencing enjoyment at both hedonic levels (e.g., simple physiological forms of pleasure) and non-hedonic levels (e.g., eudaimonia and psychological well-being).

Hedonic experiences of enjoyment are likely to stem from the highly arousing nature of games in general, and are intensified by the type of presence-inducing attributes of game technology that lead to involvement and immersion. The highly-evolved graphics and sound, the haptic stimulation, the need for active player participation and the interactive nature of game controls all work together in the creation of a more physically arousing and stimulating experience. Evidence consistent with this notion can be found in research by Skalski et al. (2007), who examined the role of natural mapping on presence-induced enjoyment. In an experiment varying the control device in a racing video game, they found that the use of a realistic-tangible mapped control device (e.g., a steering wheel) produced greater spatial presence and resulted in higher levels of enjoyment. Skalski et al. argue that the play context of video games makes their use inherently an enjoyable experience, and as such the influence of presence in gaming should only enhance these types of positive encounters.

Although consideration of enjoyment associated with non-hedonic needs is quite new to entertainment theory, some early research in this area has focused specifically on presence-inducing features of video games. In a series of studies, Ryan, Rigby, and Przybylski (2006) linked the enjoyment of video game play to presence and the satisfaction of three intrinsic needs related to psychological well-being—autonomy, competence, and relatedness. Of particular relevance here, their survey findings suggested that the perceived intuitive nature of game controls (a proxy for natural mapping) can satisfy autonomy and competence needs across a variety of video games (i.e., a platform game, fighting game, rail-shooter game, and arcade-racing game). In a different study that varied the natural mapping of game controls (directional mapping and realistic-tangible mapping), Tamborini et al. (2008) built on Ryan et al.'s (2006) survey research to demonstrate experimentally that using realistic-tangible mapped controls increased the satisfaction of autonomy and competence needs, and the related feeling of enjoyment.

Anecdotal evidence suggests that the influence of natural mapping on enjoyment might be determined at least in part by the relationship between a video game and the existing mental models users have of the real world activities in the game environment. For example, an anonymous blogger at Game Journal (mygamejournal.blogspot.com) wrote this about his experiences with the Nintendo Wii Bowling video game: "The Wiimote seems to do a very good job conforming to my mental model [of bowling]. Without reading any instructions, I was able to pick up the controller and place some pretty interesting spins on the bowling ball, just as I'd wanted. The results weren't always even as good as a bowl in RL [real life], but I did a great job overall" (Ruffin, 2007, para. 2 & 3). This anecdotal evidence is consistent with data from the aforesaid study by Tamborini et al. (2008) where respondents were given a modified Wiimote formed to closely resemble a bowling ball and asked to play *Brunswick Pro Bowling* on the Wii. Representative responses from participants in this study indicated that the bowling ball controller made the game feel much more "lifelike," "easy to learn," "engaging," and "entertaining." Interestingly, participants who were randomly assigned to play the same game with a traditional game controller complained the game was "boring," "repetitive," and "not at all like bowling." Perhaps the most direct comment about the bowling ball controller was made by a male participant, who commented that: "I thought that the game was fun and engaging. It seemed pretty life-like. It represented how I would bowl in real life, which is not very well."

Mood Management   The same features of video games that contribute to their presence-inducing nature make them particularly well-suited for use in mood management processes (Bryant & Davies, 2006; Grodal, 2000). Zillmann's work on mood management—and his broader work on selective exposure—suggests that media use is determined in large part by the ability of a medium to serve the user's immediate affective needs, even if these needs are unknown (Zillmann, 2000). Mood management theory (Zillmann & Bryant, 1985) holds that people are hedonistic and driven to arrange their environment in ways that maximize pleasure and minimize pain. The theory further argues that media environments are easily-controllable, making them well suited for this task, and that decisions to use media are often motivated by their inherent capacity in this regard. According to Bryant and Davies (2006), a medium's mood-governing capacity can be understood in terms of its potential to both regulate arousal and intervene in user thought processes. We argue that the intervention potential of video games—the ability of games to intervene in our negative affective states—is strongly linked to presence-inducing quality of games.[3]

Several features of video game technology lend themselves to be high in intervention potential, but perhaps the most notable of these features deals with the highly immersive experience of video games. The vividness and interactivity inherent in video game technology makes playing games an engaging and absorbing experience; precisely the type of experience that should have great intervention potential. For example, while traditional narrative media such as television and film require the user only to set the TV tuner on a particular channel or start a VHS or DVD to view a complete narrative, video games require near-constant user feedback to progress the narrative from one point to the next. The active user involvement required by video games commands a much higher level of engagement than other media. This engagement not only prompts experiences of presence, but also results in a high capacity for the video game to intervene in rumination. Furthermore, different situational needs and motives would compel users to select behaviors that sometimes intervene in and sometimes sustain focused thought. The promise of video games is its ability to do either *within the same game* depending on conditional needs. Tamborini and Bowman (2008) note that many games can be programmed to different settings that vary the level of user involvement required, making it possible to play the same game at a setting that constantly demands an active user's full attention or as a passive observer who is essentially along for the ride. The level of involvement demanded by a video game will determine the extent to which game play intervenes in user thought processes and whether mood is likely to be perpetuated or changed.

Priming   One of the most heavily researched areas of video game effects is the short term influence of game play on priming. In most cases, the presence-inducing attributes of video game technology seem likely to do little more than facilitate or strengthen the type of priming effects we might expect from exposure to traditional entertainment media. In these instances, the immersive nature of presence should make experiences within virtual worlds highly salient upon exiting these worlds. In turn, we might expect for short periods of time an increased availability of thoughts primed by these virtual experiences, which in turn might influence behaviors in line with those thoughts primed.

Although there is ample evidence to show that violent video games prime hostility (see Anderson & Bushman, 2001), evidence suggesting the influence of presence on this relationship has been mixed. For example, two studies comparing highly immersive virtual reality technology with traditional game control failed to find that the immersive experience produced more feelings of presence or primed more hostile thoughts (Eastin, 2006; Tamborini et al., 2004). By contrast, this pattern was observed in research comparing violent game play using immersive virtual environment technology (IVET) with a less immersive desktop platform (Persky & Blascovich, 2008). Moreover, in research using only traditional game technology, the level of presence experienced by respondents playing a violent video on a standard Sony PlayStation 2 gaming console predicted hostile intentions (Nowak, Krcmar, & Farrar, 2008). It is notable that players in the two failed attempts wore head mounted displays that completely immersed them in the game environment. The authors in both cases pointed to difficultly learning to play in the virtual reality environment as a potential cause for failed predictions. In the two studies showing that feeling present predicted hostile thoughts, the technology was more easily learned.

As is apparent, more research is needed to answer questions about violent video games and the presence induced priming of hostility. The same can be said for other areas of presence and priming. Research in other areas that examines the priming effect of presence inducing video games is surprisingly negligible, yet there is good reason to believe that these influences are strong. For example, media scholars often point to video technology allowing users to adopt a first-person perspective of game play, noting how this presence inducing technology should prime users to adopt the perspective of characters they play (e.g., Tamborini et al., 2004). Regardless of whether it is a first-person shooter game that places the player in an active war zone or a first-person parkour[4] game that simply has the player moving through urban environments, this perspective is thought to produce strong primes in ways as diverse as shaping gamers' basic emotional responses to altering their sense of proprioception in ways unattainable through traditional entertainment forms. Undoubtedly, these and related areas will be to subject future study.

More Enduring Consequences from Video Game Induced Presence

Though empirical research on the long-term consequences of video games and presence has been scant, there is good reason to believe that the lasting influence of presence-inducing game experiences would be considerable. Perhaps the best examples of this are associated with the strengthening, modifying, or development of mental models and outcomes related to routines of habitual response.

The Development of Mental Models   Earlier we argued that naturally mapped video games allow players to use and/or quickly adapt their existing mental models in virtual environments, and that the ease with which this use or adaptation occurs should increase the model's accessibility and subsequent influence on both the gaming experience and the real world. Perhaps no influence is as important as the creation of new mental models, both intended and unintended. Whereas public attention to popular video games has often focused on the dysfunctional outcomes from models that foster hostility and other anti-social behaviors, in educational games the potential for learning new models associated with a variety of pro-social behaviors and academic and practice concepts is considerable. The impact of the virtual learning of models associated with activities in military and medical training, phobia treatment, sports training, workplace practices, schools, and other contexts should not be overlooked. Indeed, many scholars maintain that the learning potential afforded by the technological innovations in educational video games can be greatly improved by making these games more immersive. For example, in her discussion of learning through virtual enhancements of direct experience, Riel (1998) describes how the ability of three-dimensional models to visually represent objects with complex properties that are otherwise invisible has been used to advance student learning, noting the particular benefits of virtual reality technology that allows students to experience different settings, make choices, and see outcomes they otherwise could not see. Further research on teaching mental rotation ability by Smith and Olkun (2005) showed that technology's capacity to shape mental models stretched from grade school children to college students. For nine-year-olds and undergraduates alike, interactive participation in a virtual environment facilitated the learning of mental models and subsequent task performance beyond non-interactive observation of an animated film.

Examples of this type of virtual learning are widespread, showing that simulated encounters can combine with actual experience to create powerful mental models. Medical interns training to be surgeons use simulators that allow them to operate on virtual patients without risk of harm. Flight simulators reproduce harsh weather environments, heavy air traffic, mechanical problems, and challenging landing conditions for both novice and experienced pilots. Athletes develop their physical and mental (model) skills for all types of sports, as baseball players simu-late hitting off of virtual pitchers, golfers improve their swing, skiers improve their balance, and bicyclists or race-car drivers learn the ins and outs of different courses before they have to compete. Indeed, the influence of these models seems pervasive, affecting cognitive skills as well as the behavioral skills already described (Skalski, Tamborini, & Westerman, 2002).

Routine Use and Habitual Response   The long-term outcomes from presence-inducing games can also be seen in how exposure influences routine behavior and habitual response. Clearly, the previous discussion of mood management has considerable implications for enduring routines as well as changes in transient affect. Though mood management theory suggests that people use media to serve their immediate affective needs, it is also the case that well-learned expectations from recurrent use will result in the development of routine behaviors to satisfy recurrent needs. Indeed, seminal research on selective exposure theory grounds its reasoning in logic about how people's routine media use decisions coincide with recurrent experiences of boredom or stress that result from daily work routines (Bryant & Zillmann, 1984). Selective exposure theory holds that attributes of traditional entertainment media such as television and radio make them ideal for satisfying affective needs. Yet, as we have already stated, the vivid and interactive features of video games increase the arousing nature of this medium. In a similar manner, the same features responsible for creating experiences of spatial presence give video games the type of heightened intervention potential unlikely to be found in traditional media. Moreover, the fact that the same games can be set for play at different levels of user involvement and can be played in ways that vary their behavioral and hedonic affinity to current mood states allows games to be used either to perpetuate or intervene in various mood states depending on situational needs. All of these features suggest the manner in which presence resulting from video games works toward cultivating its routine use. Zillmann and Bryant (1985) wrote that "pleasure stamps in the preference" for future media use (pp. 159); this is perhaps no more true than when considering the pleasure of playing video games to routinely alleviate noxious mood states.

Though somewhat different than game technology's influence routine selective use, one interesting application of gaming technology is its clinical use in the gradual habituation of enduring dysfunctional behaviors. The medical use of virtual reality technology has become increasingly popular in virtual phobia treatment. Herbelin (2005) describes over 120 scientific publications between 1995 and 2004 reporting the frequent use of immersive HMD environments. Virtual reality exposure therapy (VRET) has been used to treat arachnophobia (Garcia-Palacios, Hoffmann, Carlin, Furness, & Botella, 2002; Hoffman, Garcia-Palacios, Carlin, Furness, & Botella-Arbona, 2003), acrophobia (Jang et al., 2002), agoraphobia (Vincelli et al., 2003), and post traumatic stress disorders (Rothbaum et al., 1999), as well as fears of flying (Wiederhold et al., 2002), driving (Wald, 2004), and a variety of animals (Parrott, Bowman, & Ollendick, 2004). Traditional exposure therapy has been conducted in one of two ways: either by exposing patients to the fear-inducing stimuli (called in vivo) or by asking the patient to imagine it (Kooper, n.d.). Clinicians consider virtual reality superior to other media for exposure therapy because of the active role it affords to the users, and mounting evidence seems to suggest that video games and other VRET can effectively to treat these disorders (Herbelin, 2005). Whether it is flying, spiders, animals, or other people, over time and repeated positive interactions with increasingly realistic virtual experiences, the strength of the phobic reaction should gradually habituate to a point where the dysfunctional fear of the object has dissipated. Through this therapeutic process, virtual presence with fearful stimuli in a safe media environment appears capable of altering habitual response.

Notably, the role of video games and other presence-related technology in virtual therapy is not limited to the treatment of phobia. Considerable research has been conducted on the use of virtual reality and associated technologies for disability therapy in the areas of visual and hearing impairment, learning disability, and motor impairment (Cobb & Sharkey, 2007). Work on motor impairment, in particular, shows how advances in presence-inducing video games have been used in virtual therapy aimed at the rehabilitation of motor control (Joyce & Phalangas, 1998). Early research on user immersion in virtual environments has shown evidence of increased mobility (Kizony, Katz, Weingarden, & Weiss, 2002) and later work with stroke patients has demonstrated the role of presence-inducing technology in recovery (Kizony, Katz, & Weiss, 2004). Research comparing the use of virtual reality systems developed specifically for virtual therapy with the Sony EyeToy has shown that elderly patients preferred the EyeToy to these other systems, suggesting the potential value for developing games more specifically for rehabilitation (Rand, Kizony, & Weiss, 2004).

The manner in which immersion and interaction play a role in how video games serve the therapy needs of phobic patients or help to train soldiers and medical interns is quite distant from the playful functions that we typically associate with games. If nothing else, this shows the far-reaching outcomes for presence in video games. Some influences are as ephemeral as a prime or feelings of enjoyment and briefly felt moods. Others are more enduring forms of learning, the development of routines, or change in habitual response. Taken together, we see that the experience of presence in video games plays a surprisingly important role in many parts of our lives beyond mere enjoyment.

Conclusion

This chapter has focused on the presence-inducing features of video games, discussing how the vivid and interactive nature of video game technology is particularly well suited for creating the experience of spatial presence, how advances in natural mapping strengthen spatial presence and the development of mental models, and how these presence-inducing attributes influence the transient and enduring outcomes of video game play. Though spatial presence is only one form of presence, it is not difficult to see the capacity of modern video game technology to facilitate the experience of self presence or social presence. Indeed, separate chapters could be written about self or social presence in video games (cf. Tamborini & Skalski, 2006). Questions related to the social aspects of game play abound concerning such wide-ranging issues as the social settings in which games are played, the social relations formed in online game play, the social capital costs in real and virtual worlds, and the social facilitation influence of real and virtual audiences. Questions of self presence are almost as numerous addressing issues such as how modeling is influenced by strong identification with characters, or how self presence games can affect the self-images we have of our body or our social identity.

At the same time, the qualities that make video games unique from other forms of media are more central to the experience of spatial presence. It is not hard to imagine how feelings of social presence might be even stronger in on-line chat rooms or in sophisticated telepresence conference settings than they are in online fantasy role playing games. And while technology can certainly increase identification with game characters and the sense of self presence players experience during video game play, the strength with which people identify with characters in traditional media entertainment forms signals to us that the unique technological features of games may be less central to identification than the type of character development and narrative techniques that good writers use to make readers feel as though the story is about them. However, the same cannot be said about spatial presence and the player decisions and actions that afford gamers control over the virtual environment, the way haptic features of technology allow players to physically sense the game environment, or the way natural mapping makes players feel immersed in and familiar with the game environment. And while game technology has already made great advancements in the ability to generate experiences of spatial presence, there is little doubt that that the future holds even greater innovations with the promise of more immersive experience. While this does not mean that the holodeck of *Star Trek* fame is just around the corner, or that mobile augmented reality games will soon replace home video game consoles, developments in presence-inducing video game technology will continue. The likelihood that we are done seeing advances in game technology's capacity to induce spatial presence is about the same as the likelihood that we will see *Mario* shave his mustache.

Notes

1. In this discussion, we purposely avoid using Lombard and Ditton's (1997) often quoted phrase that defines presence as the "perceptual illusion of nonmediation." This was done to preclude giving readers the impression that we define presence as a form of illusion. While debate over this issue is beyond the scope of this chapter, the authors consider presence a virtual experience that need not be identified as illusionary.
2. For a more detailed discussion of social and self presence, both in general and as related to video games specifically, see Tamborini and Skalski (2006).

3. Though arousal regulation is less central to issues related to presence, Tamborini and Bowman (2008) argue that the arousal regulating capacity of video games is greater than traditional entertainment media because games can be set at different challenge levels, making it possible for the same game to be played in a manner that is arousing or relaxing to suit a user's need.

4. "Parkour" (also known as "free running") is an activity in which participants try to overcome obstacles—usually in an urban environment—in the quickest and most efficient way possible (McLean, Houshain, & Pike, 2006; Miller & Demoiny, 2003). This activity has been featured in several new video games, most notably *Mirror's Edge* (www.mirrorsedge.com), in which the gamer is required to use their speed and decision-making skills to swiftly navigate a dangerous urban environment. Although *Mirror's Edge* is the most prominent example of parkour in video games, other types of games can also be played in a parkour style. For example, Bogost (2007) talks about gamers using *Grand Theft Auto III* as a virtual parkour playground, and mentions that ostensibly any sandbox-style video game (that is, any video game with a non-linear narrative structure and environment) can be played in a parkour manner.

References

Anderson, C. A., & Bushman, B. J. (2001). Effects of violent video games on aggressive behavior, aggressive cognition, aggressive affect, physiological arousal, and prosocial behavior: A meta-analytic review of the scientific literature. *Psychological Science, 12,* 353–359.

Biocca, F. (1992). Virtual reality technology: A tutorial. *Journal of Communication, 42*(4), 23–72.

Biocca, F. (1997). The cyborg's dilemma: Progressive embodiment in virtual environments. *Journal of Computer Mediated Communication, 3(2).* Retrieved November 19, 2008, from http://jcmc.indiana.edu/vol3/issue2/biocca2.html

Biocca, F., Harms, C., & Burgoon, J. K. (2003). Toward a more robust theory and measure of social presence: Review and suggested criteria. *Presence: Teleoperators and Virtual Environments, 12*(5), 456–480.

Bogost, I. (2007, November 29). Persuasive games: Video game Zen. Retrieved March 13, 2009, from http://www.gamasutra.com/view/feature/2585/persuasive_games_video_game_zen.php

Braun, C., & Giroux, J. (1989). Arcade video games: Proxemic, cognitive and content analyses. *Journal of Leisure Research, 21,* 92–105.

Bryant, J., & Davies, J. (2006). Selective exposure to video games. In P. Vorderer & D. Zillmann (Eds.), *Playing video games: Motives, responses, and consequences* (pp. 181–194). Hillsdale, NJ: Erlbaum.

Bryant, J., & Zillmann, D. (1984). Using television to alleviate boredom and stress: Selective exposure as a function of induced excitational states. *Journal of Broadcasting & Electronic Behavior, 28,* 1–20.

Cobb, S. V. G., & Sharkey, P. M. (2007). A decade of research and development in disability, virtual reality and associated technologies: Review of

ICDVRAT 1996–2006. *The International Journal of Virtual Reality, 6(2)*, 51–68.

Craik, K. (1943). *The Nature of Explanation*. Cambridge, England: Cambridge University Press.

Demming, G. (2004). Sony EyeToy: Developing mental models for 3-D interaction in a 2-D gaming environment. *Lecture Notes in Computer Science: Computer-Human Interaction, 575–582*.

Dill, K. E., & Dill, J. C. (1998). Video game violence: A review of the empirical literature. *Aggression and Violent Behavior: A Review Journal, 3,* 407–428.

Diniz-Sanches, J. (2004). EyeToy: Groove. *Edge, 132,* 103.

Eastin, M. S. (2006). Video game violence and the female game player: Self and opponent gender effects on game presence and aggressive thoughts. *Human Communication Research, 32,* 351–372.

Game Informer (2008, June). Nintendo's software problem. *Game Informer Magazine, 18(6), 18–20.* Grapevine, TX: GameStop.

Garcia-Palacios, H., Hoffmann, S. K., Carlin, A., Furness, T. A., & Botella, C. (2002). Virtual reality in the treatment of spider phobia: A controlled study. *Behaviour Research and Therapy, 40,* 983–993.

Gearan, A. (1996, July 7). *'Doom' training keeps Marines out of the muck. Los Angeles Daily News*.

Gigerenzer, G., Hoffrage, U., & Kleinbolting, H. (1991). Probabilistic mental models: A Brunswikian theory of confidence. *Psychological Review, 98(4),* 506–528.

Grodal, T. (2000). Video games and the pleasures of control. In D. Zillmann & P. Vorderer (Eds.), *Media entertainment: The psychology of its appeal* (pp. 197–214). Hillsdale, NJ: Erlbaum.

Heeter, C. (1992). Being there: The subjective experience of presence. *Presence: Teleoperators and Virtual Environments, 1(2),* 262–271.

Herbelin, B. (2005). *Virtual reality exposure therapy for social phobia*. Thesis No. 3351, VRLab, Faculté informatique et communications, Institut des systèmes informatiques et mutlimédias, EPFL, Switzerland. Retrieved October 12, 2008, from http://www.google.com/search?hl=en&rlz=1T4SKPB_enUS 232US284&q=video+game+virtual+therapy+phobia&btnG=Search

Hoffman, H., Garcia-Palacios, A., Carlin, A., Furness, T., & Botella-Arbona, C. (2003). Interfaces that heal: Coupling real and virtual objects to treat spider phobia. *International Journal of Human-Computer Interaction, 16,* 283–300.

Ijsselsteijn, W. A., de Ridder, H., Freeman, J., & Avons, S. E. (2000). Presence: Concept, determinants, and measurement. *Proceedings of the SPIE, Human Vision and Electronic Imaging V, 3959–3976*.

Jang, D. P., Ku, J. H., Choi, Y. H., Wiederhold, B. K., Nam, S. W., Kim, I. Y., et al. (2002). The development of virtual reality therapy (VRT) system for the treatment of acrophobia and therapeutic case. *IEEE Transactions on Information Technology in Biomedicine, 6(3),* 213–217.

Johnson-Laird, P. N., Girotto, V., & Legrenzi, P. (1998, April 7). *Mental models: A gentle guide for outsiders*. Retrieved November 17, 2008, from http://www.si.umich.edu/ICOS/gentleintro.html

Joyce, A. W., & Phalangas, A. C. (1998). Implementation and capabilities of a virtual interaction system. In P. M. Sharkey, F. D. Rose, & J.-I. Lindström (Eds.), *Proceeding of the 2nd European Conference on Disability, Virtual Reality and Associated Technologies* (pp. 237–245). Mount Billingen, Skövde, Sweden.

Kizony, R., Katz, N., Weingarden, H., & Weiss, P. L. (2002). Immersion without encumbrance: adapting a virtual reality system for the rehabilitation of individuals with stroke and spinal cord injury. In P. M. Sharkey, C., Sik Lányi, & P. J. Standen (Eds.), *Proceeding of the 4th International Conference on Disability, Virtual Reality and Associated Technologies* (pp. 55–61). Veszprém, Hungary.

Kizony, R., Katz, N., & Weiss, P. L. (2004). Virtual reality based intervention in rehabilitation: relationship between motor and cognitive abilities and performance within virtual environments for patients with stroke. In P. M. Sharkey, R. J. McCrindle, & D. Brown (Eds.), *Proceeding of the 5th International Conference on Disability, Virtual Reality and Associated Technologies* (pp. 19–26). Oxford, England.

Klimmt, C., & Vorderer, P. (2003). Media psychology "is not yet there": Introducing theories on media *entertainment to the presence debate. Presence: Teleoperators and Virtual Environments, 12*(4), 346–359.

Kooper, R. (n.d.). *Virtual reality exposure therapy.* Retrieved November 12, 2002, from http://www.cc.gatech.edu/gvu/virtual/Phobia/phobia.html

Lee, K. M. (2004). Presence, explicated. *Communication Theory, 14*(1), 27–50.

Lee, K. M., Park, N., & Jin, S. (2006). Narrative and interactivity in computer games. In P. Vorderer & J. Bryant (Eds.), *Playing video games: Motives, responses, and consequence* (pp. 259–274). Mahwah, NJ: Erlbaum.

Lombard, M., & Ditton, T. (1997). At the heart of it all: The concept of presence. *Journal of Computer Mediated Communication, 3*(2). Retrieved November 17, 2008, from http://jcmc.indiana.edu/vol3/issue2/lombard.html

McLean, C., Houshain, S., & Pike, J. (2006). Paediatric fractures sustained in Parkour (free running). *Injury, 37*(8), 795–797.

Miller, J., & Demoiny, S. (2003). Parkour: A new extreme sport and a case study. *The Journal of Foot and Ankle Surgery, 47*(1), 63–65.

Nintendo. (2008). *Consolidated Financial Statements* [corporate Web page]. Retrieved May 29, 2008, from http://www.nintendo.co.jp/ir/pdf/2008/080424e.pdf#page=22

Nowak, K. L., Krcmar, M., & Farrar, K. M. (2008). The causes of and consequences of presence: Considering the influence of violent video games on presence and aggression. *Presence: Teleoperators and Virtual Environments, 17*(3), 256–268.

Parrott, M., Bowman, D., & Ollendick, T. (2004). A methodology for designing specific animal phobia stimuli for virtual reality exposure therapy. *Cyberpsychology & Behavior, 7*(3), 300–301.

Persky, S., & Blascovich, J. (2008). Immersive virtual video game play and presence: Influences on aggressive feelings and behavior. *Presence: Teleoperators and Virtual Environments, 17*(1), 57–72.

Rafaeli, S. (1988). Interactivity: From new media to communication. In R. P. Hawkins, J. M. Wiemann, & S. Pingree (Eds.), *Advancing communication science: Merging mass and interpersonal process* (pp. 110–134). Newbury Park, CA: Sage.

Rand, D., Kizony, R., & Weiss, P. L. (2004). Virtual reality rehabilitation for all: Vivid GX. versus Sony PlayStation II EyeToy. In P. M. Sharkey, R. J. McCrindle, & D. Brown (Eds.), *Proceeding of the 5th International Conference on Disability* (pp. 87–94). Oxford, England: New College.

Rheingold, H. (1991). *Virtual reality.* New York: Summit Books.

Riel, M. (1998, May). *Education in the 21st century: Just-in-time learning or learning communities.* Paper presented at the 4th annual conference on the Emirates Center for Strategic Studies and Research, Abu Dhabi.

Roskos-Ewoldsen, D. R., Roskos-Ewoldsen, B., & Dillman Carpentier, F. R. (2002). Media priming: A synthesis. In J. B. Bryant & D. Zillmann (Eds.), *Media effects: Advances in theory and research* (pp. 97–120). Mahwah, NJ: Erlbaum.

Rothbaum, B. O., Hodges, L., Alacorn, R. D., Ready, D., Shahar, F., Graap, K., et al. (1999). Virtual reality exposure therapy for PTSD Vietnam Veterans: A case study. *Journal of Traumatic Stress, 12(2),* 261–271.

Ruffin. (2007, April 28). Wii Sports: Mental models and bowling. [Blog posting]. *Game Journal.* Retrieved on November 17, 2008, from http://mygame-journal.blogspot.com/2007/04/wii-sports-mental-models-and-bowling.html

Rosser, J. C., Lynch, P. J., Cuddihy, L., Gentile, D. A., Klonsky, J., & Merrell, R. (2007). The impact of video games on training surgeons in the 21st century. *Archives of Surgery, 142(2),* 181–186.

Ryan, R. M., Rigby, C. S., & Przybylski, A. (2006). The motivational pull of video games: A self-determination theory approach. *Motivation and Emotion, 30(4),* 344–360.

Salen, K., & Zimmerman, E. (2004). *Rules of play: Game design fundamentals.* Cambridge, MA: MIT Press.

Skalski, P. (2004, October). *The quest for presence in video game entertainment.* Paper presented at the Central States Communication Association Annual Conference, Cleveland, OH.

Skalski, P., Tamborini, R., Lange, R., & Shelton, A. (2007, May). *Mapping the road to fun: Natural video game controllers, presence, and game enjoyment.* Paper presented at the Annual Meeting of the International Communication Association, San Francisco.

Skalski, P., Tamborini, R., & Westerman, D. (2002, November). *The development of scripts through virtual environments.* Paper presented to the social cognition division at the 88th annual convention of the National Communication Association, New Orleans, LA.

Smith, G. G., & Olkun, S. (2005). Why interactivity works: Interactive priming of mental rotation. *Journal of Educational Computing Research, 32(2),* 93–111.

Sowa, J. (1984). *Conceptual structures: Information processing in mind and machine.* Reading, MA: Addison-Wesley.

Steuer, J. (1992). Defining virtual reality: Dimensions determining telepresence. *Journal of Communication, 42(2),* 73–93.

Tamborini, R. (2000, November). *The experience of telepresence in violent video games*. Paper presentation at the Annual Conference of the National Communication Association, Seattle, WA.

Tamborini, R., & Bowman, N. D. (2008). *Selective exposure in video games*. Unpublished manuscript, Michigan State University.

Tamborini, R., Bowman, N. D., Eden, A., Grizzard, M. N., & Organ, A. (2008). *The effects of natural mapping and audience presence on intrinsic motivations in video games*. Unpublished manuscript, Michigan State University.

Tamborini, R., Eastin, M., Skalski, P., Lachlan, K., Fediuk, T. & Brady, R. (2004). Violent virtual video games. *Journal of Broadcasting & Electronic Media, 48*(3), 335–357.

Tamborini, R., & Skalski, P. (2006). The role of presence in the experience of electronic games. In P. Vorderer & J. Bryant (Eds.), *Playing video games: Motives, responses, and consequences* (pp. 225–240). Mahwah, NJ: Erlbaum.

Van Lent, M. (2008). The business of fun. *Computer, 41*(2), 101–03.

vanDijk, T. A. (1998). *Ideology: A multidisciplinary approach*. London: Sage.

Vincelli, F., Anolli, L., Bouchard, S., Wiederhold, B. K., Zurloni, V., & Riva, G. (2003). Experiential cognitive therapy in the treatment of panic disorders with agoraphobia: A controlled study. *Cyberpsychology & Behavior, 6*(3), 321–328.

Vorderer, P. (2000). Interactive entertainment and beyond. In D. Zillmann & P. Vorderer (Eds.), *Media entertainment: The psychology of its appeal* (pp. 21–36). Mahwah, NJ: Erlbaum.

Wald, J. (2004). Efficacy of virtual reality exposure therapy for driving phobia: A multiple baseline across-subjects design. *Behavior Therapy, 35*(3), 621–635.

Waxberg, S. L., Schwaitzberg, S. D., & Cao, C. G. L. (2005). Effects of videogame experience on laproscopic skill acquisition. *Proceedings of the Human Factors and Ergonomics Society, 49*, 1047–1052.

Wiederhold, B. K., Jang, D. P., Gervitz, R. G., Kim, S. I., Kim, I. Y., & Wiederhold, M. D. (2002). The treatment of fear of flying: A controlled study of imaginal and virtual reality graded exposure therapy. *IEEE Transactions on Information Technology in Biomedicine, 6*(3), 218–223.

Zahorik, P., & Jenison, R. L. (1998). Presence as being-in-the-world. *Presence: Teleoperators and Virtual Environments, 7*(1), 78–89.

Zillmann, D., & Bryant, J. (1985). Affect, mood, and emotion as determinants of selective exposure. In D. Zillmann & J. Bryant (Eds.), *Selective exposure to communication* (pp. 157–190). Hillsdale, NJ: Erlbaum.

Zillmann, D. (2000). Mood management in the context of selective exposure theory. In M. E. Roloff (Ed.), *Communication Yearbook 23* (pp. 103–123). Thousand Oaks, CA: Sage.

Part II

Telepresence and Effects of Media

Chapter 6

Telepresence and Persuasion

Terry Daugherty, Harsha Gangadharbatla,
and Laura Bright

Introduction

Technological innovations have poised marketing communication professionals to deliever multi-sensory media that engage consumers in active
experiences intended to increase the effectiveness of persuasive content
online (Li, Daugherty, & Biocca, 2001, 2002, 2003). As such, the Internet has become an important mainstream channel adept at facilitating
entertainment via informative and interactive simulations (Burke, 1996)
rich in both experiential and rational information (Novak, Hoffman,
& Duhachek, 2003). The result is a medium capable of creating a sense
of presence from content designed to influence consumer attitudes and
behaviors via persuasive appeals (Daugherty, Li, & Biocca, 2005, 2008).
The purpose of this chapter is to examine the existing body of work linking persuasion with presence and present a conceptual model illustrating
these connections. While an exhaustive account of all research in this
area is not possible here, the proceeding sections summarize key antecedents and outcomes associated with stimulating presence for persuasive purposes. An examination these relationships is important to both
academicians and professionals in a number of fields, such as entertainment media, gaming, ecommerce, advertising, marketing, psychology,
and communication. After presenting a conceptual model, conclusions
and future directions for research are discussed.

Persuasion and Media

Persuasion is characterized as simply human communication designed
to influence the beliefs and attitudes of others (Simons, 1976, p. 21).
As a communication paradigm, persuasion research is multidisciplinary
spanning across numerous academic fields with the core focus remain-
ing the intentional effort to influence another's mental state, evaluated
by cognitive, affective, and conative outcomes (O'Keefe, 2002, p. 5).
Classic models of persuasion include Involvement (Krugman, 1965),

Elaboration Likelihood (Petty & Cacioppo, 1981), Dual-Coding (Paivio, 1986), and the Availability-Valence Hypothesis (Kisielius & Sternthal, 1984), among others.

While early persuasion research considered information processing primarily rational in nature, more recent work has acknowledged the limitations of this view to explore the experiential characteristics of behavior (Hoch & Loewenstein, 1991; Holbrook & Hirschman, 1982). Ultimately, influence from one system over the other in directing behavior is determined by a consumer's degree of motivation, availability of processing resources and emotional involvement with the persuasive message. The greater the elaboration of information, the more available it is for attitudinal evaluation resulting in persuasive messages that rely on vivid content, positive verbal copy, and imagery serving to enhance memory associations causing information to be more salient (Kisielius & Sternthal, 1986). Although numerous variations of these models have emerged over the years, the basic principal remains that when presented with information, typically through the mass media via persuasion oriented disciplines (i.e., advertising, public relations, marketing, political and health communication, etc.), our awareness levels differ and are influenced in stages leading toward a behavior outcome.

The mass media has certainly experienced changes in the past 50 years that have continued to impact the creation and delivery of persuasive messages. Some of the most dramatic are the technological innovations that have lead to the creation of interactive digital media (i.e., computers, networking, the Internet, graphics, etc.). The emergence of new media, as well as the alteration of existing media, has lead researchers to question not only the effects of use, but also consumption motivations and how people incorporate media technologies into their daily lives. Early work in persuasion considers media consumption as a passive act, defined as an audience willing to accept whatever information or content is presented, store it into memory, and then act upon it. Researchers now have begun to understand that people do actively seek media content, use what they need from the media, and experience different levels of persuasion, especially in the area of interactive media (Li et al., 2001; Daugherty et al., 2005).

Consuming forms of interactive media certainly represents a deliberate, active behavior in which audiences seek content according to their internal motivations (Eastin & Daugherty, 2005). These internal elaborations represent functional sources designed to meet specific consumer needs and serve as the foundation for persuasion effects, such as advertising (O'Keefe, 2002). In fact, both academicians and practitioners have been vociferous in singing the praises of the Internet as an interactive medium for informing and persuading consumers. Much of this praise originated from early research touting the effectiveness of banner ads for increasing customer loyalty, brand awareness, and consumer perceptions (Briggs & Hollis, 1997). Certainly, as millions of Internet users continue to venture online every month, it is vital for companies to understand a non-intrusive way of informing and persuading consumers via this channel (Macias, 2003). As a result, the establishment and maintenance of an online presence through a well designed website has become increasingly important to companies and brands with consumers regularly examining product offerings, advertising, and consumer opinions online. For any business to survive in a marketplace this diverse, it must build a sustainable competitive advantage by creating a differential value from its competitors. For this reason, companies are placing an emphasis on increasing the bond between the consumer and brands online by bringing in new 'interactive' elements into this medium.

In addition to advertising, persuasion literature also concerns health communication, political communication, and various non-profit messages aiming to influence attitudes, intentions, and behavior by persuading individuals via mass media. For example, Dahlgren (2005) examines the role of Internet in political communication; Sundar, Kalyanaraman, and Brown (2003) investigated the role of web site interactivity in political campaigns; and several studies looked at the role of Internet in health communication (Cassell, Jackson, & Cheuvront, 1998; Stout, Villegas, & Kim, 2001).

Connecting Persuasion and Presence

In the physical world, we normally generate a mental model of external space from our senses. Likewise, within mediated environments our senses interpret patterns of energy designed to simulate experiences and activate the same automatic perceptual processes (Biocca, 1997). Through the combination of vividness, interactivity, and sensory stimuli, media are able to create a sense of presence in the minds of users within mediated space. An initial and much broader conceptualization of *presence* is as an experience of "being there" in a mediated environment, and early researchers suggest that it is generated from sensory input, mental processes, and past experiences assimilated together in a current state (Steuer, 1992). All media generate a sense of being in another place by bringing the experience and objects closer to us, allowing us indirectly to meet and experience other objects, other people, and the experiences of others. As a result, researchers classify presence as a psychological state originating from attending to and evaluating incoming mediated sensory information (Barfield, Sheridan, Zeltzer, & Slater, 1995; Draper, Kaber, & Usher, 1998). While the illusion of presence may be a product of all media, interactive media are able to generate the most compelling sense of presence (Barfield & Weghorst, 1993).

Lombard and Ditton (1997) describe presence as "the perceptual illusion of non-mediation." In other words, it is the extent to which a person fails to acknowledge the existence of a medium during an artificially mediated experience. Researchers have continued to deconstruct presence across multiple dimensions with two prominent distinctions classified as physical and social presence (Freeman, 1999, Lombard & Ditton, 1997; Skalski & Tamborini, 2007). While the physical dimension refers to the perception of being located in the environment or "being there," the social dimension represents the feeling of being together and communicating with someone, "being with." Social and physical presence are both related in some ways and also meaningfully different in the sense that consumers may experience a high degree of physical presence without the transmission of any kind of reciprocal communicative signals (i.e., social presence). Alternatively, one can experience a high degree of social presence in virtual environments that only supply minimal physical representations, for example, Internet chat rooms (Lessiter, Freeman, Keogh, & Davidoff, 2000). Nevertheless, research has identified factors influencing consumers' responses to websites and suggests that the presence of web-based interactive features lead to enhanced experiences and favorable attitudinal responses among consumers (McMillan, Hwang, & Lee, 2003).

Understanding what presence represents is an important step in conceptualizing the foundation of a theoretical framework. However, this first juncture is primarily descriptive in the sense that it simply reflects an active psychological state experienced from using interactive media. To develop a framework that offers persuasion researchers prescriptive connections, researchers must examine both the antecedents and outcomes of this psychological experience. Most media theories in this regard offer explanations of human behavior via a structure linking individual user characteristics with environmental factors (i.e., media) and situational influences (i.e., experience) that result in observed outcomes (Bandura, 2001). In the following sections, the antecedents and outcomes are detailed as identified from the persuasion literature. Readers should note that presence as examined in relation to persuasion is narrowly limited to advertising and marketing literature in the current chapter. This is not to suggest that the role of presence is only prominent in advertising. There have been numerous other studies that examine the role of presence in, for example, the areas of video games (Ivory & Kalyanaraman, 2007), agent-based persuasion (Skalski & Tamborini, 2007), the treatement of phobias (Hodges et al., 1994; Schuemie et al., 2000), to name a few.

Antecedents

Although the terminology may vary, three broad categories into which the determinants of presence can be classified from are user characteristics, media factors, and situational content. This framework is commonly found in the presence research and parallels other classification schemas that divide the determinants of presence into "external" (objective) and "internal" (subjective) modes (Slater, Steed, McCarthy, & Maringelli, 1998; Slater & Usoh, 1994; Slater & Wilbur, 1997).

User Characteristics

While individual traits and prior experiences are common elements understood to influence media consumption, very little work in the combined areas of persuasion and presence have examined these constructs. Nevertheless, parallels can be drawn that induce presence, which are: (a) a user's perceptual, cognitive, and/or motor abilities; (b) prior experience with media; (c) mood state; and (d) personality traits, such as willingness to suspend belief (Slater & Usoh, 1994; Witmer & Singer, 1998). In addition, relevant individual characteristics are likely to vary depending upon the age and gender of the user (Lessiter et al., 2000; Freeman, Lessiter, & IJsselsteijn, 2001).

Other factors that are likely to play a role in affecting an individual's sense of presence are mental health conditions, such as depression, anxiety, and psychotic disorders (Huang & Alessi, 1999). While consumers with such disorders are not specifically targeted by persuasive messages, these factors do affect an individual's experience of the real world so it is logical that a similar effect would occur during mediated environments. Further, because presence is an experiential state like mood (Sheridan, 1992a, 1992b), there is a possibility of variation within the same individual given the same physical conditions on separate occasions (Lessiter et al., 2000; Freeman et al., 2001).

To understand these variations, researchers have looked into the relationship between presence and individuals who are visually oriented who are more likely to experience presence in a visual environment than users whose primary representation systems are auditory or kinesthetic (Lessiter et al., 2000). The number of actors in a mediated environment may also enhance a sense of presence because we are accustomed to interacting with others in real life situations. As a result, it is expected that the presence of other individuals in a mediated environment should enhance the experience of presence (Steuer, 1992).

Finally, individual levels of skill and efficacy within mediated environments, such as virtual worlds, video games or even the Internet, can also play a role in elevating a consumer's arousal, attention and ability to enter a state of mental consciousness capable of "being there." Hoffman and Novak (1996) characterize this as flow, which has been seen as containing similar properties with presence, and is described as "the state occurring during network navigation, which is characterized by: 1) a seamless sequence of responses facilitated by machine interactivity, 2) intrinsically enjoyable, 3) accompanied by a loss of self-consciousness, and 4) self-reinforcing" (p. 57).

Media Factors

Media factors are broadly divided into two main categories–form and content– each containing multiple influences (Ijsselsteijn, de Ridder, Freeman, & Avons, 2000). Within the media form dimension, two of the most common determinants of presence are how rich in sensory information a medium is, also known as *vividness*, and how *interactive* the medium is. Daft and Lengel (1986) define *media richness* as the potential information-carrying capacity of a communication medium. A medium is considered rich if its information provides a substantial new understanding. Using a broader framework often associated with interactive media, Steuer (1992) defines media richness as the intensity, or vividness, in which a mediated environment is able to present information to the senses. Vivid content stimulates sensory experiences in consumers by evoking memories and previous sensations, which typically results in the generation of mental imagery. Sheridan contends that a media system supporting these elements will make a mediated experience indistinguishable from the real world and thus elicit a high level of presence (Sheridan, 1992a, 1992b, 1996).

How "vivid" or "rich" interactive media are is determined from the clarity and ability of the medium to produce a sensory experience and is generally thought to be more persuasive (Daugherty et al., 2005). For example, Biocca (1992) contends that forms of digital media have the ability to increase both the breadth and depth of a mediated experience, thereby contributing greatly to the level of presence. The implications of such technologies that achieve experiences that are perceptually indistinguishable from real-life experiences blur the distinction between real and represented worlds (Steuer, 1992). Empirical work in this area has shown that presence tends to increase as the fidelity of a reproduction or simulation of the real world increases. The more close a visual representation is to the real world (Ijsselsteijn et al., 1998), and more natural a user's interaction within a mediated system is (Hendrix & Barfield, 1996), have been shown to correlate with the state of presence. Thus, media rich in breadth and depth help facilitate a natural cognitive state that could be potentially beneficial for persuasion. This is because high fidelity representations are also considered less distracting. Furthermore, virtual representations might sometimes exceed direct experience by providing access to information that may not be readily available in real life (Skalski, Tamborini, & Westerman, 2002).

In a recent experimental study, Hopkins, Raymond, and Mitra (2004) found that an increase in media richness indeed elevates the level of perceived presence. This is consistent with previous findings of Coyle and

Thorson (2001) and Klein (2003), both indicating that an increase in presence is a result of an increase in the richness, as well as interactivity, of an online environment. These findings imply that interactive media that utilize elevated levels of sensory information are able to create a heightened sense of presence. Li, Daugherty, and Biocca (2002) have found that rich media in the form of virtual experience advertising is more likely to generate a feeling of presence among consumers. As a result, rich media have the potential to induce presence and generate compelling online experiences. The premise lies in the assumption that messages appealing to multiple perceptual systems are better perceived than those that call on single or fewer perceptual systems, which enhances a sense of presence.

Interactivity

Interactivity is a multidimensional construct often associated with the Internet and has been described as both the ability to communicate with people (person interactivity) and access information (machine interactivity; Hoffman & Novak, 1996). Notable among the many definitions are (a) Rafaeli's (1988) interpersonal view of interactivity, (b) Heeter's (1989) six dimensions of interactivity, (c) Steuer's (1992) three dimensions of interactivity, and (d) Ha and James' (1998) five dimensions of interactivity. As a form of communication, interactivity is measured in terms of the level of responsiveness between users along a continuum ranging from one-way discourse to the reactive interaction of two-way communication (Rafaeli & Sudweeeks, 1997). This perspective acknowledges that interactivity can occur either through a medium or without and is differentiated by the extent to which the communicator and audience facilitate each other's communication needs (Ha & James, 1998).

While interpersonal communication is an important advantage of the Internet compared with traditional media, interface properties and the method in which information is accessed are the most applicable for creating a sense of presence. Thus, the difference between interactivity capable of inducing a sense of presence and two-way communication is that interactivity in this sense is focused on the properties of the mediated environment and the relationship of individuals with that environment, rather than on specific messages, engagement and/or involvement. Three main factors that contribute toward this type of interactivity are speed, range, and mapping, which are characterized as the responsiveness of a medium. Speed refers to the rate at which information can be assimilated into the mediated environment. Range refers to the number of possibilities for action at any given time within the environment, and mapping is the ability of a system to map its controls to changes in the mediated environment in a natural and predictable manner (Steuer, 1992).

Interactive media foster more active participation by users, which can potentially transfer to persuasive messages embedded within, such as forms of advertising. In fact, most basic forms of advertising online allow consumers to choose when and how to interact with such messages. It is the nature of the online medium, meaning interactivity, which allows for greater consumer control over content in addition to the order and duration of persuasive messages consumed. This allowance of choice in turn helps consumers make better purchase decisions, have better product knowledge and memory, and be more confident about their decisions (Ariely, 2000). Most websites employ some form of interactivity, although sites differ on the degree and nature of interactivity employed. For example, Internet retail sites often differ across three dimensions of interactivity—connectedness, information collection, and reciprocal communication (Ha & James, 1998). The degree and nature of this interactivity significantly affects the perceived quality of the websites, but the greater the interactivity the more likely a site will be perceived positively (Ghose & Dou, 1998).

According to Huang (2003), a successful website induces experiential flow through engaging experiences that alter user perceptions of content in a playful and exploratory manner. Consumers who exhibited the highest experiential flow are found to be impacted by varying website designs across both hedonic and utilitarian dimensions. In particular, the level of "flow experience" that consumers feel within a website is closely linked to the level of interactivity (low, medium, or high) present within the website when interactivity is identified as "the extent of information exchange between a website and its users as determined in the conceptual domains of responsiveness, individualization, navigability, reciprocity, synchronicity, participation, and demonstrability" (p. 490). Coyle and Thorson (2001) report similar findings on the positive effects of increasing levels of interactivity within online environments. That is, consumers' perceived presence was enhanced as the level of interactivity in a website increased. In addition, interactive features designed to enhance navigation experiences and create a sense of presence in the minds of consumers are more likely to elicit favorable brand attitudes (Becker-Olsen, 2003; Daugherty, 2009). Given the complex nature of interactivity and its effect on persuasion, most researchers argue for a reconstruction of this function as digital media begin to provide rich consumer experiences (Hoffman & Novak, 1997).

Klein's (2003) research, designed to evaluate the effects of media characteristics on presence, suggests that interactive user control is positively related to the creation of presence. Furthermore, the presence created was found to have a significant positive relationship with persuasion (Klein, 2003). Apart from user control, a variety of other user characteristics play an important role in the determination of presence. In fact, Bezjian-

Avery, Calder, and Iacobucci (1998) define interactivity as the "fundamental ability to control information" (p. 24) and have found that certain forms of interactive advertising are superior to more passive formats common in traditional media. Ariely's (2000) work supports this belief with findings that indicate interactive control causes information to have higher value and a substantially more positive impact on consumers' ability to integrate, remember and understand evaluative judgments when adequate resources are met. Likewise, Lombard and Snyder-Duch (2001) emphasize that the concept of control is central to the idea of interactivity and includes control over not only the amount of information presented but also over the actual composition of that information.

Li and colleagues (2001, 2002, 2003; Daugherty et al., 2008) refer to a more recent conceptualization of user controlled interactive content as a virtual product experience. A virtual product experience provides visual and motor sensory feedback allowing consumers to freely rotate, zoom-in or out, and examine an interactive 3D representation of a product along each axis. This form of product interactivity offers non-immersive user control over many aspects of a simulated product essentially altering the viewing depth and perspective of the object. Furthermore, this degree of interactivity represents a simulation of the consumption experience in the sense that consumers generally learn about most products by examining the visual shape, texture, and perceived function of a product. Compared with traditional product representations online, a virtual experience from 3D product visualization is an active form of product interactivity allowing consumers to directly alter and control the content in a dynamic fashion using a computer mouse. While this form of product interactivity provides the greatest amount of control over the product, additional 3D visualization features such as animation, visual translation and rotation provide varying degrees of control ultimately inducing a strong sense of presence (Li et al., 2001). For instance, passive control allows a limited visual translation of a product through the activation of dynamic animation designed to rotate a product. This type of animation is commonly used to illustrate motion and can be activated by selecting an action button. On the other hand, reactive control provides a degree of visual translation indirectly through mediated interface mechanisms with levers or sliding bars used to control the movement of the object.

The notion of control is extremely pivotal to human behavior and media consumers in particular, especially in light of new media technologies that allow for more control by consumers with regard to content consumption. Past work has connected the control construct with media use. For instance, Schutz (1966) suggests, "three interpersonal needs—inclusion, affection, and control—influence all aspects of communication between people" (in Rubin, 1993, p. 161). Further, Rubin (1993) has linked external control (related to the belief of fate and chance occurrence) with passive audiences and internal control (related to the belief of self-determinism) with active media audiences. In the field of interactive media, Wu (2006) demonstrates that control, as an individual/personality trait, is related to media use. Furthermore, Alpert, Karat, Karat, Brodie, and Vergo (2003) examined the environment of e-commerce and note that the issue of control is pivotal to a consumer's media experience: "the clearest result to emerge from our studies is users' fervent desire to be in control" (Alpert et al., 2003, p. 385). Within the context of interactive media, Liu and Shrum (2002) have developed a theoretical model for interactivity and found that a user's desire for control is also a key factor in obtaining satisfaction from the interactive process. They suggest that people who have a high desirability of control will be more satisfied with interactivity than people who have a low desirability of control. In the case of presence, it is logical to believe a positive linkage exists between not only control factors within interactive media, but also an individual desire to control an experience when consuming forms of media technology.

Situational Content

While the form elements of media play a strong role in stimulating presence, probably one of the oldest determinants is simply the situational element of media content itself. For instance, Sheridan (1992a, 1992b) classifies media content to include objects, actors and events represented by the medium. This classification refers to the overall theme or narrative depicted via the content through either visual or verbal systems (Usoh, et al., 1999; Freeman et al., 2000; Freeman & Avons, 2000). It is the actual content of any media that lead users to immerse themselves in the story and generate mental imagery long before interactive media emerged. Under the right conditions, the content can provide an "escape" from reality with higher levels of immersion resulting in an elevated sense of presence (Slater & Wilbur, 1997). Perhaps this is not surprising considering imagery is very similar to presence in that it is considered a dynamic conscious cognitive process by which sensory information is represented in memory (MacInnis & Price, 1987). Bugelski (1983) describes the process of generating imagery as a neural activity resulting from sensory responses. Thus, external information from the environment is processed through our senses evoking imagery in working memory. The assumption of conscious imagery is that it enables each person to experience internal simulations of thoughts, actions, and/or ideas through vivid and clear mental representations (Marks, 1999). Along the same lines, Green and Brock (2000, 2002) suggest that individuals engage in media such as books by transporting themselves into the narrative world. This transportation into a narrative world appears to provide superior persuasion compared to persuasion that relies on arguments and no mental imagery (Green & Brock, 2002).

Social elements are also strong facets of media content that help facilitate a sense of presence. Meaning, the acknowledgement by the user of others present within media, either virtual or real, is an important determinant of experiencing presence, especially social presence. As such, a user's sense of presence (or social presence) is influenced by media content that presents and promotes interaction among the participants, rather than simply static behavior (Freeman et al., 2001). In this same context, interactivity plays a significant role as the social dynamics of group computer-mediated communication (Rafaeli & Sudweeks, 1997) indirectly influence social presence. Other tools within media content, especially online, that encourage forms of interaction are recommendation agents and comparison matrices. For example, Haubl and Trifts (2000) found that the use of avatars in an online shopping environment impacted both the quality and efficiency of consumer purchase decisions. While it is easy to understand the influences from interactive media, content designed to socially engage the audience is a standard practice used by advertisers for many years by having actors or spokespersons talk directly to the camera as if speaking to the user.

Outcomes

While understanding key antecedents of presence associated with persuasion research is an important step, it unfortunately only represents the first half of the media equation and does not fully explain the media consumption process. To this end, a primary goal of persuasion research is to understand outcomes, or effects of media use. Presence research addressing this area is very limited and the complete effects are somewhat unclear (Lombard & Ditton, 1997). Schuemie, Straaten, Krijn, and Van Der Mast (2001) contend that effects of presence can be classified into three categories: (a) subjective responses (cognitive), (b) sensations and emotions (affective), and (c) task performance (behavioral). Similarly, the effectiveness of consuming persuasive messages is also ascertained from cognitive, affective, and/or behavioral dimensions (Beerli & Santana, 1999; Hutchinson & Alba, 1991; MacInnis & Jarworski, 1989; Petty & Cacioppo, 1981).

Cognitive

In the area of outcomes of presence, one of the frequently mentioned effects is that on cognitive learning. Cognitive measures are used to determine the ability of persuasive media or content to attract attention and ultimately transfer information to memory. This element is fundamental in generating awareness, establishing knowledge, and increasing comprehension of the persuasive messages. The observation of cognition is essential in determining the amount of information an individual has obtained from persuasive content and can be measured from actual knowledge (recall) or perceived knowledge (self-reported) (Bettman & Park, 1980). In the e-commerce literature, Risden et al. (1998) measured recall of product information for web advertisements presented in both interactive and non-interactive situations. Findings from this study suggest that consumers have significantly higher recall of persuasive messages when exposed to an interactive situation. Kim and Biocca (1997) also found that an increased level of presence in consumers led to increased memory for product-relevant information.

While persuasion researchers have often treated forms of online advertising and direct product experiences as two opposing ends of the mediated communication spectrum (Klein, 1998), work has emerged recognizing virtual product experiences, afforded by the experience of presence, are capable of simulating a sense of "being there" within interactive environments (Li et al., 2001, 2002, 2003). Klein (1998) claims that an online experience holds the potential to provide product information much similar in form and comparable to individuals' direct experiences rather than product information obtained via traditional media sources (e.g., radio or television). This makes online experiences, especially those that induce presence through interactivity, similar to that of direct experiences, which are often used in effectiveness comparisons. Fundamentally, it is the interactive and vivid nature of 3D product visualization in these environments that stimulates a consumer's mental processing when experiencing a sensory rich mediated environment. Higgins (1996) refers to this process as an activation of accessible knowledge via salient influences that serve to prime individuals during a stimulus event. Salient experiences in turn are capable of raising attention (Roskos-Ewoldsen & Fazio, 1992), affecting memory (Higgins, Roney, Crowe, & Hymes, 1994), provoking judgments (Higgins & Brendl, 1995), and ultimately influence behavior when information is contextually accessible (Higgins & Chaires, 1980). The implication for individuals experiencing the feeling of presence when examining goods and environments online is that knowledge is made accessible and applicable and thus more likely to have a positive impact on learning, to evaluation and behavior. The result is heightened perception from the experience serving as a simulation heuristic generated from the imagery created (Schlosser, 2003).

Affective

Affect as an outcome is associated with presence and persuasion to identify emotional responses as well as measure individual attitudes toward messages or products. In fact, affective measures are frequently used to identify either established or created attitudes from marketing communication stimuli, with brand attitude serving as the most commonly used effectiveness measure (Fazio, Powell, & Williams, 1989; MacKenzie & Lutz, 1989). A person's attitude represents a psychological tendency, expressed by evaluating a particular object, and can serve various motivations (Eagly & Chaiken, 1993). According to Eastin and Daugherty (2005), the act of consuming media constitutes a deliberate, active behavior in which audiences seek content according to their internal motivations. Thus, the premise behind this effect is based on the belief that persuasive messages that are found to be the most pleasing produce a positive transfer affect and are better received (Mehta, 2000).

By manipulating the sensory saturation of a consumer's visual perception, Kim and Biocca (1997) were able to detect significant differences in confidence levels regarding brand preference. More specifically, the sense of presence resulted in a stronger experience with subjects becoming more confident in their attitudes toward the product information presented. Kim and Biocca (1997) concluded that the virtual experience created by presence simulated a direct experience resulting in increased persuasion. This finding supports previous research that indicates the sense of presence created in a mediated environment will cause a user to believe the experience occurred first hand, resulting in the same effect as direct experience (Lombard, 1995). The most widespread findings so far have been that presence can invoke similar affective reactions and emotions as real life experiences (Li et al., 2001). As a result, the experience of presence significantly influences consumer responses to persuasive messages, with individual level of involvement moderating these affects (Hopkins, Raymond, & Mitra, 2004). Certainly, the importance of individual attitudes and the relevant associated measures have been linked to evaluating the effectiveness of interactive media (Chen & Wells, 1999).

Macias' (2003) work shows that interactivity is an important factor in both a consumer's comprehension of and attitude toward forms of persuasive messages online. Meaning, the better an individual understands an interactive persuasive message, the more positive his or her attitude toward that message or product will be in the end (Macias, 2003). This is consistent with other findings that suggest interactive media lead to more positive attitudes about products and brands advertised.

Behavioral

Finally, media technology researchers in this area of work are generally very cognizant of behavioral responses attributed to presence with a variety of measures serving as desired outcomes. One such variable is time spent with a mediated environment. Undeniably, an expenditure of time is involved each instance any form of media is consumed, and as a result "time" is an important behavioral factor in understanding interactive media and presence. The reason is because when a user chooses to consume media they are making a decision about how to allocate a scarce resource–time. Numerous studies have dealt with understanding the way people make use of their time resources, make time allocation decisions, and choose time consuming activities (McKechnie, 1974; Duncan, 1978; Gronau, 1977). Within consumer psychology, the generally accepted belief is that time allocation decisions are governed by the combination of the temporal activity itself, psychological characteristics, and situational factors (Feldman & Hornik, 1981). In terms of behavioral effects, Babin, Darden, and Griffin (1994) indicate that interactive and entertaining shopping experiences are significantly linked to an increase in time spent within online retailing, amount spent, and impulse purchases. In fact, the goals of many design experiences within interactive media are to impact, involve, and/or enable human interaction as easy as possible in a timely manner (Heeter, 2000). Novak and colleagues have found that individuals are able to experience a state of flow via the Internet because of interactivity and presence, resulting in a loss of self-consciousness during use (Novak, Hoffman, & Yung, 2000). This psychological experience results from media content and is considered intrinsically enjoyable and self-reinforcing (Hoffman & Novak, 1996).

While observing actual behavior via monitoring time spent with a medium is possible, not all desired behavioral outcomes within persuasion research are immediate, so conative measures designed to anticipate a response are often collected. These measures generally involve some type of self-reported task (Brucks, 1985; Hoch & Ha, 1986; Levin & Gaeth, 1988) with the most widely used measure representing intention to purchase (Beerli & Santanal, 1999; Andrews, Akhter, Durvasula, & Muehling, 1992). Indeed, Li et al. (2001, 2002) contend that presence is capable of affecting purchase intention within forms of interactive advertising, and in certain circumstances mediate the relationship between content and behavior. Proponents of presence certainly consider this psychological experience as able to form causal relationships between numerous task performance measures (Welch, 1999). Not surprisingly, Erouglu and colleagues (2001) assert that atmospheric cues within online retailing, such as individual differences and interactivity, do influence behavior outcomes, with each of these factors previously identified as antecedents of presence. In fact, in today's online environment it is argued that the goal of most Internet retailers should be to seek a company's website, spend time there fulfilling their needs, and experience a level of satisfaction from their experience (Coyle & Thorson, 2001). This belief highlights the importance of such a website as the final destination of a consumer's online journey. Unlike portal or search engine sites that mediate and redirect the passage of navigation among consumers, it is critical for a company's website to retain their visitors within the site and keep them from leaving until they obtain what they look for from the site. Inducing a sense of presence within users can help facilitate this process.

Conceptual Model

Based on the literature presented, a theoretical model is proposed (Figure 6.1) with presence resulting from user characteristics, media factors, and situational content that serve to transmit persuasive messages designed to influence cognitive, affective and behavioral outcomes. The foundation of the model is that the experience of presence is capable of facilitating effective forms of persuasive communication. Examining these relationships associated with persuasion and presence allows both academic researchers and media professionals to understand important antecedents for inducing presence, as well as the potential persuasive outcomes associated with this psychological experience. Further, the identification of key variables associated with presence and persuasion is important as interactive media continue to proliferate society with marketing communication messages.

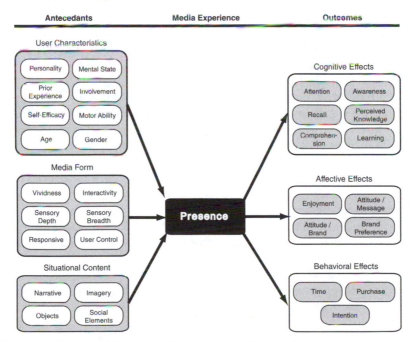

Figure 6.1 Conceptual framework for presence and persuasion.

Conclusions and Future Implications

Never before throughout human history have we experienced the level of media evolution currently encompassing our daily lives. Technological innovations in computers and data transmission have initiated the development of the Internet toward a more multi-sensory medium incorporating high quality visuals, stereo sound, and imagery (Soukup, 2000). Information can now be presented online in mediated virtual environments in which consumers may interact with three-dimensional products, animated graphics, video, and audio. The result is a more dynamic and realistic experience presenting information in an active and engaging environment. User characteristics, media factors, and situational content all have the ability to work together and potentially create compelling experiences rich in stimulating sensations of presence. While mainstream media have moved through lifecycles since their inception, interactive media also represent unlimited potential for delivering persuasive messages. By leading the way, the Internet has emerged as an outlet in which traditional forms of media entertainment have converged to offer users interactive content at the time and place most convenient for them. As a result, media scholars acknowledge that traditional media models may no longer adequately represent digital media (Perry, 2002). These changes signify both an opportunity and need for media scholars to introduce new theoretical frameworks, such as presence, as interactive experiences and immersion become conventional elements associated with digital media.

As a research paradigm, presence is certainly multidisciplinary spanning across numerous academic fields, including communication, advertising, psychology, human-computer interaction, cognitive science, and marketing, among others. While an exhaustive account of the connection between persuasion and presence is beyond the scope of this chapter, an overview of the key areas applicable for how presence is capable of facilitating persuasive messages has been presented. Through examination of both the determinants and effects of presence, work in the area of persuasion will continue to grow. The conceptual model presented represents an initial attempt to draw attention to this important area. As interactive media continue to develop and gain in prominence within society, understanding how individuals are affected by persuasive messages within presence-rich media becomes important for media technology researchers.

Nevertheless, there remains much uncertainty associated with presence and its links to persuasion. Presence, when defined as a subjective sensation, can be a goal in itself for certain applications such as video games and movies (Schuemie et al., 2001). Although the effect of presence on task performance is a controversial area, this area has significant implications for marketing communication professionals, as suggested by Li et al. (2001, 2002, 2003).

Contrary to these findings are those conducted by Bezjian-Avery, Calder, and Iacobucci (1998), which suggest that under certain conditions interactivity actually hinders the persuasion process. For example, users in their study spent less time viewing ads in the interactive system and were less likely to purchase products featured in such systems. These contradictory findings suggest an inverse relationship between interactivity and persuasion. Thus, it is more than likely naïve to always assume positive effects, and the novelty of such environments also warrants critical examination (Edwards & Gangadharbatla, 2001).

Media technology professionals need to understand that the relationship between presence and persuasion is perhaps U-shaped. For instance, playfulness associated with interactivity is often suggested to have detrimental effects on task completion when present in extreme quantities. Meaning, interactive systems may be so fun and enjoyable that users might forget their primary task or objective (Webster, Trevino, & Ryan, 1993). This is in tune with Hoffman and Novak's (1996) claim that too much "flow" results in distraction of consumers from purchase-related behavior. Nevertheless, the general consensus in the persuasion literature is that virtual environments, high in presence levels, are more effective at persuasion than traditional media (Grigorovici, 2003). At a minimum, this indicates we need to better understand the causes and effects of presence on the persuasion process.

Although this chapter has presented what the authors believe are significant research areas associated with persuasion and presence, it is important to note that several areas of substance were not included. Future areas of research exploring presence and persuasion must continue to build on the dominant themes and areas outlined. Specifically, exploring additional user and situational characteristics associated with presence are needed, such as the effects of control and mobile communication. Certainly, interactive media present new and unique opportunities for marketing communication professionals to generate compelling customer experiences that significantly affect the consumer persuasion process. Each of these issues present opportunities for researchers as well as practitioners in the areas of entertainment, virtual reality, ecommerce, advertising, and public health communication. Nonetheless, the purpose of this chapter was simply to introduce persuasion as an area of consideration as scholars continue to rely on interactive media to deliver persuasive messages to consumers.

References

Alpert, S. R., Karat, J., Karat, C., Brodie, C., & Vergo, J. G. (2003). User attitudes regarding a user-adaptive eCommerce web site. *User Modeling and User-Adapted Interaction, 13,* 373–396.

Andrews, J. C., Akhter, S. H., Durvasula, S., & Muehling, D. (1992). The effects of advertising distinctiveness and message content involvement on cognitive and affective responses to advertising. *Journal of Current Issues and Research in Advertising, 14,* 45–58.

Ariely, D. (2000). Controlling the information flow: Effects on consumers' decision making and preferences. *Journal of Consumer Research, 27*(2), 233–249.

Babin, B. J., Darden, W. R., & Griffin, M. (1994). Work and/or fun: Measuring hedonic and utilitarian shopping value. *Journal of Consumer Research, 20*(4), 644–656.

Bandura, A. (2001). Social cognitive theory of mass communication. *Media Psychology, 3,* 265–299.

Barfeld, W., Sheridan, T., Zeltzer, D., & Slater, M. (1995). *Presence* and performance within virtual environments. In W. Barfield &T. Furness III (Eds.), *Virtual environments and avanced interface design* (pp. 473–513). New York: Oxford University Press.

Barfield, W., & Weghorst, S. (1993). The sense of *presence* within virtual environments: a conceptual framework. In G. Salvendy & M. Smith (Eds.), *Human computer interaction: Software and hardware Interfaces* (pp. 699–704). Amsterdam: Elsevier.

Becker-Olsen, K. L. (2003). And now, a word from our sponsor—A look at the effects of sponsored content and banner advertising. *Journal of Advertising, 32*(2), 17–32.

Beerli, A., & Martin Santana, J. D. (1999). Design and validation of an instrument for measuring advertising effectiveness in the printed media. *Journal of Current Issues and Research in Advertising, 21*(2), 11–30.

Bezjian-Avery, A., Calder, B., & Iacobucci, D. (1998). New media interactive advertising vs. traditional advertising. *Journal of Advertising Research, 38*(4), 23–32.

Bettman, J. A., & Park, W. C. (1980). Effects of prior knowledge and experience and phase of the choice process on consumer decision making processes: A protocol analysis. *Journal of Consumer Research, 7,* 234–248.

Biocca, F. (1992). Virtual reality technology: A tutorial. *Journal of Communication, 42*(4), 23–72.

Biocca, F. (1997). Cyborg's dilemma: Progressive embodiment in virtual environments. *Journal of Computer Mediated-Communication, 3*(2). Retrieved May 5, 2002, from www.ascusc.org/jcmc/vol3/issue2/biocca2.html

Briggs, R., & Hollis, N. (1997). Advertising on the web: Is there response before click-through? *Journal of Advertising Research, 37,* 33–45.

Brucks, M. (1985, June). The effects of product class knowledge on information search behavior. *Journal of Consumer Research, 12,* 1–16.

Bugelski, B. R. (1983). Imagery and the thought processes, In A. A. Sheikh (Ed.), *Imagery: Current theory, research, and application* (pp. 72–95). New York: Wiley.

Burke, R. R. (1996). Virtual ahopping: Breakthrough in marketing eesearch. *Harvard Business Review, 74*, 120–131.

Cassell, M. M., Jackson, C., & Cheuvront, B. (1998). Health communication on the Internet: An effective channel for health behavior change? *Journal of Health Communication, 3*(1), 71–79.

Chen, Q., & Wells, W. D. (1999). Attitude toward the site. *Journal of Advertising Research, 39*(5), 27–37.

Coyle, J. R., & Thorson, E. (2001). The effects of progressive levels of interactivity and vividness in web marketing sites. *Journal of Advertising, 30*(3), 65–77.

Dahlgren, P. (2005). The internet, public spheres, and political communication: Dispersion and deliberation. *Political Communication, 22*(2), 147–162.

Daft, R. L., & Lengel, R. H. (1986). Organizational information requirements, media richness and structural design. *Management Science, 32*(5), 554–571.

Daugherty, T. (2009). Need for cognition: Understanding the influence of individual differences on virtual product experiences. *International Journal of Internet Marketing & Advertising, 5*(4), 272–286.

Daugherty, T., Li, H., & Biocca, F. (2005). Experiential ecommerce: A summary of research investigating the impact of virtual experience on consumer learning. In C. Haugtvedt, K. Machleit, & R. Yalch (Eds.), *Online consumer psychology: Understanding and influencing consumer behavior in the virtual world* (pp. 457–490). Mahwah, NJ: Erlbaum.

Daugherty, T., Li, H., & Biocca, F. (2008). Consumer learning and the effects of virtual experience relative to indirect and direct product experience. *Psychology and Marketing, 25*(7), 568–586.

Draper, J. V., Kaber, D. B., & Usher, J. M. (1998). *Telepresence. Human Factors, 40*(3), 354–375.

Duncan, D. J. (1978). Leisure types: Factor analyses of leisure profiles. *Journal of Leisure Research, 10*, 113–125.

Eastin, M. S., & Daugherty. T. (2005). Past, current, and future trends in mass communication. In A. Kimmel (Ed.), *Marketing Communication: Emerging trends and developments* (pp. 23–40). Oxford, UK: Oxford University Press.

Eagly, A. H., & Chaiken, S. (1993). *The psychology of attitudes*. Fort Worth, TX: Harcourt Brace..

Edwards, S. M., & Gangadharbatla, H. S. (2001). The novelty of 3D product presentations online. *Journal of Interactive Advertising, 2*(1). Retrieved from http://www.jiad.org

Erouglu, S. A., Machleit, K. A., & Davis, L. M. (2001). Atmospheric qualities of online retailing: A conceptual model and implications. *Journal of Business Research, 54*, 177–184.

Fazio, R. H., Powell, M. C., & Williams, C. J. (1989). The role of attitude accessibility in the attitude-to-behavior process. *Journal of Consumer Research, 16*, 280–288.

Feldman, L. P., & Hornik, J. (1981). The use of time: An integrated conceptual model. *Journal of Consumer Research, 7*, 407–419.

Freeman, J. (1999). *Subjective and objective approaches to the assessment of presence*. Unpublished doctoral dissertation, University of Essex, Colchester, England.

Freeman, J., Avons, S.E. (2000). Focus group exploration of presence through advanced broadcast services. *Proceedings of the SPIE: Human Vision and Electronic Imaging*, pp. 3959–3976.

Freeman, J. & Avons, S. E. Meddis, R. Pearson, D. E, & IJsselsteijn, W. A. (2000). Using behavioral realism to estimate presence: A study of the utility of postural responses to motion stimuli. *Presence: Teleoperators and Virtual Environments, 9*(2), 149–164.

Freeman, J., Lessiter J., & IJsselsteijn, W. A. (2001). An introduction to *presence*: A sense of being there in a mediated environment. *The Psychologist, 14*, 190–194.

Ghose, S., & Dou, W. (1998). Interactive functions and their impacts on the appeal of internet presence sites. *Journal of Advertising Research, 38*(2), 29–43.

Green, M. C., & Brock, T. C. (2000). The role of transportation in the persuasiveness of public narratives. *Journal of Personality and Social Psychology, 79*, 701–721.

Green, M. C., & Brock, T. C. (2002). In the mind's eye: Transportation-imagery model of narrative persuasion. In M. C. Green, J. J. Strange, & T. C. Brock (Eds.), *Narrative impact: Social and cognitive foundations* (pp. 315–341). Mahwah, NJ: Erlbaum.

Grigorovici, D. (2003). Persuasive effects of *presence*. In G. Riva, F. Davide, & W. A Ijsselsteijn (Eds.), *Immersive virtual environments, being there: Concepts, effects and measurement of user presence in synthetic environments* (pp. 191–207). Amsterdam, The Netherlands: Ios Press.

Gronau, R. (1977). Leisure, home production, and work: The theory of the allocation of time revisited. *Journal of Political Economy, 85*, 1099–1123.

Ha, L., & James, E. L. (1998). Interactivity reexamined: A baseline analysis of early business web sites. *Journal of Broadcasting & Electronic Media, 42*(4), 457–474.

Haubl, G., & Trifts, V. (2000). Consumer decision making in online shopping environmnets: The effects of interactive decision aids. *Marketing Science, 19*(1), 4–21.

Heeter, C. (1989). Implications of new interactive technologies for conceptualizing communication. In J. L. Salvaggio & J. Bryant (Eds.), *Media use in the information age* (pp. 217–235). Hillsdale, NJ: Erlbaum.

Heeter, C. (2000). Interactivity in the context of designed experience. *Journal of Interactive Advertising, 1*(1). Retrieved June 5, 2002, from http://www.jiad.org/vol1/no1/heeter/index.html

Hendrix, C., & Barfield, W. (1996). Presence within virtual environments as a function of visual display parameters. *Presence: Teleoperators and Virtual Environments, 5*(2), 274–289.

Higgins, E. T. (1996). Knowledge activation: Accessibility, applicability, and salience. In E. T. Higgins & A. W. Kruglanski (Eds.), *Social psychology: Handbook of basic principles* (pp. 133–168), New York: Guilford.

Higgins, E. T., & Brendl, M. (1995). Accessibility and applicability: Some "activation rules" influencing judgment. *Journal of Experimental Social Psychology, 31*, 218–243.

Higgins, E. T., & Chaires, W. M. (1980). Accessibility of interrelational constructs: Implications for stimulus encoding and creativity. *Journal of Experimental Social Psychology, 16*, 348–361.

Higgins, E. T., Roney, C., Crowe, E., & Hymes, C. (1994). Ideal versus ought predilections for approach and avoidance: Distinct self-regulatory systems. *Journal of Personality and Social Psychology, 66*, 276–286.

Hoch, S. J., & Ha, Y. W. (1986). Consumer learning: Advertising and the ambiguity of product experience. *Journal of Consumer Research, 13*, 221–233.

Hoch, S. J., & Loewenstein, G. F. (1991). Time-inconsistent preferences and consumer self-control. *Journal of Consumer Research, 17*, 492–507.

Hodges, L., Rothbaum, B. O., Kooper, R., Opdyke, D., Meyer, T., de Graaf, J. J., et al. (1994). *Presence as the defining factor in a VR application* (Technical report GIT-GVU-94-5). Georgia Institute of Technology.

Hoffman, D. L., & Novak, T. L. (1997). A new marketing paradigm for electronic commerce. *The Information Society, 13*, 43–54.

Hoffman, D. L., & Novak, T. P. (1996). Marketing in hypermedia computer-based environments: Conceptual foundations. *Journal of Marketing, 60*, 50–68.

Holbrook, M. B., & Hirschman, E. C. (1982). The experiential aspects of consumption: Consumer fantasies, feelings, and fun. *Journal of Consumer Research, 9*, 132–140.

Hopkins, C., Raymond, M. A., & Mitra, A. (2004). Consumer responses to perceived telepresence in the online advertising environment: The moderating role of involement. *Marketing Theory, 4*(1–2), 137–162.

Huang, M. (2003). Designing website attributes to induce experiential encounters. *Computers in Human Behavior, 19*(4), 425–442.

Huang, M., & Alessi N. E. (1999). Mental health implications for *presence*. *CyberPsychology and Behavior, 2*, 15–18.

Hutchinson, J. W., & Alba., J. W. (1991). Ignoring irrelevant information: Situational determinants of consumer learning. *Journal of Consumer Research, 18*, 325–345.

IJsselsteijn, W. A., de Ridder, H., Freeman, J., & Avons, S. E. (2000). *Presence: Concept, determinants and measurement*. Presented at Photonics West Conference in the Human Vision and Electronic Imaging Division, San Jose, CA, 23–28 Jan., 2000.

Ivory, J., & Kalyanaraman, S. (2007). The effects of technological advancement and violent content in video games on players' feelings of presence, involvement, physiological arousal, and aggression. *Journal of Communication, 57*(3), 532–555.

Kim, T., & Biocca, F. (1997). Telepresence via television: Two dimensions of telepresence may have different connections to memory and persuasion. *Journal of Computer-Mediated Communication, 3*(2).

Kisielius, J., & Sternthal, B. (1984). Detecting and explaining vividness effects in attitudinal judgments. *Journal of Marketing Research, 21*, 54–64.

Kisielius, J., & Sternthal, B. (1986). Examining the vividness controversy: An availability-valence interpretation. *Journal of Consumer Research, 12*, 418–431.

Klein, L. R. (1998). Evaluating the potential of interactive media through a new lens: Search versus experience goods. *Journal of Business Research, 41,* 195–203.

Klein, L. R. (2003). Creating virtual product experiences: The role of telepresence. *Journal of Interactive Marketing, 17*(1), 41–55.

Krugman, H. E. (1965). The impact of television advertising: Learning without involvement. *Public Opinion Quarterly, 29,* 349–356.

Lessiter, J., Freeman, J., Keogh, E., & Davidoff, J. (2000). *Development of a new cross-media presence questionnaire: The ITC-sense of presence.* Paper presented at the *Presence* 2000 workshop, Techniek Museum, Delft, 27–28, March, 2000.

Levin, I., & Gaeth, G. J. (1988r). How consumers are affected by the graming of attribute information before and after consuming the product. *Journal of Consumer Research, 15,* 374–378.

Li, H., Daugherty, T., & Biocca, F. (2001). Characteristics of virtual experience in e-commerce: A protocol analysis. *Journal of Interactive Marketing, 15*(3), 13–30.

Li, H., & Daugherty, T., & Biocca, F. (2002). Impact of 3-D advertising on product knowledge, brand attitude, and purchase intention: The mediating role of presence. *Journal of Advertising, 31*(3), 43–58.

Li, H., Daugherty, T., & Biocca, F. (2003). The role of virtual experience in consumer learning. *Journal of Consumer Psychology, 13*(4), 395–405.

Liu, Y., & Shrum, L. J. (2002). What is interactivity and is it always such a good thing? Implications of definition, person, and situation for the influence of interactivity on advertising effectiveness. *Journal of Advertising, XXXI*(4), 53–64.

Lombard, M. (1995). Direct responses to people on the screen: Television and personal space. *Communication Research, 22*(3), 288–324.

Lombard, M., & Ditton, T. (1997). At the heart of it all: The concept of presence. *Journal of Computer Mediated Communication, 3*(2). Retrieved from http://www.ascusc.org/jcmc/vol3/issue2/lombard.html

Lombard, M., & Snyder-Duch, J. (2001). Interactive advertising and presence: A framework. *Journal of Interactive Advertising, 1*(2). Retrieved June 15, 2002, from http://www.jiad.org

McKechnie, G. E. (1974). The psychological structure of leisure: Past behavior. *Journal of Leisure Research, 6,* 27–35.

Macias, W. (2003). A beginning look at the effects of interactivity, product involvement and web experience on comprehension: Brand web sites as interactive advertising, *Journal of Current Issues and Research in Advertising, 25*(2), 31–44.

MacInnis, D. J., & Price, L. L. (1987). The role of imagery in information processing: Review and extensions. *Journal of Consumer Research, 13,* 473–491.

MacKenzie, S. B., & Lutz, R. J. (1989). An empirical examination of the structural antecedents of attitude toward the ad in an advertising pretesting context. *Journal of Marketing, 53,* 48–65.

Marks, D. F. (1999). Consciousness, mental imagery and action. *British Journal of Psychology, 90*(4), 567–585.

McMillan, S. J., Hwang, J. S., & Lee, G. (2003). Effects of structural and perceptual factors on attitude toward the website. *Journal of Advertising Research, 43,* 400–409.

Mehta, A. (2000). Advertising attitudes and advertising effectiveness. *Journal of Advertising Research, 40*(3), 67–72.

Novak, T. P., Hoffman, D. L., & Duhachek, A. (2003). The influence of goal-directed and experiential activities on online flow experiences. *Journal of Consumer Psychology,* 13(1/2), pp. 3–16.

Novak, T. P., Hoffman, D. L., & Yung, Y. F. (2000). Modeling the flow construct in online environments: A structural modeling approach. *Marketing Science,* 19(1), 22–42.

O'Keefe, D. J. (2002). *Persuasion theory and research.* Thousand Oaks, CA: Sage.

Paivio, A. (1986). *Mental Representations: A dual coding approach.* New York: Oxford University Press.

Perry, D. K. (2002). *Theory and research in mass communication: Contexts and consequences* (2nd ed.). Mahwah, NJ: Erlbaum.

Petty, R. E., & Cacioppo, J. T. (1981). *Attitudes and persuasion: Classic and contemporary approaches.* Dubuque, IA: William C. Brown.

Rafaeli, S. (1988). Interactivity: From new media to communication, In R. P. Hawkins, J. M. Wiemann, & S. Pingree (Eds.), *Sage annual review of communication research: Advancing communication science,* 16 (pp. 110–134). Beverly Hills, CA: Sage.

Rafaeli, S., & Sudweeks, F. (1997). Networked interactivity. *Journal of Computer-Mediated Communication,* 2(4). Retrieved June 10, 2002, from http://www.ascusc.org/jcmc/vol2/issue4/rafaeli.sudweeks.html

Risden, K., Czerwinski, M., Worley, S., Hamilton, L., Kubiniec, J., Hoffman, H., Mickel, N., & Loftus, E. (1998). Interactive advertising: Patterns of use and effectiveness. In C. M. Karat, A. Lund, J. Coutaz, & J. Karat (Eds.), *Proceedings of the ACM CHI — Human Factors in Computing Systems Conference,* April 18–23 (pp. 219–224). Los Angeles, CA: Association for Computing Machinery.

Roskos-Ewoldsen, D. R., & Fazio, R. H. (1992). On the orienting value of attitudes: Attitude accessibility as a determinant of an object's attraction of visual attention. *Journal of Personality and Social Psychology,* 63(2), 198–211.

Rubin, A. M. (1993). The effect of locus of control on communication motivation, anxiety, and satisfaction. *Communication Quarterly,* 41, 161–171.

Schlosser, A. E. (2003). Experiencing products in a virtual world: The role of goals and imagery in influencing attitudes versus intentions. *Journal of Consumer Research,* 30, 184–198.

Schutz, W. C. (1966), *The interpersonal underworld.* Palo Alto, CA: Science and Behavior Books.

Schuemie, M. J., Bruynzeel, M., Drost, L., Brinckman, M., de Haan, G., Emmelkamp, P. M. G., et al. (2000). Treatment of acrophobia in virtual reality: A pilot study. In F. Broeckx & L. Pauwels (Eds.), *Proceedings of the Euromedia 2000* (pp. 271–275), May 8–10 in Antwerp, Belgium. Ostend, Belgium: EUROSIS – ETI Publications.

Schuemie, M. J., Straaten P. V., Krijn, M., & Van Der Mast, C. (2001). Research on presence in VR: A survey. *Journal of Cyberpsychology and Behavior,* 4(2), 183–201.

Sheridan, T. B. (1992a). Musings on telepresence and virtual presence, telepresence. *Presence: Teleoperators and Virtual Environments, 1,* 120–126.

Sheridan, T. B. (1992b). Defining our terms. *Presence: Teleoperators and Virtual Environments, 1*(2), 272–274.

Sheridan, T. B. (1996). Further musings on the psychophysics of presence. *Presence: Teleoperators and Virtual Environments, 5,* 241–246.

Simons, H. W. (1976). *Persuasion: Understanding, practice and analysis.* Reading, MA: Addison-Wesley.

Skalski, P., & Tamborini, R. (2007). The role of social presence in interactive agent-based persuasion. *Media Psychology, 10*(3), 385–413.

Skalski, P., Tamborini, R., & Westerman, D. (2002). *The Development of scripts through virtual environments.* Paper presented at the 88th annual meeting of the National Communication Association, New Orleans, LA.

Slater, M., & Wilbur S. (1997). A Framework for Immersive Virtual Environments (FIVE): Speculations on the role of presence in virtual environments. *Presence: Teleoperators and Virtual Environments, 6*(6), 603–616.

Slater, M. & Usoh, M. (1994). Body Centered Interaction in Immersive Virtual Environments. In Thalmann & Thalmann (Eds.) *Artificial Life and Virtual Reality* (pp. 125–147). Chichester, UK: Wiley.

Soukup, C. (2000). Building a theory of multi-media CMC. *New Media & Society, 2*(4), 407–425.

Steuer, J. (1992). Defining virtual reality: Dimensions determining telepresence. *Journal of Communication, 42*(4), 73–93.

Stout, P. A., Villegas, J., & Kim, H. (2001). Enhancing learning through use of interactive tools on health-related websites. *Health Education Research, 16*(2), 721–733.

Sundar, S., Kalyanaraman, S., & Brown, J. (2003). Explicating web site interactivity: Impression formation effects in political campaign sites. *Communication Research, 30*(1), 30–59.

Usoh, M., Arthur, K., Whitton, M. C., Bastos, R., Steed, A., Slater, M., & Brooks Jr., F. P. (1999). Walking > Walking-in-Place > Flying in Virtual Environments. In *Proceedings of SIGGRAPH.* (pp. 359–364). Los Angeles, CA: Association for Computing Machinery.

Webster, J., Trevino, L. K., & Ryan, L. (1993). The dimensionality and correlates of flow in human-computer interactions. *Computers in Human Behavior, 9,* 411–426.

Welch, B. (1999). How can we determine if the sense of presence affects task performance? *Presence: Teleoperators and Virtual Environments, 8*(5), 574–577.

Witmer, B. G., & Singer, M. J. (1998). Measuring presence in virtual environments: A presence questionnaire. *Presence: Teleoperators and Virtual Envrionments, 7*(3), 225–240.

Wu, G. (2006). Conceptualization and measuring the perceived interactivity of websites. *Journal of Current Issues and Research in Advertising, 28,* 87–104.

Chapter 7

Telepresence and Media Entertainment

Tilo Hartmann, Christoph Klimmt, and Peter Vorderer

Most popular media have become popular because they offer opportunities for entertainment. The majority of television programming worldwide serves entertainment purposes, radio's favorite content is popular music, and the best-sold print media are novels such as *Harry Potter*. Clearly, there is a close connection between media popularity and entertainment content (see chapters 1 and 5, this volume). Most of these entertainment media have always tried to facilitate a sense of presence in their users, and their communicators either implicitly or explicitly regarded this kind of experience as condition for successful entertainment. Television, for instance, has invented different form and content elements (e.g., reality-based programming; Nabi, Biely, Morgan, & Stitt, 2003) that are intended to bring the depicted events as close as possible to viewers. Successful authors such as J.K. Rowling have been applauded for their imagination-stimulating language and their ability to create a whole fictional world in readers' inner eyes. So the connection between entertainment and Presence has been important to popular media for a long time, and advancements in media technology such as high definition television continue this history of conjunction (Bracken, 2005). The relationship between media enjoyment and a sense of Presence is probably even more pronounced in next generation entertainment media, especially video games (Vorderer & Bryant, 2006) which nicely mirror early visions of interactive, multimodal, three-dimensional virtual environments (e.g., Minski, 1980; Steuer, 1992).

In this chapter, we elaborate on the link between Presence and media entertainment. While there are relevant bodies of literature on the theory of Presence (e.g., Lee, 2004; Lombard & Ditton 1997; Wirth et al., 2007) and on entertainment theory (Vorderer & Bryant, 2006; Vorderer, 2003), only few conceptual bridges between them have been built so far (Klimmt & Vorderer, 2003; Green, Brock, & Kaufman, 2004; Sherry, 2004; Vorderer & Hartmann, 2009). To advance this conceptual integration, we first outline fundamentals of media entertainment theory and then discuss links between Presence and entertainment in detail.

Finally, we draw conclusions on future entertainment media and directions for a better empirical integration of Presence and entertainment research.

Conceptualizing Presence: "Being There" and With Others

Presence has been used as an umbrella term for different experiences. The shared characteristic of all addressed experiences is that users are considered to be temporarily less aware or unaware of the mediated origin of their experience (ISPR, 2001). Instead, users perceive media content as an "apparent reality" (Zillmann, 2006, p. 218). This chapter draws on the prominent distinction of Spatial Presence and Social Presence. In addition, we consider a third class of Presence-phenomena that covers users' involvement (Wirth, 2006), transportation (Green, Brock, & Kaufman, 2004), and flow (Sherry, 2004).

Spatial Presence

In short, Spatial Presence refers to a user's "feeling of being there" in the mediated environment (Biocca, 1997; Sheridan, 1992; Riva, Davide, & Ijsselsteijn, 2003; Lee, 2004). It can be defined as "a binary experience, during which perceived self-location and, in most cases, perceived action possibilities are connected to a mediated spatial environment, and mental capacities are bound by the mediated environment instead of reality" (Wirth et al., 2007, p. 497; Slater, 2002). Typical technological determinants of Spatial Presence are the degree of interactivity of a mediated spatial environment, the breadth of human sensory channels addressed by the environment, and the naturalness of provided spatial information across sensory channels (Biocca, 1997; Steuer, 1992). Typical user-based determinants are a person's interest in and attention to the mediated spatial environment, user's arousal level (Baumgartner, Valco, Esslen, & Jancke, 2006), and his or her cognitive-spatial abilities (Wirth et al., 2007).

Social Presence

Social Presence can be defined as a "sense of being together" with one or more other social beings, although the others are not physically present (Bente, Rüggeberg, & Krämer, 2005; Biocca, Harms, & Burgoon, 2003; Blascovich et al., 2002; Schroeder, 2002). Social Presence includes a feeling of co-awareness and mutually adapted interpersonal behavior (Biocca et al., 2003). Social Presence may be also accompanied by the natural normative underpinnings of interpersonal encounters. For example, research by Yee, Bailenson, Urbanek, Chang, and Merget (2007) suggests that under conditions of Social Presence users tend to apply the same interpersonal norms as in real-world situations. Based on this and related findings, researchers suggested that intense experiences of Social Presence may result in a stronger adherence to norms, which in turn may lead to less playful and care-free behaviors than in parasocial encounters in which users stay aware of the mediated nature of the other (Reeves & Nass, 1996; Hartmann, 2008). Among the most often named determinants of Social Presence are "eye-gazing" and other addressing verbal or non-verbal behavior of mediated others (Bente, Krämer, & Eschenburg, 2008). Drawing on ideas of Mar and Macrae (2006), it may be further speculated that to create a sense of Social Presence, an entity must be perceived as an intentional agent that seems capable to observe the current behavior of a user and to interactively adapt to it.

Other Experiences of Non-Mediation

Researchers in various disciplines suggested different terms for phenomena that can be regarded as sensations of Presence as well. In this chapter, we focus on involvement (Wirth, 2006), transportation (Green, Brock, & Kaufman, 2004), and flow (Sherry, 2004, Csíkszentmihályi, 1990). All three phenomena have in common that the quality that is experienced as non-mediated is less specifically conceptualized than the spatial sensation in Spatial Presence or the social sensation in Social Presence. Rather, all three phenomena deal with a general sensation "to get lost in" or "to get absorbed by" mediated content. *Involvement* can be understood as the responsiveness of users' cognitive, affective, and behavioral processes to the "apparent reality" offered by a media content: "During media exposure, involvement is understood as the perceived connection between an individual and the mass media content on the one hand, and the degree to which the individual interacts psychologically with a medium or its message, on the other" (Wirth, 2006, pp. 200–201). Accordingly, involved users do not think and feel about a media message, but within a media message (Liebes & Katz, 1986; Tan, 1996; Vorderer, 1993). Involvement is said to depend strongly on a user's interest in the content, and the resulting attention allocation. In a similar fashion, *transportation* is defined as the "phenomenological experience of being absorbed in a story" (Green, Garst, & Brock, 2004, p. 167). In contrast to Social Presence or Spatial Presence, transportation requires a narrative. Similar to involved users, transported users "see the action of a story unfolding before them" (Green, Garst, & Brock, 2004, p. 168). As Green, Garst, and Brock (2004) point out, transportation builds strongly on how much users find a narrative plausible, which in turn also depends on how much they are willing and able to suspend any disbelief. *Flow*, in turn, is understood as an intrinsically pleasurable experience that users can experience if clearly defined tasks imposed by a media environment match exactly their skills (Sherry, 2004; Sweetser & Wyeth, 2005). If this is the case, users will neither feel bored (too easy tasks), nor frustrated (too complicated tasks), but may get lost in the interaction with the media environment.

In sum, the concept of Presence circles around the idea that users temporarily believe in the apparent reality provided by a media offering. Users may believe in an apparent spatial or social reality, or they may simply lose focus on the actual reality. In general, both automatic and voluntary processes seem to trigger the sensation of Presence. Users may automatically respond to content-factors, i.e., cues provided by the media that accurately mimic natural cues, giving rise to a feeling that "this is real" (Schubert, 2009; Skalski, Lange, Tamborini & Shelton, 2006). In addition, users may also be motivated to get lost in an apparent reality (user-factors). Accordingly, they may spend effort to maintain a belief in the world presented by a medium.

The distinction between automatic and voluntary processes in the formation of Presence warrants further discussion. Media offerings vary in their immersive capabilities (Witmer & Singer, 1998) and thus in their potential to automatically trigger Presence. Highly immersive technologies foster Presence in two ways, by displaying meaningful and natural cues and by limiting user's possibilities to withdraw attention (Witmer & Singer, 1998). Natural depictions may automatically create sensations of an apparent reality (Schubert, 2009; Zillmann, 2006). It may be hard, if not impossible, for users to fully suppress such natural sensations. A simple drawing of a three-dimensional cube may always lead to the perception of depth, for example, although everybody knows that this is just a mediated illusion. In a similar fashion, more complex spatial sceneries, if accurately displayed, may automatically induce a feeling of Spatial Presence, just like simple social cues (e.g., eye-gazing) can automatically trigger a feeling of Social Presence (Bente et al., 2008). Users may be as successful to regulate such immediate sensations of apparent reality as they are in regulating other highly automatic processes, like preventing a sneeze, for example. Still, if users are *motivated* to regulate their Presence experiences, some opportunities exist (Schramm & Wirth, 2008; Zillmann, 2006). One regulation strategy is that users simply start to recall that "this is not real", maybe by switching to a critical reception mode and by starting to identify inaccuracies in the depiction. Such a strategy may be less successful, however, the more media content becomes immersive and accurate, convincing and believable (Witmer & Singer, 1998). Imagine a user being placed in the totally immersive and believable holodeck envisioned in *Star Trek*: Recalling that "this is not real" would not be a very effective strategy to suppress or modify upcoming sensations of apparent reality. However, users of most contemporary media technologies are still able to return to reality quite easily, simply by withdrawing attention. Turning to another stimulus, closing eyes, shutting ears are simple but powerful strategies for users to disrupt the feeling of apparent reality. In sum, the more immersive an application, the more powerful it may be in automatically establishing a sense of Presence. At the same time, the more immersive the application, the more voluntary effort users need to invest to regulate their induced feeling of Presence.

Conceptualizing Media Entertainment

Experiences of entertainment have most often been described as positive feelings (Vorderer & Bryant, 2006; Vorderer & Hartmann, 2009; Klimmt & Vorderer, in press). Of what nature these feelings are is still under discussion, though, as over the past 10 to 15 years both communication science and media psychology have developed various conceptualizations that try to identify, differentiate and elaborate these emotional responses more specifically.

There seems to be some a growing consensus, however, that media users feel entertained if they manage two things, to regulate physiological homeostasis and to enhance their personal capabilities (self-enhancement or personal growth; Vorderer & Hartmann, 2009; Zillmann, 1988). The regulation of physiological homeostasis deals with users' balance-keeping of various bodily resources, including arousal and mood (Zillmann, 1988). Physiological imbalance is aversive, and restoring balance by "exploiting" the effect of environmental stimuli provides pleasurable relief. Self-enhancement, in turn, is about people's growth of personal skills and capabilities, i.e., learning (Ryan & Deci, 2000). Driven by curiosity and interest (Silvia, 2006), people voluntarily enter "unknown territory," i.e., engage in risky challenges or encounter puzzling incongruities, to enhance their abilities. Self-enhancement may often come at the cost of physiological resources (e.g., depletion of voluntary resources, loss of physical energy, a lowered mood; Baumeister, Bratslavsky, Muraven, & Tice, 1998). But the mastery of challenges or the resolution of incongruities is also often deeply satisfying (Ryan & Deci, 2000; Vorderer, Steen, & Chan, 2006; Ryan, Rigby, & Przybylski, 2006). In sum, it can be argued that people "exploit" environmental stimuli, including available media environments, to maintain both physiological homeostasis and personal growth.

Research from the Psychology of emotions suggest that both mechanisms are hierarchically organized: regulation of physiological imbalance seems to be of primary concern; people only engage in "risky" personal growth activities if they have sufficient resources to stand a failure (mood-as-a-resource; Raghunathan & Trope, 2002; broaden-and-build theory of emotion, Fredrickson, 2004). Only with necessary resources ready at hand, people engage in challenges. For example, a positive mood urges people to engage in playful and adventurous exploratory behavior (Fredrickson, 2004). People may also "invest" positive mood to learn about self-threatening but highly relevant issues (Raghunathan & Trope, 2002). With respect to media entertainment, people may thus feel entertained by a media stimulus, because it provides pleasurable relief, i.e., restores imbalanced physiological resources, but they may also feel entertained, because the stimulus provides interesting challenges (Vorderer & Hartmann, 2009). A feeling of being entertained may become complex, if the media stimulus is both painfully demanding but also deeply gratifying (Oliver, 2008). A shocking horror movie, a suspenseful video game, or a irritating book, for example, may come at the cost of physiological resources and may even foster negative emotions. At the same time, however, these costs seem to be accepted or even appreciated by the user as a reasonable spending in the light of his or her challenge-seeking or perception of mastery of challenges (c.f., re-appraisals or meta-emotions; Bartsch, Vorderer, Mangold, & Viehoff, 2008; Oliver, 2008; Schramm & Wirth, 2008).

Linking Presence and Entertainment

One of the most striking overlaps between Presence and entertainment is that users need to believe in a media-induced reality if they want to feel entertained and if they want to feel present (Klimmt & Vorderer, 2003; Wirth, 2006; Green, Garst, & Brock, 2004). Accordingly, some researchers argue that a sensation of Presence is actually a prerequisite of entertainment (Vorderer & Hartmann, 2009) or that Presence is just entertaining in itself (Green, Brock, & Kaufman, 2004; Sherry, 2004). In contrast to the reception of art, which has been traditionally considered to be appreciated "from a distance" (Cupchik, 2002), the reception of media entertainment offerings has been typically characterized by a user's lack of distance and heightened involvement (Vorderer, 1993). Past empirical research shows that Presence and entertainment experiences are indeed highly correlated sensations (Green, Garst, & Brock,, 2004; Hartmann & Klimmt, 2005; Tamborini & Skalski, 2006; Sherry, 2004; Lombard, Reich, Grabe, Bracken, & Ditton, 2000; Ravaja et al., 2006; Skalski et al., 2006).

Causal Relationships between Presence and Entertainment

Several causal links between Presence and entertainment may underlie their positive correlation (Figure 7.1). Both phenomena may only cor-

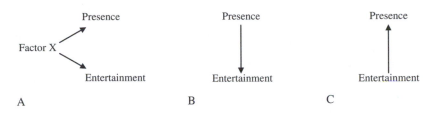

Figure 7.1 Possible causal relationships between Presence and entertainment experiences.

relate, because they build on the same factors (A), like, for example, user's attention allocation. It may be also fun in itself, however, to get lost in a media environment. A sensation of Presence may thus directly enhance users' entertainment experience (B). Vice versa, users may get lost in a media environment more easily, because they feel entertained. Accordingly, users' entertainment experience may influence the sensation of Presence (C).

To prove direct causal influences between Presence and entertainment (see B and C in Figure 7.1), one needs to show that either one or the other constructs precedes the other in time (Figure 7.2). For example, it may be argued that users of a virtual environment quickly establish a feeling of Presence, which then supports a more slowly developing entertainment experience (c.f., Zillmann, 2006). Vice versa, users could initially start to enjoy a medium, which then supports the formation of Presence.

As the analytic approach shows, possible causal relations between Presence and entertainment may underlie the found correlation between both phenomena. However, the analysis also shows that it is a difficult challenge to analytically and empirically disentangle *specific* causal relations. Literature and empirical research that conceptually linked and empirically examined both constructs is growing, but still rare (e.g., Green, Brock, & Kaufman, 2004; Hartmann & Klimmt, 2005; Tamborini & Skalski, 2006; Sherry, 2004; Lombard, Reich, Grabe, Bracken, &

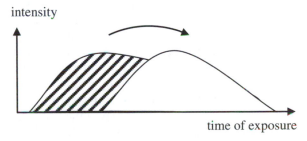

Figure 7.2 Causal influence of either Presence (shaded area) preceding entertainment (white area) in time, or entertainment (shaded area) preceding the formation of Presence (white area).

Ditton, 2000; Ravaja et al., 2006; Skalski et al., 2006; Lombard & Ditton, 1997). Because of the preliminary status of the field, a discussion of the specific causal relations between both constructs can easily become speculative. We will therefore reduce complexity in the remainder of the chapter. Drawing on past literature, we will primarily discuss general reasons why Presence and entertainment may be interrelated, but we will only marginally speculate about specific causal relationships.

Potential Factors Underlying the Correlation of Presence and Entertainment

Automatic Natural Perceptions Presence and entertainment both appear to build on natural depictions, which *automatically* trigger the sensation of an apparent reality. A display of accurate spatial or social cues, as well as a natural mapping of users' input (Skalski et al., 2007), seems to effectively trigger Presence experiences (Wirth et al., 2007). Even fictional narratives can incorporate depictions that evoke such natural perceptions (Oatley, 1999; Zillmann, 2006). Natural cues may not only foster Presence, but also users' entertainment experiences. Vorderer and Hartmann (2009) argue that entertainment conveys feelings of enjoyment and interest. According to appraisal theories of emotion, emotions result from the detection and evaluation of *relevant* stimulus events (Scherer, 2005; Smith & Kirby, 2001). Enjoyment and interest should therefore particularly occur during media exposure if the events depicted in the media are relevant to the user (Silvia, 2008). If users do not perceive any relevant stimulus events in the media, they likely remain unaffected by the depiction. Therefore, it may be argued that things are emotionally more significant if they are *accurately* displayed in the media, than if they are depicted in an inaccurate manner (i.e., contain errors or inconsistencies). First, depictions that do not conform to natural occurrences could result in a quick discounting of immediate emotional responses, as their artificiality becomes clear (Zillmann, 2006). Second, media depictions that depart from naturalistic sensations, like modern art, will also most likely result in a psychologically distant user (Cupchik, 2002). Users that are psychologically distant perceive the media content as external observers. They stay aware of the mediated nature of the stimulus, tend to approach it in an analytical manner, and do not affectively respond to events happening within the mediated world (Tan, 1996; Vorderer, 1993). That is, while perceiving the same media offering, the psychologically distant user may subjectively perceive quite different events than an involved user, namely less relevant emotion-eliciting stimulus events. Accordingly, entertainment experiences of uninvolved users may be weakened.

In sum, a display of natural cues therefore seems to promote both entertainment and Presence. Examples of technology applications that seem to apply this principle are plenty. A popular example is *Shrek-4D*, a movie attraction at Universal theme parks that features an original 3-D film, plus an extra dimension of special effects like drops of water splashed in the faces of the viewers, wobbling movie chairs leading to a sensation of gravity, etc. The only empirical study we know of, however, that examined all three constructs at a time has been conducted by Skalski et al. (2006). The study shows that a natural mapping of users' input in a video racing game (steering wheel instead of keyboard) indeed increases both Spatial Presence and game enjoyment.

Attention Allocation and Interest   A related similarity of Presence and entertainment is that both build on approach behavior (cf. Tamir & Diener, 2008). Approach behavior includes users' motivation to process the media content by paying attention. Interest can be an emotion that drives approach behavior and attention allocation, especially if individuals encounter unknown or unfamiliar things (Silvia, 2008). As Silvia (2008, p. 58) puts it: "Interest attracts people to new, unfamiliar things, and many of these things will turn out to be trivial, capricious, dangerous, or disturbing.... Interest is thus a counterweight to feelings of uncertainty and anxiety."

Interest in new and unfamiliar worlds of a media offering seems to guide people's attention allocation. Interest may thus ensure that people stay connected to the ongoing presentation of the media offering. Research has shown that users' attention allocation, in turn, precedes and accompanies Presence experiences (Wirth et al., 2007; Draper, Kaber, & Usher, 1998). An attention focus reduces user's processing of external information that else could undermine the emergence of Presence. An attention focus also ensures that Presence-evoking cues are readily perceived by a user. The same applies for entertainment, which requires and promotes attention to the stimulus as well. For example, if people do not pay sufficient attention, they may miss an important part of a joke or any other potentially enjoyable narrative or presentation. Accordingly, they may feel less entertained.

Escapism   Users may not only be motivated to process a media offering, they may sometimes have the specific motivation that a media offering induces a sensation of apparent reality. That is, users may be especially interested to be stimulated by media offerings that accurately mimic real-world stimuli. A related motivation has been addressed as "escapism" in Communication Research (Henning & Vorderer, 2001; Katz & Foulkes, 1962; Moskalenko & Heine, 2003). According to Katz and

Foulkes (1962), people turn to fictional media content in order to forget about their troubling life situation. In a similar fashion, Moskalenko and Heine (2003) show that television is an "effective stimulus to direct the focus away from oneself and to render people less aware of how they are falling short of their standards" (p. 76). Research by Henning and Vorderer (2001) further demonstrates that some people escape to the media particularly to avoid situations where they have nothing else to do, because such "unfilled" situations would urge them to engage in thinking. In sum, good evidence exists that people sometimes escape to the media to avoid or alleviate noxious experiences (see also Zillmann, 1988, 2000).

Existing conceptualizations of escapism are not really specific about the type of Presence troubled people seek from the media, however. People escape to the media to block their previous noxious moods or thoughts (Zillmann, 1988). People thus successfully escape already if they get involved and manage to distract themselves. They do not need to establish a feeling of Spatial Presence or Social Presence. Escapism therefore seems to be primarily related to involvement; and only due to involvement it is related to more sophisticated forms of Presence, like Spatial or Social Presence.

Escapism can also be linked to entertainment, although this link is not entirely clear, either. It may be argued that a relief from noxious states already establishes a feeling of entertainment. In other words, people may feel entertained, because they successfully distract themselves from existing problems (Zillmann, 1988). In sum, one way to link escapism, Presence and entertainment experiences is that people try to escape their real-life problems by engaging in distracting media offerings. If the offerings are indeed involving and noxious states are successfully blocked, people can experience pleasurable relief, which may be considered a form of entertainment (Zillmann, 1988).

An opposing argument, however, is that reducing pain or other noxious states through media use does not suffice in evoking entertainment (cf. Vorderer & Hartmann, 2009). From this perspective pain relief may be indeed pleasurable, but a feeling of entertainment may require more than the absence of negative experience. Presence, escapism, and entertainment may be linked, because if media users reach a state of Presence (for instance, a strong sensation of being present in the video game world where the player *is* a war hero), this experience may mark a perfect escape from troublesome real-life circumstances (for instance, a state of humiliation and lack of social importance), as the mediated self-experience contrasts the real-life experience. Thus, not only the social forces that caused the trouble in reality are blocked away from users' cognitions, emotions, and behavior, but users also escape towards a world that is beneficial in itself. From this perspective, escapism would not only be enjoyable as people get away from troubling life situations, but also, because they arrive in entertaining mediated worlds. Such a perspective seems to be shared by Green, Garst, and Brock (2004) who show that transportation and enjoyment strongly correlate, obviously independent of noxious states or troublesome life situations people are in. Accordingly, they argue that transportation can be considered a general desirable state, sought out by individuals on a regular basis.

Suspension of Disbelief   Next to escapism, suspension of disbelief has been highlighted as another motivational process in both Presence and entertainment research (Green, Brock, & Kaufman, 2004; Lombard & Ditton, 1997; Wirth et al., 2007). A users' disbelief in an apparent reality may be fostered by irritating, inaccurate, or inconsistent information provided by a medium. A willing suspension of disbelief, in turn, supports the maintenance of an existing Presence experience (Böcking, 2008; Green, Garst, & Brock, 2004; Wirth et al., 2007). Suspension of disbelief may therefore be linked to entertainment experiences as well. If users are forced to disbelieve in a media offering, they start to approach it from an analytical, and often critical perspective (Vorderer, 1993). As discussed above in the context of natural cues displayed by a medium, users may become emotionally less responsive to the events depicted by a medium, if they approach it from a critical perspective. Thus, their entertainment experience may be weakened. A willing suspension of disbelief, however, could help to maintain the illusion of an apparent reality and to keep the user involved. Users' suspension of disbelief may thus foster both entertainment and Presence experiences (Klimmt & Vorderer, 2003).

An applied example of this type of connection between media enjoyment and Presence are fictional video games. The successful Jedi Knight games that are related to the *Star Wars* series (cf., Pena & Hancock, 2006) are an example. The science-fiction context of these games puts combat action onto fictional planets, with fantasy weapons, magic (The Force), and continuous, striking contradictions to the laws of physics. At the same time, these game offer internally consistent 3D environments that can facilitate a sense of Spatial Presence. Players—especially fans of the *Star Wars* universe—are likely to suspend their disbelief concerning the differences between the reality of the game world and the actual reality in order to achieve pleasurable states such as the joy of parasocial closeness to admired characters or feelings of curiosity when exploring spaceships known from the movies. With this high readiness to tolerate special, social, physical, etc., problems in the game, it is highly likely that players of Star Wars shooter games enter a sense of Presence as consequence of their wish to maintain enjoyment. By fulfilling a user-related requirement of entertainment—suspension of disbelief—game players pave the way for Presence experiences to co-occur with pleasure.

Arousal   Another important factor underlying both entertainment and Presence seems to be *arousal*. Several studies suggest that arousal may foster Presence experiences (Baumgartner et al., 2006; Dillon, Keogh, Freeman, & Davidoff, 2000; Lombard et al., 2000). Baumgartner et al. (2006) provide neuropsychological evidence that arousal is positively correlated to Presence experiences (respective to related brain activities). Participants either watched an exciting or monotonous rollercoaster ride simulated on a computer. Users watching the exciting rollercoaster ride had both stronger arousal and feelings of Presence (and related brain activity) than did users watching the monotonous rollercoaster ride. The result suggests that users in a high state of arousal may tend to forget about the mediated nature of their experiences more easily.

Arousal has been considered an integral part of entertainment as well (Zillmann, 1991). Arousal underlies any suspenseful media content like movies, soccer matches, or dramatic novels (Vorderer, Wulff, & Friedrichsen, 1996). According to excitation-transfer theory (e.g., Zillmann, 1991), arousal is key to euphoria, which is aversive distress (high arousal, negative labeling) being converted into pleasurable eustress (high arousal, positive labeling). Euphoria, in turn, has been linked to the enjoyment of all kinds of dramatic narratives that result in a happy-ending, like distressing movies or video games, or close sport contests with a good ending (Zillmann, 1991).

Arousal may thus accompany both Presence and entertainment experiences (Schubert, 2009). Indeed, research by Lombard et al. (2000) shows that viewing bigger image sizes (due to bigger screens and/or smaller viewing distances) leads to a heightened arousal level of onlookers, as well as to stronger senses of Presence and enjoyment. Ravaja et al. (2006) examined users' responses of playing video games against human opponents versus the computer. The study shows that "playing against another human elicited higher Spatial Presence, [...] physiological arousal, as well as more positively valenced emotional responses" (p. 327) than playing against the computer. In sum, both studies provide evidence that arousal, Presence, and entertainment experiences are indeed related phenomena.

Conclusion   In sum, the review of the theoretical and empirical literature on Presence and entertainment shows that no approach exists so far that systematically conceptualized and examined the causal relationships between both constructs. The diversity of existing phenomena that are subsumed under the umbrella term "Presence" makes it difficult to develop such an integrative account. However, researchers already conceptualized and empirically tested links between entertainment and some of the *specific* Presence phenomena, especially transportation (Green, Brock, & Kaufman, 2004) and flow (Sherry, 2004). With respect to flow experiences this may be less surprising, as flow has been *defined* as an intrinsically pleasurable experience. By definition, flow is entertaining.

In contrast, the definition of transportation does not entail pleasurable experiences. As Green, Garst, and Block (2004) argue, people may become fully engaged in a story without necessarily enjoying it. Still, transportation and enjoyment tend to be highly correlated. They explain the correlation by drawing on similar factors as the ones discussed above. Like transportation, conceptualizations of Spatial Presence and Social Presence also do include enjoyment or entertainment experiences. Still, both Presence experiences seem to be positively correlated with entertainment. Again, the factors discussed in this section: natural cues, user's interest, attention allocation, arousal, and motivation to believe, may explain this correlation.

Direct Mutual Effects between Presence and Entertainment

So far, we highlighted factors that potentially underlie the positive relationship between Presence and entertainment. Less has been said, however, about how these factors may be embedded in causal relationships between Presence and entertainment (cf. Figure 7.1). For example, whereas users' willing suspension of disbelief seems to foster both Presence and entertainment, it may be that users first feel present and then suspend disbelief, giving rise to a feeling of entertainment (Zillmann, 2006), or, vice versa, that users feel entertained and thus motivated to suspend disbelief, giving rise to a feeling of Presence (see Figure 7.2). As argued above, sketching the exact causal relationships between both constructs is difficult and, given that research on this topic is still rare, necessarily leads to speculative assumptions. Still, we think some general speculations on how Presence may directly affect entertainment, and entertainment may directly affect Presence, are worthwhile.

Presence Fosters Entertainment Entertainment may become more likely, after users entered a state of Presence. Several researchers have argued that Presence, especially Spatial Presence, is a binary state (Slater, 2002; Vorderer, 1993; Wirth et al., 2007). Users can be either present or not present. Users that feel present probably start to perceive and experience things displayed by a medium differently than users that do not feel to be present. If users feel present, the formation of entertainment may be affected by their altered perception.

If users feel present, they allocate their attention onto the media stimulus, their sensory channels primarily perceive input generated by the media technology, and they tend to incorporate incoming information into their overall belief that "this is true." In such a state, several of the factors discussed in the previous section may be pronounced, increasing the likelihood that users feel entertained. For example, the media environment may become emotionally more significant. For instance, immediate dangers (like a displayed spider or snake) may be initially perceived as real dangers, and even more abstract or symbolic threats (like an upcoming nuclear strike) may be less critically reflected and more immediately perceived. Accordingly, users may become more aroused and excited, which holds the potential to increase their overall entertainment.

A major difference between entertainment and Presence experiences exists, however. Presence seems to increase the more users get involved and immersed in a medium. In contrast, it only requires a certain involvement for users to be entertained. For an optimal entertainment experience, users may sometimes need to regulate their emotions that are automatically induced while they are in an involved mode. If emotions get too intense, they may counteract enjoyment. If emotions get aversive (e.g., panic caused by an approaching snider), users need to be able to break the illusion and to distance themselves in order to regulate their emotions and to maintain their entertainment experience (Schramm & Wirth, 2008; Vorderer & Hartmann, 2009). Therefore, some media offerings that display highly accurate cues may trigger Presence, but diminish entertainment. At the same time, there may be many situations when entertainment is intensified when Presence is *reduced*—at least temporarily.

For instance, television stations hope to intensify affective audience responses to sports broadcasts by delivering high definition images (HDTV) that are much more rich in details, natural, and perceptually impressive (Bracken, 2005). Such displays may not only promise to increase Presence, but also viewer enjoyment, because they may trigger stronger arousal and excitement, for example, in broadcasted sport contests (Zillmann, Bryant, & Sapolsky, 1989). At the same time, however, a dramatic match presented in HDTV may increase moments where excitement gets exceedingly high, and even aversive, urging users to manage their arousal level. Consequently, users may actively reduce their sensation of Presence, to keep their arousal on a pleasurable level and to maintain their entertainment experience.

Entertainment Fosters Presence   If users start to feel entertained by a medium, they may more readily accept it to be further drawn into the mediated world. Again, several of the factors discussed in the previous section may be pronounced, due to a rising feeling of entertainment.

Building on motivational concepts of media entertainment such as mood management theory (Zillmann, 1988) or the concept of entertainment as play (Klimmt & Vorderer, 2009; Steen & Owens, 2001; Vorderer, 2003), it can be argued that people display a strong preference to enter and sustain pleasurable states. Zillmann (1988) refers to this motivational disposition as hedonic premise; in positive psychology, reaching and holding a state of well-being is construed as fundamental human motivation (Kahneman, Diener, & Schwarz, 1999). For the present research issue, these general motivational considerations imply that once media users experience enjoyment, they will in many cases intend to continue this state and to avoid shifts to less pleasurable conditions. Viewers of a television comedy who feel exhilarated during the first five minutes are likely to continue exposure, for instance, and players of video games who have acquired sufficient skill to be successful will continue game play in order to capitalize on their abilities in terms of fun (e.g., Klimmt, 2003).

Positive experiences facilitated by an entertaining medium may increase the likelihood that events portrayed by the medium are perceived to be relevant. A media message may thus become more interesting to media users, because it facilitates enjoyment. An interesting message, in turn, intensifies users' readiness to continue exposure. Continuation of exposure implies attention allocation to the message; that is, people focus their information processing resources on the message as long as they find it relevant and interesting (e.g., Lang, 2000). Continuation of exposure with sustained or even increased attention, in turn, ensures that those natural spatial or social cues that facilitate a sense of Presence are readily perceived by the user.

Entertained users may also engage more in playful and exploratory behavior. According to the broaden-and-build theory of positive emotions (e.g., Fredrickson, 2004), positive emotions broaden and expand an individual's attention and mind-set. Joy, for example, creates an urge to play, to push the limits, and to become creative. Accordingly, users that enjoy an interactive media offering may be more willing to play around with certain features, to test out new things, and to explore the environment. Via exploratory behavior, users may become more engaged. Presence experiences may thus be fostered or further intensified.

The intention to prolong and protect media enjoyment may also strengthen users' willingness to suspend any disbelief. If media users adjust their mode of media information processing in order to preserve enjoyment, they may more readily tolerate inconsistencies (Green, Garst, & Brock, 2004). Thus, the likelihood that Presence experiences emerge from further message processing substantially increases. If media users actively and tolerantly consume the entertainment message, they also utilize Presence-relevant content (e.g., descriptions of a building in a novel) in a constructive, benevolent manner—they let the message establish a sense of Presence in their mind. A non-critical mode of information processing that may results from the desire to maintain media enjoyment could render Spatial or Social Presence follow-up consequences of (initial) entertainment experiences (Green, Garst, & Brock, 2004).

Conclusion

First-hand impressions of how most popular media work render the assumption of integral connections between Presence and entertainment experiences more than obvious. Much contemporary development in media entertainment technology (such as HDTV, or graphics cards for PC gaming) seems to pursue an increase in audience experiences of Presence as route towards more or more sustainable enjoyment. From a theoretical perspective, however, the systematic elaboration of how these two concepts are interrelated is much more complex, which is caused by several reasons. One is the diversity of entertainment experiences (e.g., Klimmt & Vorderer, 2009); some modes of media enjoyment will be affected by Presence, others will not. Some of them may affect Presence, others may not. Moreover, the emergence of Presence depends on a broad range of media and user characteristics, and depending on the model of Presence one intends to apply (e.g., Lee, 2004; Schubert, 2009; Wirth et al., 2007), the conceptual elements where entertainment can be connected are different. Finally, interrelations between Presence and entertainment are likely to be technologically and psychologically specific for different popular media: Such connections may operate primarily though visual-perceptual processes in HDTV, user-medium interaction in video games, and involved imagination when reading a fictional story (see the "book problem" in Presence research in Schubert & Crusius, 2002), for instance.

The present chapter has discussed the relationship between Presence and entertainment at a general level and has, for the reasons mentioned, found only modest clarity concerning causal and temporal dependencies between the two concepts. More specific insight may be achieved if Presence and entertainment processes are elaborated on with a focus on a specific media message delivered through a specific media technology. For such smaller units of conceptualization, one specific theory of media entertainment may be applicable that allows to define the relationship between Presence and entertainment with more precision and predictive clarity to guide empirical investigations. For instance, crime drama presented in HDTV would be a case where Presence could be linked to entertainment evoked through psychological mechanisms explicated by affective disposition theory (Zillmann, 2006). Social presence with media characters could then be discussed in terms of how it affects the social-emotional viewer responses to the media characters that drive the entertainment experience. For such specific settings, less generalizable, but more detail-rich construals of links between Presence and entertainment are likely to be emerge in future research on popular media.

While case-based theory connection remains a task for future work, the present chapter concludes that Presence and entertainment share various conceptual roots and/or characteristics. Both can only emerge if sufficient user motivation is available, and both depend on compatibility between media factors and user attributes, including skills, expectations, and thematic knowledge. There are also various lines of theory that support the assumption of Presence in general being a pathway towards entertainment, either because of causal facilitation of enjoyment or by dependence of both experiential processes from the same determinants.

At the general level of elaboration that has been pursued in this chapter, then, a conceptual vision of cyclic dependencies between Presence and entertainment seems to be the logical conclusion. Such a vision can be substantiated by discussing different cases of Presence and entertainment, collecting empirical evidence, and drawing generalized conclusions of how this cyclic dependency becomes manifest across different popular media technologies, message types, users, and situations of media use. In sum, the link between Presence and entertainment, as obvious and intuitive as it may appear, needs further conceptual work and empirical exploration before every-day observations and intuition can be replaced by solid theory with explanatory and predictive power.

References

Bartsch, A., Vorderer, P., Mangold, R., & Viehoff, R. (2008). Appraisal of emotions in media use: Toward a process model of meta-emotion and emotion regulation. *Media Psychology, 11*, 7–27.

Baumeister, R. F., Bratslavsky, E., Muraven, M., & Tice, D. M. (1998). Ego depletion: Is the active self a limited resource? *Journal of Personality and Social Psychology, 74*(5), 1252–1265.

Baumgartner, T., Valco, L., Esslen, M., & Jancke, L. (2006). Neural correlate of spatial presence in an arousing and non-interactive virtual reality: An EEG and psychophysiology study. *Cyberpsychology & Behavior, 9*, 30–45.

Bente, G., Krämer, N. C., & Eschenburg, F. (2008). Is there anybody out there? In E. A. Konijn, S. Utz, M. Tanis, & S. B. Barnes (Eds.), *Mediated interpersonal communication* (pp. 131–157). New York: Routledge.

Bente, G., Rüggeberg, S., & Krämer, N. C. (2005). Virtual encounters. Creating social presence in net-based collaborations. In M. Slater (Ed.), *Proceedings of the 8th International Workshop on Presence* (pp. 97–102). London: University College.

Biocca, F. (1997). The cyborg's dilemma: progressive embodiment in virtual environments. *Journal of Computer-Mediated Communication, 3*(2). Retrieved from http://jcmc.indiana.edu/vol3/issue2/biocca2.html

Biocca, F., Harms, C., & Burgoon, J. (2003). Toward a more robust theory and measure of social presence: Review and suggested criteria. *Presence: Teleoperators and Virtual Environments, 12*(5), 456–480.

Blascovich, J., Loomis, J., Beall, A., Swinth, K., Hoyt, C., & Bailenson, J. N. (2002). Immersive virtual environment technology as a methodological tool for social psychology. *Psychological Inquiry, 13*, 103–124.

Böcking, S. (2008). *Grenzen der Fiktion? Von Suspension of Disbelief zu einer Toleranztheorie für die Filmrezeption* [Boundaries of fiction]. Köln, Germany: von Halem Verlag.

Bracken, C. C. (2005). Presence and image quality: The case of high-definition television. *Media Psychology, 7*(2), 191–206.

Csíkszentmihályi, M. (1990). *Flow: The psychology of optimal experience.* New York: Harper and Row.

Cupchik, G. C. (2002). The evolution of psychical distance as an aesthetic concept. *Culture & Psychology, 8*(2), 155–187.

Dillon, C., Keogh, E., Freeman, J., & Davidoff, J. (2000). *Aroused and immersed: The psychophysiology of presence.* Paper presented at the 3rd Annual International Workshop on Presence, Delft, The Netherlands.

Draper, J. V., Kaber, D. B., & Usher, J. M. (1998). Telepresence. *Human Factors, 49*(3), 354–375.

Fredrickson, B. L. (2004). The broaden-and-build theory of positive emotions. *Philosophical Transactions of the Royal Society London, 359*, 1367–1377.

Green, M. C., Brock, T. C., & Kaufman, G. F. (2004). Understanding media enjoyment: The role of transportation into narrative worlds. *Communication Theory, 14*, 311–327.

Green, M. C., Garst, J., & Brock, T. C. (2004). The power of fiction: Determinants and boundaries. In L. J. Shrum (Ed.), *The psychology of media entertainment* (pp. 161–176). Mahwah, NJ: Erlbaum.

Hartmann, T. (2008). Parasocial interaction and paracommunication with new media characters. In E. A. Konijn, S. Utz, M. Tanis, & S. B. Barnes (Eds.), *Mediated interpersonal communication* (pp. 177–199). New York: Routledge.

Hartmann, T., & Klimmt, C. (2005). Ursachen und Effekte Parasozialer Interaktionen im Rezeptionsprozess: Eine Fragebogenstudie auf der Basis des PSI-Zwei-Ebenen-Modells [Causes and effects of parasocial interactions]. *Zeitschrift für Medienpsychologie, 17*(3), 88–98.

Henning, B., & Vorderer, P. (2001). Psychological escapism: Predicting the amount of television viewing by need for cognition. *Journal of Communication, 51*, 100–120.

ISPR. (2001). What is Presence? Retrieved from http://www.temple.edu/ispr/frame_explicat.htm

Kahneman, D., Diener, E., & Schwarz, N. (Eds.). (1999). *Well-being: The foundations of hedonic psychology.* New York: Sage.

Katz, E., & Foulkes, D. (1962). On the use of the mass media as "escape": Clarification of a concept. *The Public Opinion Quarterly, 26*(3), 377–388.

Klimmt, C. (2003). Dimensions and determinants of the enjoyment of playing digital games: A three-level model. In M. Copier & J. Raessens (Eds.), *Level Up: Digital Games Research Conference* (pp. 246–257). Utrecht, The Netherlands: Faculty of Arts, Utrecht University.

Klimmt, C., & Vorderer, P. (2003). Media psychology "is not yet there": introducing theories on media entertainment to the presence debate. *Presence: Teleoperators and Virtual Environments, 12*(4), 346–359.

Klimmt, C., & Vorderer, P. (in press). Media entertainment. In C. Berger, M. Roloff, & D. Roskos-Ewoldsen (Eds.), *Handbook of Communication Sscience* (2nd ed.). London: Sage.

Lang, A. (2000). The information processing of mediated messages: A framework for communication research. *Journal of Communication, 50*, 46–70.

Lee, K. M. (2004). Presence, explicated. *Communication Theory, 14*(1), 27–50.

Liebes, T., & Katz, E. (1986). Patterns of involvement in television fiction: A comparative analysis. *European Journal of Communication, 1*, 151–171.

Lombard, M., & Ditton, T. B. (1997). At the heart of it all: The concept of presence. *Journal of Computer-Mediated Communication, 3*(2). Retrieved from http://jcmc.indiana.edu/vol3/issue2/lombard.html

Lombard, M., Reich, R. D., Grabe, M. E., Bracken, C. C., & Ditton, T. B. (2000). Presence and television: The role of screen size. *Human Communication Research, 26*, 75–98.

Mar, R. A., & Macrae, C. N. (2006). Triggering the intentional stance. In G. Bock & J. Goode (Eds.), *Empathy and Fairness* (pp. 110–119). Chichester, England: Wiley.

Minsky, M. (1980). Telepresence. *Omni*, June, 45–51.

Moskalenko, S., & Heine, S. J. (2003). Watching your troubles away: Television viewing as a stimulus for subjective self-awareness. *Personality and Social Psychology Bulletin, 29*(1), 76–85.

Nabi, R. L., Biely, E. N., Morgan, S. J., & Stitt, C. R. (2003). Reality-based TV programming and the psychology of its appeal. *Media Psychology, 5*(4), 303–330.

Oatley, K. (1999). Why fiction may be twice as true as fact: Fiction as cognitive and emotional simulation. *Review of General Psychology, 3*, 101–117.

Oliver, M. B. (2008). Tender affective states as predictors of entertainment preference. *Journal of Communication, 58*, 40–61.

Pena, J., & Hancock, J. T. (2006). An analysis of socioemotional and task communication in online multiplayer video games. *Communication Research, 33*(1), 92–109.

Raghunathan, R., & Trope, Y. (2002). Walking the tightrope between feeling good and being accurate: Mood as a resource in processing persuasive messages. *Journal of Personality & Social Psychology, 83*(3), 510–525.

Ravaja, N., Saari, T., Turpeinen, M., Laarni, J., Salminen, M., & Kivikangas, M. (2006). Spatial Presence and emotions during video game playing: Does it matter with whom you play? *Presence: Teleoperators and Virtual Environments, 15*(4), 381–392.

Reeves, B., & Nass, C. I. (1996). *The media equation: How people treat computers, television, and new media like real people and places*. Stanford, CA: CSLI Publications.

Riva, G., Davide, F., & IJsselsteijn, W. (Eds.). (2003). *Being there: Concepts, effects and measurement of user presence in synthetic environments*. Amsterdam: IOS Press.

Ryan, R. M., & Deci, E. L. (2000). Self-determination theory and the facilitation of intrinsic motivation, social development, and well-being. *American Psychologist, 55*, 68–78.

Ryan, R. M., Rigby, S., & Przybylski, A. (2006). The motivational pull of video games: A Self-Determination Theory approach. *Motivation and Emotion, 30*, 344–360.

Scherer, K. (2005). What are emotions? And how can they be measured? *Social Science Information, 44*, 695–729.

Schramm, H., & Wirth, W. (2008). A case for an integrative view on affect regulation through media usage. *Communications: The European Journal of Communication Research, 33*(1), 27–46.

Schroeder, R. (2002). Social interaction in virtual environments: Key issues, common themes, and a framework for research. In R. Schroeder (Ed.), *The social life of avatars: Presence and interaction in shared virtual environments* (pp. 1–18). London: Springer-Verlag.

Schubert, T. (2009). A new conception of Spatial Presence: Once again, with feeling. *Communication Theory, 19*(2), 161–187.

Schubert, T. W., & Crusius, J. (2002). Five theses on the book problem. Presence in books, film, and VR. In F. R. Gouveia & F. Biocca (Eds.), *Proceedings of the fifth international workshop on Presence* (pp. 53–59). Porto, Portugal: Universidad Fernando Pessoa.

Sheridan, T. B. (1992). Defining our terms. *Presence: Teleoperators and Virtual Environments, 2*, 272–274.

Sherry, J. L. (2004). Flow and media enjoyment. *Communication Theory, 14*(4), 328–347.

Silvia, P. J. (2006). *Exploring the psychology of interest.* New York: Oxford University Press.

Silvia, P. J. (2008). Interest — the curious emotion. *Current Directions in Psychological Science, 17*(1), 57–60.

Skalski, P., Lange, R., Tamborini, R., & Shelton, A. (2007). *Mapped-quest: Natural video game controllers, presence, and game enjoyment.* Paper presented at the 57th Annual Conference of the International Communication Association, San Francisco.

Slater, M. (2002). Presence and the sixth sense. *Presence: Teleoperators and Virtual Environments, 11*(4), 435–439.

Smith, C. A., & Kirby, L. D. (2001). Toward delivering on the promise of appraisal theory. In K. R. Scherer, A. Schorr, & T. Johnstone (Eds.), *Appraisal processes in emotion: Theory, methods, research* (pp. 121–138). New York: Oxford University Press.

Steen, F. F., & Owens, S. A. (2001). Evolution's pedagogy: An adaptionist model of pretense play and entertainment. *Journal of Cognition and Culture, 1*(4), 289–321.

Steuer, J. (1992). Defining virtual reality: Dimensions determining telepresence. *Journal of Communication, 42*(4), 73–93.

Sweetser, P., & Wyeth, P. (2005). Game flow: A model for evaluating player enjoyment in games. *ACM Computers in Entertainment, 3*(3), 1–24.

Tamborini, R., & Skalski, P. (2006). The role of presence in the experience of electronic games. In P. Vorderer & J. Bryant (Eds.), *Playing video games. Motives, responses, and consequences* (pp. 225–240). Mahwah, NJ: Erlbaum.

Tamir, M., & Diener, E. (2008). Approach-avoidance goals and well-being: One size does not fit all. In A. J. Elliot (Ed.), *Handbook of approach and avoidance motivation* (pp. 415–430). Mahwah, NJ: Erlbaum.

Tan, E. S. (1996). *Emotion and the structure of narrative film. Film as an emotion machine.* Mahwah, NJ: Erlbaum.

Vorderer, P. (1993). Audience involvement and program loyalty. *Poetics. Journal of Empirical Research on Literature, the Media and the Arts, 22,* 89–98.

Vorderer, P. (2003). Entertainment theory. In J. Bryant, D. R. Roskos-Ewoldsen, & J. Cantor (Eds.), *Communication and emotion: Essays in honor of Dolf Zillmann* (pp. 131–154). Mahwah, NJ: Erlbaum.

Vorderer, P. & Bryant, J. (Eds.). (2006). *Playing video games: Motives, responses, and consequences.* Mahwah, NJ: Erlbaum.

Vorderer, P., & Hartmann, T. (2009). Entertainment as media effect. In J. Bryant & M.B. Oliver (Eds.), *Media effects: Advances in theory and research* (3rd ed., pp. 532–550). New York: Routledge.

Vorderer, P., Steen, F. F., & Chan, E. (2006). Motivation. In J. Bryant & P. Vorderer (Eds.), *Psychology of entertainment* (pp. 3–18). Mahwah, NJ: Erlbaum.

Vorderer, P., Wulff, H. J., & Friedrichsen, M. (Eds.). (1996). *Suspense: Conceptualizations, theoretical analyses, and empirical explorations.* Hillsdale, NJ: Erlbaum.

Wirth, W. (2006). Involvement. In J. Bryant & P. Vorderer (Eds.), *Psychology of entertainment* (pp. 199–213). Mahwah, NJ: Erlbaum.

Wirth, W., Hartmann, T., Boecking, S., Vorderer, P., Klimmt, P., Schramm, H., et al. (2007). A process model of the formation of spatial presence experiences. *Media Psychology, 9,* 493–525.

Witmer, B. G., & Singer, M. J. (1998). Measuring presence in virtual environments: A presence questionnaire. *Presence: Teleoperators and Virtual Environments, 7*(3), 225–240.

Yee, N., Bailenson, J. N., Urbanek, M., Chang, F., & Merget, D. (2007). The unbearable likeness of being digital: The persistence of nonverbal social norms in online virtual environments. *CyberPsychology & Behavior, 10*(1), 115–121.

Zillmann, D. (1988). Mood management: Using entertainment to full advantage. In L. Donohew, H. E. Sypher, & E. T. Higgins (Eds.), *Communication, social cognition, and affect* (pp. 147–171). Hillsdale, NJ: Erlbaum.

Zillmann, D. (1991). Television viewing and physiological arousal. In B. J. & D. Zillmann (Eds.), *Responding to the screen: reception and reaction process* (pp. 103–133). Hillsdale, NJ: Erlbaum.

Zillmann, D. (2000). Basal morality in drama appreciation. In I. Bondebjerg (Ed.), *Moving images, culture, and the mind* (pp. 53–63). Luton, England: University of Luton.

Zillmann, D. (2006). Dramaturgy for emotions from fictional narration. In J. Bryant & P. Vorderer (Eds.), *Psychology of entertainment* (pp. 215–238). Mahwah, NJ: Erlbaum.

Zillmann, D., Bryant, J., & Sapolsky, B. S. (1989). Enjoyment from sports spectatorship. In J. H. Goldstein (Ed.), *Sports, games, and play: Social and psychological viewpoints* (pp. 241–278). Hillsdale, NJ: Erlbaum.

Chapter 8

Telepresence and Media Effects Research

Paul D. Skalski, James Denny, and Ashleigh K. Shelton

It was just when the Martians were spraying the people at Grovers Mill with the heat ray. At first we couldn't believe it was happening but it was so real...

(Koch, 1970, p. 90)

The above quote could be that of a person who had just visited some exciting, futuristic virtual environment, or someone who had recently played the latest high-definition video game. But in reality, as any media scholar might guess, it comes from a college student who had listened to the *War of the Worlds* radio broadcast at a party on Halloween Eve, 1938. This famous incident of millions of Americans being panicked by a radio dramatization highlights the power of the mass media to affect audiences, which has received a great deal of scholarly attention. The scientific study of media effects has a rich history dating back to investigations of such high-profile phenomena as World War II propaganda (Hovland, Lumsdaine, & Sheffield, 1949) and the *War of the Worlds* broadcast itself (Cantril, 1940). Although this early research did not include the concept of telepresence, it seems plausible that telepresence played a key role, for example, in the fright reactions observed following the "invasion from Mars." Radio listeners who were especially frightened may have felt more "in" the invasion (spatial presence) or "with" Martians (social presence), causing them to be more fearful of the broadcast. The concept of telepresence has the potential to help explain fright reactions such as these as well as a host of other media effects, making it a valuable consideration for media scholars and anyone else interested in the ability of presence to affect outcomes of technology use.

This chapter focuses on the potential for telepresence to influence media effects that have received recurring attention in the mass communication literature. Beyond the role of telepresence in entertainment and persuasion covered in the two prior chapters, theory and empirical evidence suggests that telepresence may also affect other important outcomes of media exposure, such as aggression and fear. Although research linking telepresence to these areas is scant compared to that on enjoyment and persuasion, this chapter discusses the likely relationship between telepresence and media theory and illustrates how the concept may shape outcomes of media exposure in three prominent content domains: violent media, frightening media, and sexual media/pornography. The goal of this chapter is to highlight the importance of the concept of telepresence in empirical considerations of media effects, both negative and positive.

Media Theory and Telepresence

How do media affect people? Although individual studies can identify important variables in this process, such as telepresence, nothing helps to advance knowledge better than theory. Good theories help to explain and predict empirical phenomenon as well as generate new hypotheses, thereby advancing science (Chaffee & Berger, 1987). As Kurt Lewin (1951) famously put it, "there is nothing so practical as a good theory" (p. 169). In the area of mass communication, several theories have been formulated over the years in an effort to elucidate the various influences media may have on audiences.

The first major "theory" of media effects, although never formally stated, has become known as the *magic bullet* (or *hypodermic needle*) *model of mass communication* (Sparks, 2006). This perspective emerged in the early twentieth century as a result of the dual emergence of mass society and mass media, the latter of which was viewed by some as dangerous and a threat to social order (Lowery & DeFleur, 1995). In line with this thinking, the idea behind magic bullet/hypodermic needle theory was that the media messages could "shoot" or "inject" mass audiences with direct and powerful effects on their thoughts and behaviors. This perspective treated media users as uniform and undifferentiated, and it seemed supported by early studies like the Payne Fund Studies of film (e.g., Blumler, 1933) and aforementioned research on the *War of the Worlds* radio broadcast (Cantril, 1940). The grim view of magic bullet theory was that media affected everyone the same and could be used to control the masses if it got into the wrong hands. However, later research such as the People's Choice study (Lazarsfeld, Berelson, & Gaudet, 1948), which showed the media had a weak influence on voting behavior, largely debunked this idea and pointed to more limited or subtle effects, paving the way for considerations of moderating variables such as telepresence.

Indeed, more recent media theories have adopted a more sophisticated view that takes the medium, message, audience, and type of effect into account in determining the extent to which people are affected (Sparks,

2006). Cultivation theory, for example, which emerged in the late 1960s, suggested that television messages may influence viewer perceptions of social reality, with the effect being strongest among heavier viewers and those who have real-world experience with the content (Gerbner, Gross, Morgan, Signorielli, & Shanahan, 2002). Other, functional approaches to mass communication such as parasocial interaction (Horton & Wohl, 1956) and uses and gratifications (Katz, Blumler, & Gurevitch, 1974) called attention to the idea that the way in which we experience media is important (Tamborini, 2000). Instead of treating audiences as passive like magic bullet theory, functional theories view audience members as more active in determining the effects media have on them. The move to an active view of audiences is supported in media research meta-analyses, which clearly demonstrate that certain types of individuals or situations are associated with particular effects (Allen & Casey, 2007).

The notion of an "active audience" has taken on new meaning in recent years due to technological advances such as interactivity. Moreover, as Tamborini (2000) points out, "with technology's promise to blur the distinction between reality and virtual reality to a point where we can no longer take for granted our ability to separate the two, researchers have been forced to focus their attention on subtle differences in the complex process of media experience" (p. 11). The primary way in which this has happened is through considerations of telepresence, "the perceptual illusion of nonmediation" (Lombard & Ditton, 1997), and related concepts such as spatial presence, social presence, immersion, and realism. The rise of telepresence as a research area has not only furthered understandings of how highly advanced media technologies affect users, but it has also called attention to the potential of this type of psychological experience to shape outcomes of exposure to everyday media, as this volume shows.

Given the emergent and growing importance of telepresence as an individual difference variable affected in part by technology form and content, an important next step is to connect it to existing theories of media effects in order to better explain and predict future outcomes. Scholars have already attempted to do this in the relatively new area of entertainment theory (see chapter 7, this volume), but few have examined more established media theories through the lens of telepresence. As Bryant and Cummins (2007) note, "one of the most pressing needs in communication research is the greater development, testing, and synthesis of communication theories" (p. 9). Linking these theories to telepresence, where relevant, should help their development immensely given the profound changes that have occurred in everyday media technologies and use since classic effects theories were formulated. A full consideration of these linkages is beyond the scope of this chapter, but it will illustrate in depth how one prominent media effects theory, social learning theory, relates to the experience of non-mediation as an example of how telepresence can be integrated into theories and models attempting to explain the media's impact.

Application: Social Learning Theory and Telepresence Research

A general effect of great interest to media researchers is learning, and one of the most well-known theories of how media affect learning is social learning theory (SLT), formulated by Albert Bandura (1977). In simple terms, this theory explains how people may model behaviors observed in the media. SLT was most famously tested through Bandura's classic "Bobo doll" studies in the 1960s, designed to show that children may imitate violent behavior viewed on television. In one early experiment (Bandura, Ross, & Ross, 1961), a random group of children were shown a film of a model aggressing against a punching bag-like Bobo doll while another group was shown a non-aggressive model. Both groups were then left to play with a Bobo doll and other toys. Results showed that the children who saw the aggressive model were more likely to play aggressively themselves, sometimes even imitating the exact behaviors they observed in the film such as bashing the Bobo doll with a hammer. This research established that observational learning may occur and laid the foundation for what would become social learning theory. Subsequent studies by Bandura and colleagues varied features such as whether the model was rewarded or punished to further refine the perspective (Sparks, 2006), and it has since been used as a theoretical basis for numerous investigations of media effects. SLT is the most frequently cited mechanism by which violent video games may cause aggressive behavior, for example (Sherry, 2007), and it has also been applied in prosocial contexts such as entertainment education (Smith, 2002).

Social learning theory has clearly been useful to media researchers, and a closer look at the complex process by which it works reveals several possible linkage points with telepresence and related research. According to Bandura (2002), observational learning is governed by four subfunctions, each of which may include a number of influencing factors. The first, *attentional processes*, determine what modeling influences are observed and extracted from ongoing modeled events. These are determined in part by characteristics of modeled events such as salience and complexity and also by observer attributes such as cognitive capabilities. The second subfunction, *retention processes,* involves the coding and remembering of modeled events. Influential factors at this level include cognitive construction and rehearsal. Third, *behavioral production processes* involve translating symbolic conceptions into courses of action, and the final subfunction, *motivational processes*, has to do with incentives for performing observed behaviors. Overall, the subfunctions

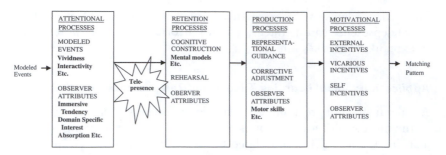

Figure 8.1 Linkage points between the subfunctions governing observational learning and influential factors from telepresence research.

and factors involved in observational learning mediate the relationship between modeled events and matching performances of observers (Tan, 1986), and the first two—attentional and retention processes—are particularly relevant from a telepresence standpoint, as shown in Figure 8.1.

The model depicted in Figure 8.1 is adapted from work by Bandura (2002) and shows the relationship between the four subfunctions governing observational learning and categories of influential factors. The specific influential factors in Bandura's work, however, have been replaced by selected concepts from the telepresence literature that may also play into these processes, in an attempt at theoretical intension. At the attentional processes stage, "modeled events" may be expanded to include concepts from scholarship attempting to explain dimensions of technology affecting telepresence, such as Steuer's (1992) work on vividness and interactivity and Lombard and Ditton's (1997) enumeration of media form variables. In line with the concept of *salience* identified by Bandura, the expectation is that these characteristics will relate positively to attention through increased sensory or (in the case of interactive media) motor engagement. As for "observer attributes," several works have attempted to identify user characteristics influencing attention to telepresence-inducing media, and these may also be added to the observational learning model, including immersive tendency (Witmer & Singer, 1998), domain specific interest (i.e., content interest), and absorption (Wirth et al., 2007). Next, telepresence itself has been added as a potential mediating (or moderating) variable between attentional and retention processes. Attention has been suggested to be a precursor of spatial presence experiences (Wirth et al., 2007), and the spatial situation models created in response to attention, as specified by Wirth and colleagues, should influence retention of observed events in the form of more enduring *mental models*, discussed elsewhere as cognitive representations of situations in real or imagined worlds (Roskos-

Ewoldsen, Roskos-Ewoldsen, & Dillman Carpentier, 2002; Tamborini & Bowman chapter 5, this volume). These mental models for behavior can be thought of as "cognitive constructions" (to use Bandura's term) that may be strengthened through repeated media exposure. And, in the case of mental models formed in response to naturally mapped interactive media experiences, they may even affect motor skills for performing the behavior (Tamborini & Skalski, 2006), identified in the model as a production processes "observer attribute."

The revised observational learning model illustrates several possible linkage points between social learning theory and telepresence, showing how the concept may facilitate social learning theory effects. Further work along these lines could help increase the explanatory power of the theory in the wake of the profound technological changes that have occurred since the Bobo doll experiments of the 1960s. As Bandura himself recently observed, "whereas previously modeling influences were confined to the behavior patterns exhibited in one's immediate environment, the accelerated growth of video delivery technologies has vastly expanded the range of models to which members of society are exposed to day in and day out" (Bandura, 2002, p. 127). These words ring especially true following the rise of YouTube, mobile video devices, and similar applications and technologies. The potential to learn behaviors both good and bad through media has never been greater. Expanding theories such as SLT to include telepresence and related concepts can reinvigorate these powerful tools and help them maintain their relevance in the digital age.

Other Media Theories and Telepresence

Beyond social learning, several other media theories could benefit from a consideration of telepresence. Rubin and Haridakis (2001) identified the dominant theoretical perspectives in mass communication at the turn of the century and they included agenda setting, diffusion of innovations, social cognition, uses and gratifications, cultivation, gap hypothesis, critical/cultural studies, framing, and third person effects. Although these perspectives encompass different approaches to the study of communication, most are studied at a level conducive to adding the concept of telepresence as an additional explanatory mechanism, as in the following brief examples:

Cultivation Theory and Telepresence As previously discussed, cultivation theory says that television consumption affects perceptions of social reality (Gerbner et al., 2002). The perspective has recently been explained in terms of cognitive processes underlying the effect.

Specifically, this newer work argues that cultivation happens when viewers are unmotivated to process information systematically and instead rely on cognitive heuristics to arrive at a judgment (Shrum, 2002). One factor that makes constructs more accessible for making judgments is *vividness*, which in this domain has to do with the extent to which something is "concrete and imagery provoking, and proximate in a sensory, temporal, or spatial way" (Nisbett & Ross, 1980, p. 45). Although not exactly the same, this treatment of vividness is very similar to how the term is used in the telepresence literature, with the same implications. One would expect more vivid media of either type to create a sense of presence with "constructs" such as those relating to violence (e.g., the extent to which certain places are dangerous) or social roles (e.g., the number of people in real life who are police officers), making those constructs more accessible and likely to be used in making reality judgments. Of all media theories, cultivation theory has one of the clearest linkages to telepresence, since both have to do with differences between mediated experiences and real ones. The more mediated experiences seem nonmediated, all other things being equal, the stronger cultivation effects should be.

Agenda Setting Theory and Telepresence   Agenda setting refers to the ability of news media "to influence the salience of topics on the public agenda" (McCombs & Reynolds, 2002, p. 1). It says that the amount of coverage the press gives to particular issues gives "salience cues" as to their relative importance (Wantra & Ghanem, 2007), telling people what to think about. The frequent appearance of terms related to "salience" in the agenda setting literature suggests a linkage point to telepresence. Salience may be defined as an orienting motive that directs attention toward specific aspects of a stimulus environment (Zillmann & Brosius, 2000). Aspects of a stimulus environment can be made more salient by the manner in which they are presented through media technology, and this may affect their perceived importance among members of the public. For example, the Vietnam War has been called the first "living-room war" because of its regular coverage by television news (Arlen, 1982). TV's ability to bring the battlefront to the home front undoubtedly contributed to the anti-war movement (agenda) at the time by making the "horrors" of war salient. More specifically, the high-telepresence evoking medium of television likely brought more attention to (and presence with) death and human casualty than older forms of media, which do not capture that aspect of the stimulus environment as well. The phrase "living-room war" itself suggests a presence-like phenomenon, and there have been efforts to reduce media access to certain images (e.g., coffins carrying fallen soldiers) in recent conflicts such as the war in Iraq (Memmott, 2006). The ability of media salience and resulting telepresence to make particular topics and issues more salient to the public is an interesting future direction for agenda setting research, particularly in light of technological advancements such as HDTV.

Uses and Gratifications and Telepresence   The uses and gratifications perspective focuses on motivations for media consumption and how people use media to meet their needs (Katz, Blumler, & Gurevitch, 1974; Rubin, 2002). As a result of years of research grounded in the approach, a great deal is now known about the reasons people choose to engage in various kinds of media use (Sparks, 2006). A scan of specific motivations uncovered in uses and gratifications studies reveals several linkage points with telepresence. In television research, *escape* and *companionship* have been identified reasons for use (e.g., Greenberg, 1974; Rubin, 1983), and these motivations seem analogous to spatial presence and social presence, in that they involve using television to feel "away from" one's physical environment or "with" others. Similarly, work on video game uses and gratifications identifies *fantasy* and *social interaction* as reasons for play (Sherry, Lucas, Greenberg, & Lachlan, 2006), and the ability of games such as World of Warcraft to create corresponding senses of spatial and social presence has already been discussed (see chapter 5, this volume). The uses and gratifications perspective calls attention to the idea that telepresence experiences are not merely a consequence of exposure to advanced media technologies but also something that audiences may actively seek. Uncovering the extent to which individuals have a "need for telepresence" along with the ability of various media to gratify this would be a valuable endeavor.

The above examples highlight just a few ways in which telepresence may inform media theory. There are many other possibilities, and the examples presented in this section call attention to some meta-considerations concerning telepresence and media theory. While none of the theories discussed above specifically mention telepresence, all include concepts that are similar to concepts in the telepresence literature, e.g., vividness, salience, escape, etc. One obvious future research direction for inquiry would be to search for more potential concept linkages in an effort to expand the scope of media theories and reconcile the telepresence and media theory literatures. A second and related avenue for inquiry would be to identify the implications of mediated experiences that seem "real" or "nonmediated" across multiple theories. This can help reduce conceptual and theoretical overlap and cut to the heart of what telepresence means for media effects. Generally, it seems to intensify effects, and perhaps a theory with broader scope can help inform this process. Exemplification theory, for example, addresses how noteworthy examples influence subsequent judgments (Zillmann & Brosius, 2000). Similar to the drench hypothesis, which says that certain portrayals stand out and may have a stronger impact on viewers (Greenberg, 1988), exemplification theory assumes a superior influence of certain types of media events (e.g., concrete or emotionally arousing ones). Telepresence seems to function similarly, with high-telepresence inducing experiences producing stronger effects by making certain stimuli more prominent. Future work should continue to examine the complex relationship between telepresence and media theory to advance knowledge of both.

Although much progress has been made in our understanding of media effects since the days of magic bullet theory, Bryant and Cummins (2007) lament the absence of theory in the mass communication literature. They cite content analyses showing that only 27% to 39% of articles in popular communication journals contain theory. They also note that many media "theories" are not true theories at this time "but rather a relatively coherent body of research guided by repeated theme and a general framework of ideas and research methods" (p. 2). Several of these bodies of research will now be discussed in light of telepresence, particularly research on media sex, violence, and fright reactions. This discussion will help further illuminate how telepresence may inform the study of media effects, with the ultimate goal of advancing both theory and research.

Telepresence and Media Effects

Telepresence and Violence Effects

Media violence has long been a theme of public concern and anxiety and is arguably the most researched topic in mass communication. The first documented scientific observation of the mass media dates back to the Payne Fund Studies of the early 1930s, which focused in large part on violence in film. Of the 12 independent studies conducted, Dale's (1935) content analysis of 1,500 films produced from 1920–1929 illustrated a substantial number of crime-related themes and incidents. Blumler's (1933) survey regarding media experiences of nearly 2,000 children also confirmed that many respondents had performed and imitated violent behaviors learned from the cinema, fueling anxieties about the medium. The early public concern over film likely stems in part from its highly immersive nature compared to other media that preceded it (see chapter 2, this volume).

Since this initial glimpse at the beginning of the 20th century, hundreds of studies have looked at the effects of media violence, guided by theories such as social learning and cultivation. The swift rise in juvenile delinquency and youth crime in the 1950s prompted U.S. congressional hearings on the effects of television violence on children (Wright et al., 2001). The ability of television to bring highly realistic (possibly presence-inducing) depictions of violence into the home undoubtedly contributed to the distress it caused. An increase in real world and televised urban crime eventually led to government funding at the University of Pennsylvania to monitor TV programming, and this resulted in a report by the National Commission on the Causes and Prevention of Violence (convened by President Johnson) citing television violence as the primary contributor to America's crime and violence epidemic (Baker & Ball, 1969). Concern about media violence among members of the scientific community, paralleling that of legislators and the public, has persisted over time. Bushman and Anderson (2001) recently argued that the statistical magnitude of the link between media violence and aggression has been clearly positive and consistently on the rise since 1975. The increase in the number and availability of telepresence-inducing technologies since then may be one reason.

Consistent with this logic, recent scholarship has focused on violence in the relatively new popular medium of the video game. A meta-analysis by Sherry (2007) of the video game violence literature indicated that there is a small but significant overall effect of violent game play on aggression ($d = .30$), though the effect was less than the effect of violent television on aggression found by Paik and Comstock (1994) of d = .65. Interestingly, however, the link between video game violence and aggression was positively correlated with the year of the study ($r = .39$), suggesting that the effect of violent video game play on aggression has *increased* over time. This finding makes sense considering the numerous advances in video game technology that have occurred throughout the history of the medium (Skalski, 2004). These advances are troubling from a violence effects standpoint given the growing ability of games to immerse players in violent scenarios in which they are active participants.

As a result, researchers have recently shifted their attention to the role of telepresence in video games violence effects (e.g., Eastin, 2006; Ivory & Kalyanaraman, 2007; Farrar, Krcmar, & Nowak, 2006; Tamborini et al., 2004). Why might telepresence in response to video games contribute to violent outcomes? Tamborini and Skalski (2006) suggest that feeling spatially present in violent games that require players to repeatedly aggress against others can foster the development of mental models for real-life aggression. This should be intensified when games have features that increase telepresence, such as naturally mapped controls (see chapter 5, this volume). Along these same lines, playing violent video games using immersive virtual environment technology (IVET) should lead to even greater telepresence and aggression compared to traditional game platforms. A few studies have examined this relationship and findings for this type of technology have been mixed. Contrary to predictions, Tamborini et al. (2004) did not find telepresence to mediate the relationship between virtual reality (VR) technology and hostile cognitions, but aggressive feelings were mediated by telepresence in a similar study using IVET by Persky and Blascovich (2008), even though aggressive behavior was unaffected. As IVET becomes less bulky and more familiar to users over time, telepresence should mediate violent outcomes more consistently.

Other research has considered additional form, individual difference, and content variables related to telepresence and violent video game effects. Ivory and Kalyanaraman (2007) investigated the impacts of technological advancements more common than IVET (e.g., whether a game is accompanied by a narrative storyline). Results indicated that both technological advancements and violent video game content were positively correlated with telepresence and arousal. Eastin (2006) explored the subject of video game violence and gender effects on telepresence and aggressive thoughts, and results indicated that females playing violent video games experience an increase in aggressive thoughts and telepresence when a gender match between the game character and self exists (an ethical issue that has further been addressed by Klimmt, Schmid, Nosper, Hartmann, & Vorderer, 2006). Moreover, Eastin found that combating a human opponent, rather than playing against the computer, increases aggressive thoughts in both males and females, perhaps due to an increase in social presence. Farrar, Krcmar, and Nowak (2006) found two separate causal paths leading to telepresence. First, males and more frequent gamers experienced more telepresence, and second, participants who played a violent video game felt more telepresence than those who played a nonviolent video game, ultimately leading to an increase in resentment, verbal aggression, and physically aggressive intentions. Lachlan and Maloney (2008) examined the role played by individual differences in generating violent content in games and found it to be highly variable across telepresence tendencies and other player characteristics.

For years, the question of whether media violence leads to aggressive behaviors or if people with naturally aggressive tendencies seek out violent media has sparked heated debates between industry figures, scholars, legislators, and the general public. Yet it's hard to deny that the diffusion of technological innovations such as high-definition (HD), surround sound, and interactive controls are increasingly immersing media users in worlds of violence, with uncertain consequences. This makes research on media violence of continued importance. Although almost all of the research on media violence and telepresence thus far has focused on video games, violent television and film should not be overlooked. These popular sources of violent content lack interactivity but offer more salient models and greater realism, features that will become more pronounced as high-resolution digital technologies continue to diffuse. These and other developments need to be considered to advance knowledge on this important topic and help inform the ongoing media violence debate.

Sexual Media and Telepresence

Although video games have received much scrutiny for their violent content, perhaps the biggest game-related controversy of 2005 concerned sexual content in the hit title *Grand Theft Auto: San Andreas*. The infamous "Hot Coffee" mini-game had the player engage in simulated sexual intercourse, and though it could only be accessed through a game hack, the Federal Trade Commission took action against the companies responsible, resulting in the title being pulled from retailer shelves for a time and an eventual settlement (Adams, 2006). The depiction of sex in the "Hot Coffee" mod was tame compared with much of the sexual media content available today (the characters were animated and mostly clothed), yet it still drew the ire of many, no doubt due to its appearance in a popular new interactive (and more telepresence-inducing) medium.

Sexuality has enjoyed a close connection with technology over the years, and, in addition to being highly controversial, their union has proven to be highly sought after by consumers. Pornography or "adult entertainment" is an estimated $12 billion dollar a year industry in the United States alone (Sloan, 2007). In line with scholarship on the topic, pornography is defined here as "media material used or intended to increase sexual arousal" (Mundorf, Allen, D'Alessio, & Emmers-Sommer, 2007, p. 181). The term "pornography" is frequently used to refer to sexually explicit media materials such as those featuring nudity and intercourse. However, as Sparks (2006) points out, the study of sexual media content is "fraught with definitional ambiguities" and could refer to anything from kissing to a brutal rape scene (p. 108). This section focuses on more explicit sexual content (which would likely be dubbed pornography) since it has received the most scholarly attention.

In addition to including a wide range of content types, sexual media has been presented in many forms over the years due to technological innovation. Lombard and Jones (2004) argue that sexual media content has often driven the development, use, and profitability of new technologies. As Steinberg (1993) notes:

[E]very new technological achievement quickly finds its way, like water flowing downhill, to a sexual application. When the photographic process was first discovered, one of its first uses was to create enticing images of naked women. When motion pictures were born, underground sex films immediately followed. One of the prime economic foundations of the home video revolution has been the sex video market.

This popular media trend has continued with the Internet, which accounted for more than 20% of adult industry revenue in 2006 (Harris

& Barlett, 2009), and even extends to mobile devices such as the iPhone now. The creators of sexual media clearly seem to want to give users a sense of being physically close to the people represented in their content (i.e., experiences of presence), and they have attempted to do this in large part through innovative applications of technology, a number of which have been identified by Lombard and Jones (2004). Presence as *realism*, for example, has been attempted by adult entertainment producers through HD videos and sex toys such as artificial genitals with lifelike skin. *Transportation* has been achieved through interactive DVDs that allow users to "come together" with mediated partners. This is similar to *social actor within medium* computer programs featuring virtual girlfriends and other "lovers." *Immersion* has been attempted through combinations of the above that engage multiple senses, e.g., video of a performer along with an external reproduction of the performer's genitals that the user can interact with. And products such as the Realdoll, which are life-sized and lifelike love dolls (one of which was memorably featured in the film *Lars and the Real Girl*), provide an example of presence as *medium as social actor* (for a more comprehensive discussion of these and other intersections of media form and sexual content, see Lombard & Jones, 2004). Aside from products such as the Realdoll, one notable aspect of the above examples is their reliance, for the most part, on popular media such as TVs, VCRs, computers, and the Internet. Sexual media has clearly come a long way in terms of its presence potential, and yet it is still rooted in everyday technologies instead of more advanced ones such as VR (or "teledildonics," a term coined to refer specifically to advanced sexual technologies).

To date, no studies have examined how telepresence relates to sexual media effects, but many studies have been done on sexual media effects in general. Research generally lumps these outcomes into three major categories: (a) arousal, (b) attitudinal changes, and (c) behavioral effects (Harris & Barlett, 2009). In terms of the first type of effect, one might expect telepresence to relate positively to sexual arousal simply by making the mediated experience more like the "real thing," which seems to be what users of sexual media content want (along with users of presence-inducing media in general; Lombard & Ditton,1997). And as suggested above, the arousal effect should increase with more sensory engagement and interactivity, especially if the latter provides genital stimulation. However, these formal features of technology are not necessary for arousal to occur. As Harris and Bartlett (2009) suggest, explicitness need not correlate highly with arousal, since viewers can fill in their own scripts for what may happen during a sex scene that is not fully shown (or shown at all). And in the case of technology, an imperfect device that has limited immersive or interactive capabilities may constrain what happens physically, whereas a person's imagination can go anywhere and do anything. This highlights the need to conduct research on the psychological experience of telepresence as it relates to a person's arousal level in response to sexual media content. Sexually explicit media has already been shown to lead to high levels of physiological arousal (Allen & D'Alessio, 1993). While it seems likely that telepresence may mediate or moderate this effect, the role of technology form and content variables in the process is more questionable and in need of further study.

The other two general types of sexual media exposure outcomes, attitudinal changes and behavioral effects, have a less intuitive connection to telepresence. Attitudinal effects that have been studied include acceptance of violence in interpersonal relationships, acceptance of the rape myth, and the view that sexual relationships are adversarial (Mundorf et al., 2007). On the behavioral side, researchers have looked at outcomes such as disinhibition of known behaviors and impact on rape and other sex crimes (Harris & Bartlett, 2009). Research in this area has tended to focus on the effects of sexually explicit material of either a nonviolent or violent nature. Meta-analysis findings indicate that exposure to this type of content (particularly violent pornography) is positively related to negative attitudes and antisocial behaviors (Mundorf et al., 2007). However, researchers have struggled to identify a coherent theoretical explanation for the observed pattern of results, and telepresence may be able to help. It has been found, for example, that simple exposure rates to sexually explicit materials do not predict criminal sexual behavior (Allen, D'Alessio, & Emmers-Sommer, 1997). Mundorf and colleagues suggest that individual differences or situations need to be taken into account, particularly how a person "reacts" to exposure.

This calls attention to the potential value of considering telepresence and related concepts in future work on this topic, since telepresence is a psychological reaction that can help explain and predict effects. Viewers who experience telepresence in response to a rape film, for example, may be more likely to engage in criminal sexual behavior after exposure (and develop strong mental models for doing so), whereas other viewers may be disgusted and break the connection, minimizing the effect. In that sense, telepresence may serve as a consumer's basis for selecting from different types of sexual media content and technologies, since they want to feel "there" or "with" content of interest. Theories such as uses and gratifications and social learning can help determine where telepresence fits in the complex interplay between exposure and effects.

On a final note, the experience of telepresence may also provide clues for what to do about the negative outcomes associated with exposure to sexually explicit materials. Meta-analysis has also been performed on studies examining educational messages designed to combat harmful effects (Mundorf et al., 2007), and these findings indicate that such messages not only eradicate negative effects but also cause a small *positive* change in attitudes! As Mundorf and colleagues explain:

> Educational efforts assume that the problem of media is the misappropriation of content to real life. A vicarious fantasy experience creates an emotional reaction. The educational material recontextualizes this experience, perhaps reminding the consumer that such material is in fact a fantasy and not a reflection of real life. (p. 194)

Although telepresence is never mentioned in this literature, the discussion of content being equated with "real life" is consistent with research on perceived reality (Potter, 1988) and seems to partially implicate it in shaping harmful effects, though it also suggests a solution. Breaking or reducing telepresence over time, as in virtual exposure therapy, may help at-risk individuals to overcome their urge to act out in violent and antisocial ways in response. Regardless, sexually explicit media is likely to remain controversial due to moral and ethical issues associated with it, as well as its ubiquity in everyday life and media.

Telepresence and Fright Effects

At the start of the chapter, a quote from a listener of the 1938 *War of the Worlds* radio broadcast illustrated that mediated messages can have adverse effects upon an audience known as fright effects. Like the reactions to the *War of the Worlds* broadcast, many fright effects are immediate in nature, meaning that they occur while the audience is attending to a frightening media presentation according to Harrison and Cantor (2000). They point out that the symptoms of these effects can include increased heart rate, sweating, trembling, shortness of breath, choking, chest pain, nausea, dizziness/faintness, and many other physiological manifestations, as well as emotional effects ranging from a feeling of losing control to crying and tantrums. Along with panic, it would seem that most of the effects stemming from the *War of the Worlds* broadcast were immediate, and that once the Martian attack was revealed to be nothing more than a radio drama, those who had fallen prey to the broadcast saw these symptoms subside. In the case of other fright effects, however, this is not always the case.

Attending to frightening media content can lead to enduring effects. As Harrison and Cantor (2000) explain, avoidance behaviors such as the avoiding of situations that are either reminiscent or merely similar to those that were presented in a frightening media message or the avoiding of that type of scary media content or form altogether can last anywhere from several hours to more than one year following exposure to such content. Other symptoms that might have a short- to long-term hold upon audience members can be an alteration of one's behavior in the areas of sleeping and eating, and obsessive talking or thinking about the frightening content. Regardless of whether the effects are immediate or enduring, such effects should not be taken lightly, and it might be important to determine if telepresence plays a role in increasing fright effects.

As mentioned in the introduction, telepresence may have had a hand in increasing the level of terror felt by the *War of the Worlds* broadcast's audience. Furthermore, it is almost certain that telepresence plays a role in the effects of other frightening media content as well. Through the examination of several of its core concepts, a better understanding of just how telepresence might increase levels of fright in those who attend to frightening stimuli can be gained.

Realism is a key component for experiencing presence. The more accurately a mediated environment can capture reality, then the greater the telepresence effects (Lombard & Ditton, 1997). Many researchers have also found that when looking at realism in terms of frightening media content, realism is one of the biggest contributors to increasing affective response in children and adults (Neuendorf & Sparks, 1988; Harrison & Cantor, 2000; Valkenburg, Cantor, & Peeters, 2000). Other than children of a very young age, viewers generally find realistic threats or events more frightening when presented in the media than fantastic threats. Harrison and Cantor (2000) discuss the principle of Stimulus Generalization, which posits that if a person is frightened by a real-life stimulus, then a mediated representation of that stimulus will elicit a fear response that is similar to that of the stimulus being represented, but to a lesser level of fear. For instance, if a person is frightened by spiders, then a film that features spiders as a threat will induce a similar fright response for the person that he or she would experience with a real-life spider, but the person will experience less anxiety with the film version. Interestingly, this tactic has been applied intentionally in the area of cybertherapy, where high telepresence-inducing technologies such as VR have been used to help people overcome fears including spider phobia (Garcia-Palacios, Hoffman, Carlin, Furness, & Botella, 2002).

Harrison and Cantor (2000) point to psychology research that categorizes frightening stimuli into five classifications, four of which are exclusively real-life objects or situations. The four real-life stimuli categories include animals, such as sharks or the aforementioned spiders; environmental, such as natural disasters; blood/injection/injury, thus capitalizing on people's fear of needles, physical harm, or queasiness at the sight of blood; and situational, such as a fear of heights or the dark. Filmmakers and television programs that utilize these stimuli are numerous, and with such realistically frightening inclusions, viewers may experience greater levels of both presence and fear.

The immersion component of presence may also elicit greater fright responses in audience members. Immersion is the aspect of presence that draws a person into a medium physically and psychologically (Lombard & Ditton, 1997). For instance, a more immersive video game would be a game where the player physically feels as if they are a part of the video game world, and while playing, shuts out much of the external world in which they reside. In the case of *The War of the Worlds* broadcast of 1938, no visual immersion could be achieved; however, many listeners were no doubt immersed into the medium of radio, perhaps like never before. The format of the presentation itself, a program that mimicked the characteristics of a musical program with breaking news bulletins that reported the invasion from Mars (Koch, 1970), was a presentation style that listeners were accustomed to, and thus it is understandable why so many listeners were drawn into what was happening before their very ears (Cantril, 1940). The broadcast boasted skilled actors, a solid script, and sound effects to further bring listeners into the apocalyptic experience. Even without the aid of visuals to draw in its listeners, the medium of radio was seemingly capable of pulling the public into its world.

Of course, motion pictures have an obvious advantage over radio in terms of achieving immersion and non-mediation due to its ability to visually pull in its audience. When looking at film, one finds a medium that has always been doing its utmost to represent the real world within its frame, and that has successfully been drawing its audience into this representational realm both physically and psychologically (see chapter 2, this volume). Also, in film one finds a medium that, soon after its inception and transformation into a narrative device (Cook, 2004), began serving up mixes of fantasy and horror to its terrified audiences (Gifford, 1973), all the while striving to attain the greatest possible immersive quality.

The horror film may work extraordinarily well as an immersive genre because of the divide between the real world and that which is in the frame. Undoubtedly, sitting in a darkened movie theater and viewing cinematic terror unfold on the screen while enveloped by darkness all around helps viewers psychologically shut out the external world and focus more attentively on the world presented on the screen. Not only is the film surrounded by darkness, but it is projected onto a giant screen, which has been found to increase viewer arousal and sense of participation, as well as excitement felt during the viewing experience (Lombard & Ditton, 1997). If the image filling this giant screen is one of horror, offering some realistic threat as was discussed earlier, and the audience is fully drawn into the world presented within the frame of the film, then it is logical to argue that the immersion aspect of presence can lead to greater fright effects in viewers. Furthermore, when looking at coping strategies that have been developed or that are instinctively practiced to reduce the effects of viewing frightening content, it is clear that many of these strategies can be successful in reducing or sometimes even eliminating viewer immersion. The behavioral control strategy of covering the eyes was found to be effective in reducing fright effects in younger children (Wilson, 1989). Of course, covering the eyes breaks any visual contact that the child has with the frightening content, and without visual contact, the level of immersion (and telepresence) naturally would be lessened.

Telepresence and Other Effects

In addition to the violence, sex, and fright reactions, there are many other media effects areas that telepresence may help inform. Spence, Lachlan, and Westerman (2009), for example, examined how presence affects responses to tragic news stories, showing how the concept may benefit journalistic research. In an earlier presence and news study, Bracken (2006) found that the improved image quality of HDTV (over standard definition) had a positive impact on source credibility and overall credibility of a newscast. Additional media effects areas that could benefit from incorporating telepresence include media portrayals (of minorities, gender, etc.), political media effects (e.g., perceptions of issues and candidates), effects of health and safety campaigns, and cultural effects of the mass media. As discussed earlier, entertainment and persuasion are also important considerations in the matrix of media effects (see chapter 7, and chapter 6, this volume).

Conclusion

The evidence presented in this chapter underscores the rich potential for telepresence to affect outcomes of media exposure. Future research should attempt to link these outcomes to both media theory and telepresence. This will help advance knowledge of how individuals and society are affected by both current and emerging popular media. Though it is true that audiences have come a long way since the *War of Worlds* broadcast of 1938, the same is true of the media that frighten them (and affect them in other ways). Scary radio and films, for example, have now been joined by the popular genre of survival horror video games, including such grisly titles as *Resident Evil, Left 4 Dead,* and *Carnevil*. These and other interactive, immersive experiences point to potentially powerful effects. They demand a reconsideration of how media impact audiences, as does the ubiquity of media in daily life and the steep rise in media use due to tethered mobile devices like cell phones. To keep up with current and future trends in popular media use and understand the array of effects it may have, new concepts are needed, and telepresence can help immensely in filling this void.

References

Adams, D. (2006). Rockstar, FTC settle over Hot Coffee. Retrieved December 3, 2008, from http://ps2.ign.com/articles/711/711788p1.html

Allen, M., & Casey, M. K. (2007). Wherefore art thou mass media theory? In R. W. Preiss, B. M. Gayle, N. Burrell, M. Allen, & J. Bryant (Eds.), *Mass media effects research: Advances through meta-analysis* (pp. 31–36). Mahwah, NJ: Erlbaum.

Allen, M., & D'Alessio, D. (1993). Comparing the physiological responses of males and females to pornography: A preliminary meta-analysis. *Women and Language, 15*(2), 50.

Allen, M., D'Alessio, D., & Emmers-Sommer, T. (1997, November). *Reactions of criminal sex offenders to pornography: A meta-analytic summary.* Paper presented at the National Communication Association Convention, Chicago, IL.

Arlen, M. (1982). *The living room war.* New York: Penguin.

Baker, R. K., & Ball, S. J. (1969). *Mass media and violence: A staff report to the National Commission on the Causes and Prevention of Violence.* Washington, DC: United States Government Printing Office.

Bandura, A. (1977). *Social learning theory.* Englewood Cliffs, NJ: Prentice Hall.

Bandura, A. (2002). Social cognitive theory of mass communication. In J. Bryant & D. Zillmann (Eds.), *Media effects: Advances in theory and research* (pp. 121–153). Mahwah, NJ: Erlbaum.

Bandura, A., Ross, D., & Ross, S. A. (1961). Transmission of aggression through imitation of aggressive models. *Journal of Abnormal and Social Psychology, 63,* 575–582. Retrieved December 3, 2008, from http://psychclassics.yorku.ca/Bandura/bobo.htm

Blumler, H. (1933). *Movies and conduct.* New York: Macmillan.

Bracken, C. C. (2006). Perceived source credibility of local television news: The impact of television form and presence. *Journal of Broadcasting & Electronic Media, 50*(4), 723–741.

Bryant, J., & Cummins, R. G. (2007). Traditions of mass media theory and research. In R. W. Preiss, B. M. Gayle, N. Burrell, M. Allen, & J. Bryant (Eds.), *Mass media effects research: Advances through meta-analysis* (pp. 1–13). Mahwah, NJ: Erlbaum.

Bushman, B. J., & Anderson, C. A. (2001). Media violence and the American public: Scientific facts versus media misinformation. *American Psychologist, 56,* 477–489.

Cantril, H. (1940). *The invasion from Mars: A study in the psychology of panic.* New York: Harper.

Chaffee, S. H., & Berger, C. R. (1987). What communication scientists do. In C. R. Berger & S. H. Chaffee (Eds.), *Handbook of communication science* (pp. 99–122). Newbury Park, CA: Sage.

Cook, D. A. (2004). *A history of narrative film* (4ᵗʰ ed.). New York: W. W. Norton.

Dale, E. *(1935). The content of motion pictures*. New York: Macmillan.

Eastin, M. S. (2006). Video game violence and the female game player: Self- and opponent gender effects on presence and aggressive thoughts. *Human Communication Research, 32*(3), 351–372.

Farrar, K., Krcmar, M., Nowak, K.L. (2006). Contextual features of violent video games, mental models and aggression. *Journal of Communication,* 6(2), 387–405.

Garcia-Palacios, A., Hoffman, H., Carlin, A., Furness, T. A., & Botella, C. (2002). Virtual reality in the treatment of spider phobia: A controlled study. *Behaviour Research and Therapy, 40,* 983–993.

Gerbner, G., Gross, L., Morgan, M., Signorielli, N., & Shanahan, J. (2002). Growing up with television: Cultivation processes. In J. Bryant & D. Zillmann (Eds.), *Media effects: Advances in theory and research* (pp. 43–67). Mahwah, NJ: Erlbaum.

Gifford, D. (1973). *A pictorial history of horror movies*. Middlesex, England: Hamlyn.

Greenberg, B. S. (1974). Gratifications of television viewing and their correlates for British children. In J. Blumler & E. Katz (Eds.), *The uses of mass communication: Current perspectives on gratifications research* (pp. 71–92). Beverly Hills, CA: Sage.

Greenberg, B. S. (1988). Some uncommon television images and the drench hypothesis. *Applied Social Psychology Annual, 8,* 88–102.

Harris, R. J., & Barlett, C. P. (2009). Effects of sex in the media. In J. Bryant & M. B. Oliver (Eds.), *Media effects: Advances in theory and research* (pp. 304–324). New York: Routledge.

Harrison, K., & Cantor, J. (2000). Tales from the screen: Enduring fright reactions to scary media. *Media Psychology, 1,* 97–116.

Horton, D., & Wohl, R. R. (1956). Mass communication and para-social interaction. *Psychiatry,19,* 215–229.

Hovland, C. I., Lumsdaine, A. A., & Sheffield, F. D. (1949). *Experiments on mass communication*. Princeton, NJ: Princeton University Press.

Ivory, J. D., & Kalyanaraman, S. (2007). The effects of technological advancement and violent content in video games on players' feelings of presence, involvement, physiological arousal, and aggression. *Journal of Communication, 57,* 532–555.

Katz, E., Blumler, J. G., & Gurevitch, M. (1974). Utilization of mass communication by the individual. In J. G. Blumler & E. Katz (Eds.), *The uses of mass communications: Current perspectives on gratifications research* (pp. 19–32). Beverly Hills, CA: Sage.

Klimmt, C., Schmid, H., Nosper, A., Hartmann, T., & Vorderer, P. (2006). How players manage moral concerns to make video game violence enjoyable. *Communications: The European Journal of Communication Research,* 31(3), 309–328.

Koch, H. (1970). *The panic broadcast: Portrait of an event*. Boston: Little-Brown.

Lachlan, K., & Maloney, E. (2008). Game player characteristics and interactive content: Exploring the role of personality and telepresence in video game violence. *Communication Quarterly, 56*(3), 284–302.

Lazarsfeld, P. F., Berelson, B. R., & Gaudet, H. (1948). *The people's choice.* New York: Columbia University Press.

Lewin, K. (1951). *Field theory in social science: Selected theoretical papers.* New York: Harper & Row.

Lombard, M., & Ditton, T. (1997). At the heart of it all: The concept of presence. *Journal of Computer Mediated Communication, 3*(2). Retrieved October 20, 2008, from http://jcmc.indiana.edu/vol3/issue2/lombard.html

Lombard, M., & Jones, M. T. (2004, October). *Presence and sexuality.* Presented at the Seventh International Workshop on Presence, Valencia, Spain.

Lowery, S. A., & DeFleur, M. L. (1995). *Milestones in mass communication research: Media effects.* White Plains, NY: Longman.

McCombs, M., & Reynolds, R. (2002). News influence on our pictures of the world. In J. Bryant & D. Zillmann (Eds.), *Media effects: Advances in theory and research* (pp. 1–8). Mahwah, NJ: Erlbaum.

Memmott, M. (2006). Reporters in Iraq under fire there, and from critics. *USA Today.* Retrieved December 3, 2008, from http://www.usatoday.com/news/world/iraq/2006-03-22-media-criticism_x.htm

Mundorf, N., Allen, M., D'Alessio, D., & Emmers-Sommer, T. M. (2007). Effects of sexually explicit media. In R. W. Preiss, B. M. Gayle, N. Burrell, M. Allen, & J. Bryant (Eds.), *Mass media effects research: Advances through meta-analysis* (pp. 181–198). Mahwah, NJ: Erlbaum.

Neuendorf, K. A., & Sparks, G. G. (1988). Predicting emotional responses to horror films from cue-specific affect. *Communication Quarterly, 36*(1), 16–27.

Nisbett, R. E., & Ross, L. (1980). *Human inference: Strategies and shortcomings of social judgment.* Englewood Cliffs, NJ: Prentice-Hall.

Paik, H., & Comstock, G. (1994). The effects of television violence on antisocial behavior: A meta-analysis. *Communication Research, 21*, 516–546.

Persky, S., & Blascovich, J. (2008). Immersive virtual video game play and presence: Influences on aggressive feelings and behavior. *Presence: Teleoperators and Virtual Environments, 17*(1), 57–72.

Potter, J. W. (1988). Perceived reality in television effects research. *Journal of Broadcasting & Electronic Media, 32*(1), 23–41.

Roskos-Ewoldsen, D. R., Roskos-Ewoldsen, B., & Dillman Carpentier, F. R. (2002). Media priming: A synthesis. In J. Bryant & D. Zillmann (Eds.), *Media effects: Advances in theory and research* (pp. 97–120). Mahwah, NJ: Erlbaum.

Rubin, A. M. (1983). Television uses and gratifications: The interactions of viewing patterns and motivations. *Journal of Broadcasting, 27*, 37–51.

Rubin, A. M. (2002). The uses and gratifications perspective of media effects. In J. Bryant & D. Zillmann (Eds.), *Media effects: Advances in theory and research* (pp. 525–548). Mahwah, NJ: Erlbaum.

Rubin, A. M., & Haridakis, P. (2001). Mass communication research at the dawn of the 21st century. *Communication Yearbook, 24*, 73–97.

Sherry, J. (2007). Violent video games and aggression: Why can't we find effects? In R. W. Preiss, B. M. Gayle, N. Burrell, M. Allen, & J. Bryant (Eds.), *Mass media effects research: Advances through meta-analysis* (pp. 245–262). Mahwah, NJ: Erlbaum.

Sherry, J. L., Lucas, K., Greenberg, B., & Lachlan, K. (2006). Video game uses and gratifications as predictors of use and game preference. In P. Vorderer. & J. Bryant (Eds.), *Playing video games: Motives, responses, and consequences* (pp. 213–224). Mahwah, NJ: Erlbaum.

Shrum, L. J. (2002). Media consumption and perceptions of social reality: Effects and underlying processes. In J. Bryant & D. Zillmann (Eds.), *Media effects: Advances in theory and research* (pp. 69–95). Mahwah, NJ: Erlbaum.

Sloan, P. (2007). Getting in the skin game. *CNNMoney*. Retrieved April 20, 2009, from http://money.cnn.com/magazines/business2/business2_archive/2006/11/01/8392016/index.htm

Skalski, P. (2004, April). *The quest for presence in video game entertainment.* Paper presented at the Central States Communication Association Annual Conference, Cleveland, OH.

Smith, D. (2002). The theory heard 'round the world. *Monitor on Psychology, 33*(9). Retrieved December 3, 2008, from http://www.apa.org/monitor/oct02/theory.html

Sparks, G. G. (2006). *Media effects research: A basic overview.* Belmont, CA: Thomson.

Spence, P., Lachlan, K., & Westerman, D. (2009). Presence, sex, and bad news: Exploring the responses of men and women to tragic news stories in varying media. *Journal of Applied Communication Research, 37*(3), 239–256.

Steinberg, D. (1993). Tech sex: For better, for worse. *Spectator Magazine.* Retrieved May 2, 2009, from http://www.sexuality.org/I/davids/cn07.html

Steuer, J. (1992). Defining virtual reality: Dimensions determining telepresence. *Journal of Communication, 42*(4), 73–93.

Tamborini, R. (2000, November). *The experience of telepresence in violent video games.* Paper presented at the 86th annual convention of the National Communication Association, Seattle, WA.

Tamborini, R., & Skalski, P. (2006). The role of presence in the experience of electronic games. In P. Vorderer & J. Bryant (Eds.), *Playing video games: Motives, responses, and consequences* (pp. 225–240). Mahwah, NJ: Erlbaum.

Tamborini, R., Eastin, M. S., Skalski, P., Lachlan, K., Fediuk, T. A., & Brady, R. (2004). Violent virtual video games and hostile thoughts. *Journal of Broadcasting & Electronic Media, 48*, 335–357.

Tan, A. S. (1986). Social learning of aggression from television. In J. Bryant & D. Zillmann (Eds.), *Perspectives on media effects* (pp. 41–55). Hillsdale, NJ: Erlbaum.

Valkenburg, P. M., Cantor, J., & Peeters, A. L. (2000). Fright reactions to television: A child survey. *Communication Research, 27*(1), 82–89.

Wantra, W., & Ghanem, S. (2007). Effects of agenda setting. In R. W. Preiss, B. M. Gayle, N. Burrell, M. Allen, & J. Bryant (Eds.), *Mass media effects research: Advances through meta-analysis* (pp. 37–51). Mahwah, NJ: Erlbaum.

Wilson, B. J. (1989). The Effects of two control strategies on children's emotional reactions to a frightening movie scene. *Journal of Broadcasting & Electronic Media, 33*(4), 397–418.

Wirth, W., Hartmann, T., Böcking, S., Vorderer, P., Klimmt, C., Schramm, H., et al. (2007). A process model of the formation of spatial presence experiences. *Media Psychology, 9*(3), 493–525.

Witmer, B. G., & Singer, M. J. (1998). Measuring presence in virtual environments: A presence questionnaire. *Presence: Teleoperators and Virtual Environments, 7*(3), 225–240.

Wright, J. C., Huston, A. C., Murphy, K. C., St Peters, M., Piñon, M., Scantlin, R., & Kotler, J. (2001). The relations of early television viewing to school readiness and vocabulary of children from low-income families: The Early Window Project. *Child Development, 72*(5), 1347–366.

Zillmann, D., & Brosius, H. (2000). *Exemplification in communication: The influence of case reports on the perception of issues.* Mahwah, NJ: Erlbaum.

Part III

The Future of Telepresence

Chapter 9

Mediated Presence in the Future

Eva L. Waterworth and John A. Waterworth

Introduction: The Evolution of Mediated Presence

Up until now, the ultimate in mediated presence has often been thought of as being totally immersed in a virtual world—with the assumption that a virtual world is an *alternative world* to the physical, and *in competition* with it. In other words, that this illusion of being—created through the experience of a medium—is more-or-less (depending on the degree of presence) the same experience as being in a similar situation in the physical world. Current widescreen surround sound cinemas and home entertainment centers are designed specifically to put the observer in the centre of the action, almost as if she were really there. This is the classic phenomenon of "being there," the perceptual illusion of non-mediation (Lombard & Ditton, 1997). But what happens as new information technologies and their applications evolve is that the world changes—and we ourselves also change. The distinction between the physical and the virtual blurs to an ever greater extent, and we become accustomed and adapt to it—in the manner in which we perceive, respond to, and generally experience the world around us.

Our everyday lives are more and more pervasively experienced through media. Everywhere in our built environments devices such as video screens, electronic access systems, and sensor-based smart environments are proliferating. Even in "the great outdoors" mobile phones, navigation and other location-aware systems mediate our experiences. There are very few places where one is out of the reach of mobile devices; thanks to this and to cross-media production of content, TV shows, movies, and web pages are accessed from almost everywhere, along with e-mail, chat, text messages, and, of course, voice telephony. Presence research will need increasingly to embrace this proliferating mediation of our everyday lives. The future won't be so much about being in a mediated or a physical reality, but about having different kinds of experiences and ways of behaving, in new situations that combine both. And yet to conceptualize and hopefully understand what is happening, we believe it is important to consider how and why we feel varying degrees of presence at all, in any kind of situation.

We see the natural, pre-media (and therefore pre-human) sense of presence as the feeling of being somewhere in the physical world, in the present. It is the means by which an organism knows when something is happening in its proximal world at the present time, and is the manifestation of an encoded ability to know when consciousness is occupied with situations in the immediate, outside world. To survive, an organism must feel directly when it is attending to the external world; this is the feeling we call *presence*. The strength of the feeling of presence reflects the extent to which *conscious attention* is focused on the non-self, *the other*. In our earlier work, we suggested that through evolution this developed into the ability to distinguish external, physical, and shared events and situations from those that are realized only internally and in a way that is specific to the individual, in thought and imagination (Riva & Waterworth, 2003; Waterworth & Waterworth, 2003a,b). This cannot be done through emotional appraisal or reality judgments, since imagined situations trigger the same emotional responses as physical situations (Russell, 2003), and may also seem real or unreal (as may physical events). When attention is mostly focused internally, our experience is one of absence from the external world (Waterworth & Waterworth, 2003a).

Both perception and imagination are uncertain processes, but we must somehow judge the significance of events as we experience them. We can and often do misperceive aspects of the environment (Gregory, 1998) and we may imagine or remember scenarios, which never did, or could, take place. Yet to survive we must try to answer, fast and unconsciously, at least three questions about situations of which we are conscious (though not necessarily in this order):

1. Is this happening in the world around me, or only in my head?
2. Is this likely to be true or is it fiction?
3. Is this good or bad for me (and how good or bad)?

We suggest that the answer to the first question is the degree of presence felt, the answer to the second question is arrived at through a reality judgment, and the answer to third is the strength of a positive or (more commonly) negative emotional response. These are the mechanisms brought into play when we experience events, whether those events are in the physical world, portrayed in media, or imagined; and they influence each other in determining our feelings about and our responses to events.

Presence mediated by information and communication technology is the feeling of being in an external world, in the realization of which that technology plays an active and direct role. To arise and persist, it requires adequate form to be directly perceived, conscious attention to that form, and content that will sustain such attention. Although presence can be distinguished from emotion, an important aspect of designing for specific degrees of presence is the evocation of explicit types of emotional state (e.g., Waterworth & Waterworth, 2006), since feelings of presence and of emotion moderate each other. The three-layer model of presence (Riva, Waterworth, & Waterworth, 2004) provides one way of thinking about presence, and its relationship to emotional experience, in terms of the fundamental psychological distinction between self and other.

The rapidly developing phenomena of mediated presence, made possible by the proliferation of digital devices and systems providing pervasive media experiences, point to a dynamically changing relationship between self and other. When we experience strong mediated presence, our experience is that the technology has become part of the self, and the mediated reality part of the other. When this happens, there is no conscious *effort of access* to information, nor *effort of action* to overt responses. The experiences and behavior of a well-practiced player of immersive, shared and action-oriented computer games provide a clear example of this. He perceives and acts directly, as if in an unmediated reality.

In the remainder of this chapter, we discuss the implications of this view and the likely course of technological innovation in the area for the future of presence and of presence research. In the next section, we consider the relationship between the body and the experience of presence through media. If the feeling of presence differentiates the self from the other, as we suggest, then any changes in how the body is experienced induced by media will have a significant effect, since body image and bodily actions are intrinsic to the way the sense of presence develops.

Action and Altered Body Experiences

Sanchez-Vives and Slater (2005) argue that the phenomenon of mediated presence may help neuroscientists in the study of consciousness, since it is essentially consciousness within a restricted domain. Since in a fully-immersive virtual reality all technical aspects affecting the experience can be controlled and replicated precisely, it would seem obvious that virtual reality provides a powerful paradigm for experimenting with the impact of various external cues on perception, with presence measures serving as dependent variables. And this could be done at different levels of detail, for both top-down and bottom-up processes. Sanchez-Vives and Slater (2005) also imply that mediated presence occurs when what is true of consciousness in general occurs within a virtual reality. But this seems to imply that if one is conscious, one will feel presence in a virtual reality, which is clearly not the case. This partly motivates our emphasis on what is not presence but is still conscious in any situation, which we have termed *absence* (Waterworth & Waterworth, 2003a)—arising when the main focus of attention is the self (the internal world), not the other (the external world, physical and/or in media).

Earlier support for the role of presence experiments in understanding the concept of minimal cues is based on the idea that there are determinable minima of, say, the number of modalities or level of scenic detail which underlie presence and, hence, perception (Slater, 2002). If a medium provides this minimum for each modality, then presence in the mediated reality will be experienced, and the observer will behave accordingly. However, this claim should be viewed with caution. While it is generally agreed that we do not need all details of a situation to be reproduced in media for a degree of presence to be experienced (and, of course, they never are or could be), and that remarkably low fidelity simulations can sometimes induce high levels of presence, it doesn't follow that this is because there are generalizable minimal cues that are the key to a convincing sense of presence.

Overt action is a strong indicator of high presence, as when participants in a virtual reality really try to run away from a portrayed dangerous situation. One might think that the richness of cues could be systematically reduced to find the minimal cues needed for this to happen. People will probably not run away from movies shown on their Apple i-Pod. But any actions that do occur depend on a host of other factors than the perceptual cues present in the medium, including who the immersant is, who they are with, how the situation is understood by them before they get into it, whether they have experienced this situation before, etc. We should remember that when the Lumière brothers first showed grainy, jumpy, black and white, but moving images of a train coming into a station, people "screamed, ducked or even ran out of the theatre" (IJsselsteijn, 2003, p. 24). And we should also keep in mind that presence is not an all or none thing. We rarely, if ever, feel totally present anywhere, whether the place physically surrounds us or is experienced through media.

While we can question the value of searching for minimal cues to *presence*, virtual realities will be valuable in searching for minimal cues for perception-based *action*, both in animals and in humans. Research on such minimal cues is beginning to use kinds of virtual reality to access the precise sensory information needed by a fly, for example, to adjust its flight adaptively to external events (New Scientist, 2008). But a fly, presumably, does not share its attention between internal and external world models. If we assume that these relatively simple animals are conscious, and that they are conscious of all they perceive, then for them perception *is* presence. (If they are not conscious, then they do not feel present at all.) This is clearly not the case with humans.

Action is not always an indicator of conscious attention, and our view implies that *presence depends on conscious attention*. Overt actions are often indicators of presence, but actions can be automatized, reflex, or otherwise unconscious—or at least not bearers of conscious intention. It is possible to feel high levels of presence without acting in the world. At the extreme, a victim of paralysis may feel extremely present—the fact of being paralyzed might be expected to maximize presence in horrific or otherwise threatening situations, just because action to leave or modify the situation is not possible. For the same reason, the presence experienced through media such as film often exceeds that of life—this is partly because the portrayed events tend to be more exciting, but also because we cannot do anything about them except close our eyes or hide behind the sofa. We often cannot act in response to media events because interaction is not supported by most media. This apparent weakness of some media, the lack of possible interaction, may sometimes strengthen the experience of presence. As a general statement, we suggest that presence in media is maximized when there is no attentional "effort of access" to information, nor attentional "effort of action" in experiencing media content.

New interaction methods directly question our understanding of what presence is and how mediated presence will evolve. So-called brain/computer interfaces (BCIs) allow a person to make direct inputs to a computer—and so to other devices—by thought. Typically, electrodes attached to the scalp or implanted on the surface of the brain allow electrical activity of the brain to control external devices (see Lebedev & Nicolelis, 2006, for a summary). With practice, a user can play a simple game (such as on-screen "pong"), move a cursor around and select from options (to compose a text message, for example) or, more, interestingly, navigate through a virtual world (or, indeed, the physical environment if seated in a computer-controlled wheelchair or other vehicle). Since there is apparently significant attentional "effort of action," we predict that the user will not feel much presence, reflecting that the technology will not be felt to be a part of the self, psychologically speaking. But with much practice, and in light of the potential for plasticity in the brain, will this continue to be the case? Will navigation and other interaction by thought then become as attentionally effortless as walking or driving a car? If it does, then the technology can be said to have modified the other—the world—while itself disappearing, and high levels of presence in the world become possible whilst also navigating, despite the fact that the physical body is not carrying out the actions.

The importance of the observational perspective provided by representations of ourselves and of others is discussed in the following section.

First-, Second-, and Third-Person Presences

We see changing experiences of the body as a key aspect of the future development of presence in media, not least the potential to experience events from a wide variety of observational perspectives. Standard perceptual effects such as the rubber hand illusion (Botvinick & Cohen, 1998) have been successfully reproduced in virtual reality and, with reduced vividness, mixed reality situations (IJsselsteijn, de Kort, & Haans, 2006). The body image can be remarkably flexible, and may be stretched well beyond the confines of the biological body. It has been known for some time that it is possible for virtual reality to achieve a kind of sensory rearrangement resulting in modified experiences of an individual's own body (Biocca & Rolland, 1998; Castiello, Lusher, Burton, Glover, & Disler, 2004; Riva, 1998; Riva, Bacchetta, Baruffi, & Molinari, 2001). More recently, methods for inducing out of body experiences have been reported (Ehrsson, 2007; Lenggenhager, Tadi, Metzinger, & Blanke, 2007), using relatively simple technology. In these cases, it has been found that if at least some tactile stimulation is correlated with visual information, the two may be psychologically integrated into a profoundly altered experience of self. In other words, we can observe media representations of ourselves from the outside while simultaneously experiencing *individual presence as the observed person*. This is a truly novel mode of experience for people in normal mental states, and opens up a wealth of new possibilities for entertainment experiences, in areas such as game-playing, sports broadcasts, and many other types of TV shows.

A first-person perspective if often seen as a key ingredient in evoking strong presence in media, and is of course the norm in classical virtual reality, where we view the mediated world as if embodied there ourselves (to some degree) and with a first-person perspective on things. Indeed, the word "media" has its roots in the Latin *medius* or middle. We are placed, perceptually, in the middle of things. We move our physical head and the virtual view changes accordingly; we move our physical arms and hands and we see a representation of these body parts depicted as if they are collocated with the internal image we have of our physical body. But just how important is this collocation? Some studies of "dextrous" work in virtual reality suggest that collocation is not a very strong factor in accurate task performance (although, of course, hand eye coordination is) whether one is working in two *or* three dimensional space (Waterworth, 2000, 2002). One reason is that we seem to be very adept at dealing with mappings of bodily actions onto the behavior of tools, as long as the behavior of the tool is closely coordinated with movements of the body. This is how we can do such a wide variety of things as use a computer mouse, drive a car, or fly a remote control model airplane without much difficulty (though only after some practice). Future research will try to understand how body-virtual image collocation, or lack of it, affects our sense of presence and the nature of our feelings of personal embodiment.

Increasingly we see ourselves represented in the third person in social virtual spaces, but generally not in a realistic way, and with minimal body-virtual image coordination—as when mouse actions or arrow buttons control gross movements and pre-programmed gestures of our avatar. In these social spaces , we can usually choose the appearance of our virtual persona from a selection of avatars or avatar parts. And these social spaces do give us a degree of co-presence with others, even though we are looking at ourselves from the outside, as a third-person self amongst the third-person selves of one or more other people. This limited embodiment has opened up many opportunities to experiment with notions of self and personal identity over the last 20 years or so (Turtle, 2005). But what happens if our physical body is closely coordinated with that of the avatar? Increasingly in animation movies and special effects movies the onscreen character's bodily actions are modeled from those of an actor (though not in real time due to the heavy computational demands of computer graphics rendering). What will happen when a person's virtual third-person avatar (or a robot in the physical world) closely mimics the bodily and facial changes of the physical person in real time? Will there be a sudden shift in the quality of presence? How does the realism of the depiction affect the sense of self and of presence? In other words, do I feel more present if my avatar looks and behaves like me, and how does this compare or perhaps interact with degree of body-avatar coordination? These are as yet open research questions, although there is at least one preliminary study in the literature (Ratan, Santa Cruz, & Vorderer, 2007).

There are few second-person, interactive, and virtual representations of self as yet (arguably the mediated mirror-image camera view provided by the Sony Eye-Toy game environment is a potentially large-scale step in that direction). This is the case where one can interact with a virtual characterization of oneself, and which—as with third-person self representational avatars—would be more or less like ones physical self. If the virtual image (or even robot) is coordinated with my body, it would be somewhat like looking in a more or less distorting mirror. How would this affect my sense of self?

To understand the mechanisms of individual presence, we will continue to experiment with different degrees of *first-person* immersion for a wide range of purposes. We know that we can simulate a situation and that people will behave as if it's a physical situation. We already know that first-person VR can be extremely powerful in diagnosis and therapy, both mental and physical, and in skills training and the arts. Virtual reality often contributes something that other media cannot, an integration of mind and body in an interactive situation. The central mystery is the interplay between the form and degree of immersion, and the content portrayed—the overall situation in which people find themselves. We will see more experimentation directed by more interesting hypotheses than in the past, where the outcomes will actually surprise us. Psychological questions will be central, for example the role of presence in attention allocation, planning and carrying out intentional action. The environmental contexts will often be novel, rather than straight simulations of similar unmediated situations.

Social Versus Individual Presence in Media?

The impact of ever more social applications of digital media will be particularly important for future research, not least in considering changes in the experience of presence over a person's lifetime. Salient research questions include: Are social and individual presence aspects of the same thing, or in conflict? In other words, does the one tend to reinforce or to negate the other? How does the experience of presence change through development, from a baby, to a child, to an adult of increasing maturity? The development of a sense of self may require both embodied perception *and* interaction with (or at least observation of) other agents (Maclaren, 2008). A very young infant seems to experience no differentiation of self from other—which includes everything perceived externally. Is that a state of total presence, or no presence at all?

If the capacity for presence diminishes as the sense of self develops through social interaction with others, social presence may be at the expense of individual presence. As the child recognizes and experiences others as agents, including real and fictional others in media and in physical reality, this will moderate how the self is experienced in relation to the other—and thus the level of presence. As the individual matures into adulthood and then old age, levels of presence habitually experienced seem to diminish. In the very old, relatively little attention seems to be directed to the world outside the individual, including the world experienced through media. The individual predominantly experiences absence, with an internal focus of attention on the self and not the other.

There is also evidence of situations that produce neither clearly individual nor social presence, but rather some form of group presence. In a cinema, our experiences are strongly influenced by the responses of those around us; there is, to some extent at least, a shared sense of presence. We have described this phenomenon in relation to an interactive and distributed virtual space (Waterworth, Waterworth, & Westling, 2002), but more pervasive media are increasingly used to support a shared sense of presence. Phenomena such as social networks, instant chat, text messaging with location awareness, and so on, all point to the increasingly shared nature of our experiences. Recent innovations such as the web-based (but mostly mobile phone- accessed) Twitter have high-lighted the strong need many people feel for constant social connection to physically-distant others. They have also been adopted in other time-sensitive and demanding situations, such as news reporting from conflict areas. The proliferation of social interconnectedness seems inevitable, but the forms this will take—and to what extent will these support a truly shared sense of *presence*—remain open questions.

Related questions revolve around second-person presences of others, often not corresponding directly to other real people. Examples include virtual characters that help us do things or entertain us, and more or less personable robots. Would these characters be improved by their having their own sense of presence (do they perhaps have one already)? Does that require or follow from having a sense of self? And what would implementing a sense of presence in virtual personalities tell us about the experience of presence in individuals and also in groups?

Whether our not our speculations turn out to be valid, it is clear that a great many questions related to individual, social, and group presence remain to be addressed by future research, as digital media, and our sense of presence, evolve together.

Digital Media and the Future Evolution of Presence

Since more and more of our experiences are now mediated by digital information and communication technology, it is reasonable to see the future development of the human sense of presence as a reflection of the rapid evolution of ever more pervasive digital technologies. This evolu-tion has been interpreted by some authors (e.g., Clark, 2003) in terms of three inter-related arguments. The first is that the technology in general is increasingly part of our bodies: not only embedded devices such as pacemakers or electrodes on the brain, but also carried devices such as mobile phones or even laptops. The second is that tangible or embodied interaction—in which physical objects stand for virtual entities and are manipulated bodily to interact with information systems—characterizes our future. And the third is that the individual is in some ways an abstrac-tion. The mind is extended by the technology beyond the body, through extended perception and distributed cognition (Hutchins, 1995). But these views are challenged when we consider the sense of mediated pres-ence as a result of the continuing significance of distinguishing self from other. Our view suggests that some kinds of digital media become part of the self; but other kinds become part of the other, the non-self.

It is true that without the media we have become used to and dependent upon, we feel at a loss, at least temporarily. The loss may feel as if some aspect of the world no longer exists. But it may also feel as if a part of memory has been erased, as when the address book on my mobile phone suddenly disappeared due to a technical fault. These are quite different psychological effects that reflect the presence faculty in operation. We do feel strong presence in some kinds of mediated environments. But we do not feel present within an electronic address book; nor would we want to. This points to, and is because of, the inherent limits of tangible interaction. Language, after all, is intangible. To feel presence, the media content must be realized externally and experienced as part of the other. Linguistic media content is realized internally, and so experienced as part of the self.

Over time, technological developments have meant that media penetrate ever more pervasively into our everyday lives. The mobile phone, now with multiple functions including internet, television and other media access, is the most obvious example, but there are many others, including those in the home, the car, and the office. When using most existing products of this type there is competition for the user's conscious attention, on a smaller scale than with virtual reality, but still representing a potentially serious conflict. This is why, for example, using a mobile phone while driving is illegal in some countries. This is sometimes a conflict between self and other, the internal and the external, presence and absence, but perhaps more often a conflict between presence here and presence there. Resolving this problem is perhaps *the* major challenge for future research.

Mixed realities, combinations of the physical and the virtual, based on technologies such as tangible interaction objects, wearable augmented reality displays, and sensor and camera-based capture of body movements and state information, are beginning to emerge as one of the most promising technological direction for presence research. Interreality systems (van Kokswijk, 2003; Gintautas & Hubler, 2007) go further than this. In these blended real-virtual realities, not only are the virtual and the physical combined into a perceptual whole, as with augmented reality, but the physical affects the virtual and—which is more challenging—the virtual affects the physical. Blended realities are combinations of the real and the virtual that affect each other and that can come to be understood as new real/virtual things in themselves. Ambient intelligent spaces are one example, though currently limited in scope and number.

There are clear technological trends indicating that presence will increasingly come to be understood as what we experience when we attend to an external world in which the physical and the virtual are somehow blended, but not in conflict as with immersive VR. Blends of the proximal and the distal already occur in some situations, such as those provided by videoconferencing systems. As of now, these happen in specific physical places. But the trend towards mobile media access seems inevitable, and we can anticipate mediated meetings of physically distant and proximal people, each experiencing a consistent blended physical-virtual reality including all participants. For this to work, media devices will need to be sensitive to both the situational context of their use, and the state of their users. Presence levels will be adjusted dynamically during the management of blended streams of incoming and outgoing information.

Conclusion

When we experience strong mediated presence, our experience is that the technology has become part of the self, and the mediated reality to which we are attending has become an integrated part of the other. When this happens, there is no conscious *effort of access* to information, nor *effort of action* to overt responses. We can perceive and act directly, as if unmediated. The extent to which we experience presence through a medium thus provides a measure of the extent to which that technology has become part of the self. This is not simply a matter of sensory replacement as addressed in classical virtual reality research—the personal significance of the mediated situation and other factors relating to content are known to cut across technological sophistication in inducing presence. It is a matter of how and where we experience the boundary between self and other. We predict that presence will increasingly be experienced and studied in *blended realities* of the physical and virtual. Our changing experiences of presence reflect the changing virtual/physical world in which we live.

A major program for future presence research will be systematically to implement and experiment with different viewpoints of media experience, involving singular and multiple first, second and third-person virtual representations of self and others. Factors such as degree of body-virtual image coordination, sensory-motor coupling and visual similarity (amongst others) will be varied and the impact on the sense of presence assessed (by means of triangulations of introspective, behavioral, and neuro-psychological data). A particular focus for the interpretation of results will be the search for indications of quantum shifts in the quality of presence in response to specific manipulations of such independent variables. Theory building will be achieved through progressive model development and hypothesis testing. A satisfactory general theory of presence will take into account not only media and technology-related aspects but also social, developmental, and evolutionary considerations.

Mediated presence is the feeling of being in an external world, in the realization of which technology plays a role. To persist, it requires adequate form to be directly perceived, conscious attention to that form, and content that will sustain such attention. When information is realized internally, as with abstract forms of representation, any technology involved is experienced as part of the other. But when information is realized externally, in or as a surrounding environment to which one can consciously attend, the medium becomes part of the self. To be part of the self, technology must create or modify an external other of which it is not perceived to be a part. This will be another in which, or with which, we can be consciously present.

It is unlikely that full-blown virtual reality, where the "immersant" is isolated from the physical world and exposed to a simulated world through maximized sensory replacement, will ever become the dominant technology for generating mediated presence. This is not the future of mediated presence. Rather, we predict that we will not experience presence in either a mediated world or in the physical world, but in a mixed reality that includes aspects of both. This has obvious advantages. Virtual reality excludes the physical world, as it must since the two are usually in complete conflict. But in most situations, such exclusion is undesirable, unsafe, and/or unsociable. The big expansions in use of digital media are likely to be seen in situations where the user is also active, and often mobile, in the physical world. This is not so strange, since the external world people experience has always been mediated. In a general sense, there is no purely physical world out there to be simulated and replaced.

References

Biocca, F. A., & Rolland, J. P. (1998). Virtual eyes can rearrange your body: Adaptation to visual displacement in see-through, head-mounted displays. *Presence: Teleoperators and Virtual Environments, 7,* 262–277.

Botvinick, M., & Cohen, J. (1998). Rubber hands 'feel' touch that the eye sees. *Nature, 391,* 756.

Castiello, U., Lusher, D., Burton, C., Glover, S., & Disler, P. (2004). Improving left hemispatial neglect using virtual reality. *Neurology, 62*(11) 1958–1962.

Clark, A. (2003). *Natural born cyborgs: Minds, technologies, and the future of human intelligence.* Oxford, England: Oxford University Press.

Ehrsson, H. H. (2007). The experimental induction of out-of-body experiences. *Science, 317*(5841), 1048.

Gintautas, V., & Hubler, A. W. (2007). *Experimental evidence for mixed reality states in an interreality system Physics. Review E., 75.* Retrieved from http://scitation.aip.org/getabs/servlet/GetabsServlet?prog=normal&id=PLEEE80000750000005057201000001&idtype=cvips&gifs=yes

Gregory, R. L. (1998). *Eye and brain: The psychology of seeing.* Oxford, England: Oxford University Press.

Hutchins, E. (1995). *Cognition in the wild.* Cambridge, MA: MIT Press.

IJsselsteijn, W. A. (2003). Presence in the Past: what can we learn from media history? In G. Riva, F. Davide, & W. A. IJsselsteijn (Eds.), *Being there: Concepts, effects and measurements of user presence in synthetic environments* (pp. 17–40). Amsterdam: IOS Press.

IJsselsteijn, W. A., de Kort, Y. A. W., & Haans, A. (2006). Is this *my* hand I see before me? The rubber hand illusion in reality, virtual reality, and mixed reality. *Presence: Teleoperators and Virtual Environments, 15,* 455–464.

Kokswijk, J. van, (2003). *Hum@n, telecoms & internet as interface to inter-reality.* Hoogwoud, The Netherlands: Bergboek.

Lebedev, M.A., & Nicolelis, M. A. (2006). Brain-machine interfaces: Past, present and future. *Trends in Neuroscience, 29,* 536–546.

Lenggenhager, B., Tadi, T., Metzinger, T., & Blanke, O. (2007). Video ergo sum: Manipulating bodily self-consciousness. *Science, 317*(5841), 1096–1099.

Lombard, M., & Ditton, T. (1997). At the heart of it all: The concept of presence. *Journal of Computer-Mediated Communication, 3*(2). Retrieved from http://jcmc.indiana.edu/vol3/issue2/lombard.html

Maclaren, K. (2008). Embodied perceptions of others as a condition of selfhood? *Journal of Consciousness Studies, 15*(8), 63–93.

New Scientist. (2008, May 1). *Virtual reality for flies puts humans in control.* Retrieved May 1, 2008, from http://technology.newscientist.com/article/dn13814-virtual-reality-for-flies-puts-humans-in-control.html

Ratan, R., Santa Cruz, M., & Vorderer, P. (2007). *Multitasking, presence & self-presence on the Wii.* Paper presented at the Proceedings of Presence 2007, Barcelona, Spain, October 25–27. Retrieved from http://www.temple.edu/ispr/prev_conferences/proceedings/2007/Ratan,%20Santa%20Cruz,%20and%20Vorderer.pdf

Riva G. (1998). Modifications of body-image induced by virtual reality. *Perceptual & Motor Skills, 86*(1), 163–170.

Riva, G., & Waterworth, J. A. (2003, April). Presence and the self: A cognitive neuroscience approach. *Presence-Connect, 3*(3). Retrieved from http://presence.cs.ucl.ac.uk/presenceconnect/articles/Apr2003/jwworthApr72003114532/jwworthApr72003114532.html

Riva, G., Waterworth, J. A., & Waterworth, E. L. (2004). The layers of presence: A bio-cultural approach to understanding presence in natural and mediated environments. *Cyberpsychology & Behavior, 7*(4), 402–416.

Riva, G., Bacchetta, M., Baruffi, M., & Molinari, E. (2001). Virtual reality-based multidimensional therapy for the treatment of body image disturbances in obesity: A controlled study. *Cyberpsychology & Behavior, 4*(4), 511–526.

Russell, J. A. (2003) Core affect and the psychological construction of emotion. *Psychological Review, 110*(1), 145–172.

Sanchez-Vives, M. V., & Slater M. (2005). Opinion: From presence to consciousness through virtual reality. *Nature Reviews Neuroscience, 6,* 332–339.

Slater, M. (2002). Presence and the sixth sense. *Presence: Teleoperators, and Virtual Environments, 11*(4), 435–439.

Turtle, S. (2005). *The second self: Computers and the human spirit, twentieth anniversary edition.* Cambridge, MA: MIT Press.

Waterworth, E. L., & Waterworth, J. A. (2006, September). *The presence of emotion: Designing the feeling of being there in interactive media experiences.* Paper presented at the Proceedings of Design and Emotion 2006, Gothenburg, Sweden.

Waterworth, J. A. (2000). Dextrous VR: The importance of stereoscopic display and hand-image collocation. In J. D. Mulder & R. van Liere (Eds.), *Virtual Environments 2000* (pp. 75–84). Vienna: Springer Computer Science.

Waterworth, J. A. (2002). Dextrous and shared Interaction with medical data: Stereoscopic vision is more important than hand-image collocation. In J. D. Westwood, H. M. Hoffman, R. A. Robb, & D. Stredney (Eds.), *Proceedings of Medicine Meets VR 2002* (pp. 560–566). Amsterdam: IOS Press.

Waterworth, J. A., & Waterworth E. L. (2003a). The meaning of Presence. *Presence-Connect, 3*(3). Retrieved from http://presence.cs.ucl.ac.uk/presenceconnect/articles/Feb2003/jwworthFeb1020031217/jwworthFeb1020031217.html

Waterworth, J. A., & Waterworth, E. L. (2003b, July). The core of presence: Presence as perceptual illusion. *Presence-Connect, 3*(3). Retrieved from http://presence.cs.ucl.ac.uk/presenceconnect/articles/Feb2003/jwworth-Feb1020031217/jwworthFeb1020031217.html

Waterworth, J. A., Waterworth, E. L., & Westling, J. (2002). Presence as performance: The mystique of digital participation. In F. R. Gouveia & F. Biocca (Eds.), *Proceedings of Presence 2002: 5th International Workshop on Presence* (pp. 174–181). Porto, Portugal: Universidade Fernando Pessoa.

Chapter 10

The Promise and Peril of Telepresence

Matthew Lombard

Human beings have attempted to create telepresence throughout recorded history, from cave paintings to virtual reality, but today these experiences are more prevalent than ever, and the trend is toward ever more effective and impactful experiences in which the roles of technology are hidden.

One common definition of "presence," a shortened version of the term "telepresence," has been "a perceptual illusion of nonmediation" (Lombard & Ditton, 1997). Lee (2006) has criticized the use of the term "illusion," noting that it has a negative connotation of deception and manipulation. But illusions can be either good or bad. For example, science fiction often previews (and motivates) the development of new technologies and provides visions of both positive and negative consequences of telepresence. Among the positive portrayals are those of the *Star Trek* franchise, where the holodeck provides the ultimate virtual space for recreation and self-actualization and where the android Data is accepted and treated as human by his colleagues and friends. In stark contrast are portrayals such as those of *The Matrix* films, in which humans dangerously fail to distinguish between reality and virtuality.

The primary telepresence technologies available to most members of Western societies in the last several decades—print, film, radio, television, video games, and computers—have been evolving increasingly quickly and, along with other newly emerging ones, are increasingly offering us useful and entertaining experiences previously impossible. But with these changes also come potential dangers. This chapter is about the promise of telepresence—how telepresence illusions are and may soon be used in nearly all aspects of our lives for good, and the peril of telepresence—the potential for unethical and harmful uses of the power of telepresence illusions in our everyday lives.

Defining Telepresence

While there are many competing and overlapping definitions and models of telepresence (Lombard & Jones, in press), the definition followed here is that of the International Society for Presence Research (2000): "a psychological state or subjective perception in which even though part or all of an individual's current experience is generated by and/or filtered through human-made technology, part or all of the individual's perception fails to accurately acknowledge the role of the technology in the experience." This definition allows for several types or dimensions of telepresence, including those in which the technology seems to become invisible (as in a "realistic" virtual environment, one that corresponds perceptually and socially to our nonmediated experiences) and those in which the technology (e.g., a computer, virtual pet, robot or android) seems to be an independent, "living" social entity.

The Promise of Telepresence

Telepresence experiences provided by current and future technologies hold great promise to improve nearly every aspect of our lives. An exhaustive discussion here is impossible, but the sections that follow provide some highlights of telepresence potential in the areas of entertainment, business, education, relationships, and health (examples in many other areas are available via International Society for Presence Research, 2000).

Entertainment

We begin with the aspect of our lives perhaps most strongly associated with telepresence. Because telepresence technologies increasingly allow media creators to produce experiences of wonder, excitement and delight, they are powerful tools for entertainment. It is sometimes hard to remember how far the entertainment experience has evolved in just the last few decades. Small, blurry, black and white images on furniture-sized television receivers have been replaced by large, detailed, vivid, color images on thin wall-mounted screens, and supplemented by a variety of interactive video game and computer-based virtual worlds.

The increasing numbers of people who watch high definition television sets, especially large ones, are experiencing representations of objects, people, and events in a new way. A common example is sports programming:

> [It's] very startling for those who haven't previously watched a [football] game in high-definition. The picture is six times more detailed than those on traditional analog sets and lacks the scan lines so visible when a viewer stands close to an analog TV. Tiny blemishes invisible on normal screens-a cut on a player's hand, a paint fleck on a helmet—are very evident in HDTV...."Since HDTV gives you

a wider shot of the field, you are able to see more action," said Scott Kemper, an HDTV set owner in Lawrence, Kan.... It makes watching football more realistic." It's not just the picture that is better, but the sound, too; the technology also accommodates digital surround sound, a format familiar to moviegoers. As Rob MacKenzie of Alexandria, Va., said, "You are surrounded by the noise of the crowd, the action on the field, the PA announcements." Even in a society where changes in technology and popular culture that once took years now take only months, the rapid move to HDTV for NFL telecasts is a dramatic metamorphosis for America's most popular TV sport. (Associated Press, 2003)

Today's HDTV is likely only a step along the way toward ever more powerful telepresence evoking technologies for the home. One possible successor to today's display technology is called high-dynamic range (HDR):

Whereas high-definition displays pump out more pixels, HDR displays provide more contrast.... [T]he brightest whites are hundreds of thousands of times brighter than the darkest blacks... "A regular image just looks like a depiction of a scene," says Roland Fleming, a research scientist at the Max Planck Institute for Biological Cybernetics, in Tübingin, Germany. "But high-dynamic range looks like looking through a window." (Greene, 2007)

NHK, the Japanese national broadcasting company, is working on something even more advanced:

Ultra High Definition Video, or UHDV, has a resolution 16 times greater than plain-old HDTV, and its stated goal is to achieve a level of sensory immersion that approximates actually being there. At a picture size of 7,680 by 4,320 pixels—that works out to 32 million pixels—UHDV's resolution trounces even high-end digital still cameras. HDTV, by comparison, has about two million pixels, and normal TV about 200,000 (and only 480 lines of horizontal resolution versus 4,000 with UHDV). Add to that UHDV's beefed-up refresh rate of 60 frames per second (twice that of conventional video). (Heingartner, 2004)

Beyond contrast, resolution, and refresh rates is 3D:

Operating like a holographic greeting card, [Phillips' prototype] combines slightly different angles of the same image to create video that appears to have different depths as your eyes scan it.... "We say

the market progression is black and white, to color, to high definition, to 3D," said Bjorn Teuwsen, demonstrating the product. (Associated Press, 2008)

Experts are even predicting that holographic television will further
enhance the illusion of objects and people entering the viewing room:

> The potential for television is mind blowing. Imagine watching a
> football game when suddenly a linebacker jumps off the screen to
> tackle a runner passing by. Or how about gazing at a documentary
> on the Pacific Ocean when a seagull circles in mid-air in the middle
> of your room. (Swann, 2007)

> [D]on't be surprised if within our lifetime you find yourself discard-
> ing your plasma and LCD sets in exchange for a holographic 3-D
> television that can put [soccer star] Cristiano Ronaldo in your living
> room or bring you face-to-face with life-sized versions of your gam-
> ing heroes. (Steere, 2008)

(For more on telepresence and television, see chapter 3, this volume.)
   Meanwhile, the film industry is transitioning to high resolution digital projection, and with its bigger budgets and the latest computer technologies can already produce or reproduce almost any experience for
movie-goers. Giant Screen Cinema formats such as IMAX and IMAX
3D provide "the ultimate movie experience. With crystal clear images
and wraparound digital surround sound, IMAX lets you feel like you're
really there" (IMAX Corporation, n.d.). The entertainment potential of
telepresence becomes even greater in simulator rides when films are combined with "4D" technologies that change room temperature, vibrate
or hydraulically move seats, shoot jets of air and water, etc. (Lombard,
2008). (For more on telepresence and film, see chapter 2, this volume.)
   Computer Generated Imagery (CGI) is evolving so quickly that creators of content for television, film, and other media are, or soon will be,
replacing real animals (Rogers, 2008), crowds of extras (Graham-Rowe,
2007), and even lead actors with technological illusions. The biggest
challenge has been to create a cgi person that doesn't appear eerily unhu-
man—the "Uncanny Valley" (Mori, 1970)—but new modeling technologies are close to crossing this long-standing barrier (Richards, 2008).
   Video games add the interactivity of nonmediated experience with
a variety of increasingly compelling peripheral devices. Nintendo's Wii
remote controller allows users to more literally play tennis and baseball
(Suellentrop, 2006), bowl (Clark, 2008), and box (Allen, 2008), among
other things. Force feedback steering wheel controllers provide the experience of driving. For example, Logitech's Driving Force Pro Force Feed-

back Wheel controller "transforms [Sony's *Gran Turismo 4*] from a good game into an honest-to-goodness simulator... The realistic turn ratio taps your real-world driving reflexes, rather than forcing you to develop a new set of motor responses for a controller" (Crowson, 2005).

The peripheral devices of the *Guitar Hero* and *Rock Band* games let users become rock guitarists: "'Everyone wants to be a rock star in this day and age,' [24-year-old Mike] Postlewaite said. 'When you plug that guitar in, turn the volume all the way up and jam out in your underwear, that's what Guitar Hero is all about'" (Wurst, 2008); the games may even be encouraging people to learn to play the real thing (Wurst, 2008).

The 3rd Space vest from TN Games contains air powered pneumatic cells that create impacts of different strengths at different locations, all corresponding to events in a video game.

> "The drama moment with this is getting shot in the back in a first-person game," [Creator and CEO Mark] Ombrellaro says. In market tests for the vest, he says, people would turn around in surprise when they felt the impact in the back, even though they knew intellectually to expect it. (Naone, 2007)

And Phillips Electronics' amBX PC system "takes a multi-sensory approach to pulling us deeper into" the experience (Taves, 2007):

> For example, while playing *V8 Supercars 3*, you can feel the breeze gaining momentum as you gain speed on the track, and changing force according to the direction of your turns. Meanwhile, rumble effects are felt through a wrist pad as you hit bumps or barriers, and ambient lighting behind and beside the screen matches the intensity of the on-screen action, dominating your peripheral vision. (Hill, 2007)

Soon we may not even need controllers:

> [T]hink about sparring with a virtual boxing opponent by doing nothing but standing up and throwing punches in the air....[3DV Systems'] new ZCam, a 3D camera that plugs directly into a PC, is designed to let gamers' hands be the only controllers they need. ... 'Imagine a game machine where you're just going to pick up the bat and swing it, or the tennis racket and swing it,' [supporter Bill] Gates said. (Terdiman, 2007)

Evolved from simple Internet Relay Chat (IRC), role-playing games in which users "moved" around a virtual area with text commands, today's Massively Multiplayer Online Role Playing Games (MMORPGs) such as *World of Warcraft* and *EverQuest* are increasingly sophisticated navigable visual and aural virtual spaces in which users control a representation (avatar) of their character and explore a world, meet other players, complete quests, and more (for more on telepresence and video games, see chapter 5, this volume). The virtual worlds aren't all game spaces—Second Life, There, and other worlds let users explore, socialize, build, buy, and sell all types of property; and pretty much do anything else they can do in the nonmediated world.

Augmented Reality (AR), in which nonmediated experience is enhanced with objects and entities superimposed over it via technology, is already providing an entertaining blurring of reality and virtuality. Simple examples can be found in sports broadcasts, in which down lines in American football and colored trails behind hockey pucks are superimposed on the fields of play. Gaming examples include Eye of Judgment for Sony's Playstation 3 and EyeToy camera, in which "High Definition 3D animated characters and vehicles come to life seamlessly into the on camera view of your tabletop" (Playstation.com, n.d.), and the experimental *Human Pacman*, a "human version of the classic arcade game *Pacman*, superimposing the virtual 3D game world on to city streets and buildings" so that "[p]layers equipped with a wearable computer, headset and goggles can physically enter a real world game space" (Sandhana, 2005; see also MXR, n.d.).

At Georgia Tech the AR Second Life project brings avatars into the real world "in life-sized form" where they interact with users and even stand in for actors in "mixed physical-virtual reality performances" of plays (Wen, 2008; see also Baard, 2007).

Combine all of these telepresence-evoking technologies—HDTV, 3D, holography, CGI, interactive computer peripheral devices, interactive immersive virtual worlds, augmented reality, and more—and, in the more distant future, it seems entirely plausible that consumers will have access to a "home holodeck," a room in which we can have a wide variety of highly compelling, entertaining, realistic (and fantastic), social, interactive telepresence experiences that will enrich our lives.

Business

Although entertainment may be the most enjoyable application of telepresence technologies, they also are already transforming our lives at work and as customers in the world of business in positive ways. In 2006, Cisco launched the "Cisco TelePresence Meeting Solution—a breakthrough 'in-person' experience for real-time, remote, business communication and collaboration." These advanced videoconferencing products use large high definition monitors, high-quality spatial audio, low latency connections, and unified room designs that make meeting participants "feel as if they are in the same room together, even though they may be located across the globe" (Cisco, 2006). Hewlett-Packard, Polycom, LifeSize, and other companies are producing competing products and the industry is growing quickly (Lichtman, 2006). Everyone benefits from this technology: Business users save the time and physical and emotional energy required by physical travel, improving their work/life balance; organizations save the costs of travel and can make important decisions more quickly; and society benefits from reduced carbon emissions and other damage to the environment.

Other technologies that evoke telepresence, even if the term isn't used, are also playing a growing role in many parts of the business world. The potential to provide the experience of being in a different location is a boon to tourism (and tourists). With Google Earth (Roush, 2007) we can seem to travel to almost anywhere on the planet; increasingly sophisticated 3D models of cities allow us to visit them as prospective tourists or for other reasons (Brinn, 2004); and IMAX movies and simulator experiences promote travel venues by taking viewers/riders everywhere from Yellowstone National Park (James & Merrill, 1994) to Antarctica (Flatman & Weiley, 1991) to India (Sanstha & Melton, 2005) to Jordan (Speetjens, 2004). The technology can even come to the consumer: *Texas on Tour* uses "virtual reality, holograms, green screen video and photography, interactive games and more" in a "53-foot mobile marketing experience that [travels] throughout the United States" and "transports the consumer to unique outdoor Texas experiences" (Langlinais, 2008).

At some travel destinations visitors are offered further adventures via telepresence. For example, at the Kawarau Bridge bungy jump site in New Zealand "the curious can experience a Hollywood-style simulation of a spine-chilling jump":

> Visitors stand on a kinetic viewing turntable (holding up to 48 people) surrounded by 130 video monitors and state-of-the-art audio and lighting systems. This provides the full range of emotional and intellectual experiences that are part of making a bungy jump. Meet this personal challenge and you are ready for the real thing. (New Zealand's Information Network, n.d.)

At Niagara Falls a virtual reality show "delivers a time-lapse lesson about the 10,000-year formation of the natural wonder complete with glacial snow, pelting rain and rumbling erosion, all building to 360-degree helicopter views unavailable from shore" (Thompson, 2008).

In the near future it will likely be possible to experience even more vivid and accurate virtual versions of possible vacations and other trips before deciding where to go in the nonmediated world.

Telepresence technology is also increasingly used in architecture, construction, and real estate to help people experience what it's like to be present in properties that are or will be built:

> Imagine using an avatar—an Internet representation of yourself—to walk through a virtual version of the new condo as if you were there, even though construction of the development has yet to begin. Or consider the possibilities of customizing the unit by changing the flooring, appliance or countertop options through the click of a button. (Severs, 2008)

These types of experiences aren't limited to buildings. Technologies that present vivid, realistic, immersive, interactive experiences are making it possible for advertisers to provide consumers a sense of what it would be like to use all kinds of products. Lombard and Snyder-Duch (2001) describe several ways interactive advertising might be designed to maximize different types of telepresence, and a growing number of studies (e.g., Choi, Miracle, & Biocca, 2001; Hopkins, Raymond, & Mitra, 2004; Klein, 2003; Schlosser, 2003) are demonstrating the connection between telepresence and purchase decisions:

> "Virtual product demonstrations that allow individuals to interact with merchandise create more vivid mental images of the consumer using the products, thereby increasing the likelihood they'll purchase the item," said Ann Schlosser, UW Business School assistant professor of marketing. "We've found that the more easily individuals can envision themselves using a product, the more likely they are to buy it." (Gardner, 2003)

Eventually with these technologies "advertisers will be able to offer consumers any experience with their product and any interaction with their company's representatives (real or technology-based) that they choose" (Lombard & Snyder-Duch, 2001); advertisers obviously will benefit, but so will (critical) consumers. (For more on telepresence and advertising, see chapter 6, this volume.)

Education

Another big part of our lives is spent learning, and here too telepresence holds great potential. Without using the term "telepresence," the major parties in education are acknowledging its importance: The Immersive Education Initiative is an international non-profit collaboration of educational and business institutions developing and promoting best practices in the use of "interactive 3-D graphics, commercial game and simulation technology, virtual reality, voice chat, Web cameras (webcams) and rich digital media [in] collaborative online course environments and classrooms"; the goal is to give participants "a sense of "being there" even when attending a class or training session in person isn't possible, practical, or desirable" and thereby enhance communication and learning (Media Grid, 2008). Educators are developing a wide variety of Virtual Learning Environments (VLEs; Selverian & Hwang, 2003) that connect classrooms not just to other classrooms but to ocean environments, Antarctica, NASA Space Centers, clinics and operating rooms, and many other locations (Meltzer, 2007; Polycom, 2008). Universities are beginning to replace primitive audio and video conferencing equipment with advanced telepresence conferencing systems like the ones discussed above (University of Missouri System, 2008).

Not only will telepresence be an increasingly common and critical part of young people's formal education, but it will be used to teach workers in nearly every profession. Simulator technologies that reproduce experience without risking the consequences of error are already being used to train people in firefighting (Photonics.com, 2007; Stair, 2005); logging (Riebe, 2005; Wendland, 2003); mining (Jafari, 2006); police work (Boyd, 2007); public safety (Raths, 2008); military combat (Crane, 2005; Kakesako, 2006; Payne, 2003); every kind of transportation including planes (Associated Press, 2006; BBC News, 2006; Blanchard, 2005), trains (Trainmaster, n.d.), and automobiles (Drive Square, 2004; Trotter, 2003); and many aspects of medical care including surgery (E-Health Insider, 2005; *Medical News Today*, 2004), physical therapy (News-Medical.Net, 2004; Wilson, 2007), and dental care (UIC, 2008). Simulators are also being used to let doctors in training learn what it's like to be a patient (WCAU, 2006) or experience the hallucinations of mental illnesses such a schizophrenia (Patch, 2004), and to teach students about the perceptual and motor impairments of driving while drunk (Standard-Times, 2005). By altering our representations in a virtual environment, Bailenson and his colleagues (e.g., Yee & Bailenson, 2007; Platoni, 2008) have demonstrated the potential of telepresence to teach us what it's like to have a different appearance (e.g., height, weight, attractiveness, age, race, or gender).

Because we "learn by doing" (formally, experiential learning; Kolb, 1984), telepresence technologies hold nearly unlimited promise to help us learn more effectively.

Relationships

Telepresence is beginning to provide new opportunities to enhance perhaps the most important area of our lives, our relationships. Supplementing letters and standard telephones, e-mail, mobile phones and web-based social networking technologies already let us stay in closer touch more of the time; web cameras combined with services such as Skype add the visual channel. All of these technologies help family members and others stay psychologically connected even when they're thousands of miles away (Pessoa, 2008).

Other new technologies may someday soon provide subtle cues to connect us over distance. With Presence Frames, designed by Matty Sallin, a motion detector in one person's picture frame triggers a light in the other person's frame via an Internet connection, indicating the first person's presence; Michael Jefferson's Slumberlight uses a similar logic but with proximity sensors under a bed (Block, 2005); and Tomitsch, Grechenig, and Mayrhofer (2007) use ceiling projections to provide "remote awareness." A variety of new technologies even allow the illusion of sexual intimacy over distance (see Lombard & Jones, 2004).

Cisco has begun using its advanced TelePresence systems to connect military personnel with their families. A wife whose husband is serving in Iraq makes the benefits clear:

> I loved feeling like my husband was sitting right across the table from me. It makes this deployment a little bit easier being able to see my husband on a huge screen. Even though my sweetheart is half way around the world, when I am in that room he is right beside me. (U.S. Troops, 2008)

Cisco plans to bring the technology to the home soon (Lawson, 2007) so that friends and relatives can "be together" despite living in different cities or countries. It seems increasingly likely that a standard feature of even middle-class homes will soon be a wall-size screen and unobtrusive speakers and microphones that allow anyone to visit, play, and live together with their significant others, family, and friends, regardless of geographical location.

Aside from these benefits of telepresence for our relationships with humans, we'll increasingly have satisfying relationships with virtual pets and maybe even artificial people. Some popular virtual pets exist online, including Nintendogs (Buffa, 2005) and GoPets (GoPets, 2005). Others exist both online and in physical reality, such as Webkinz (Cook, 2006). And others exist only in our world, such as Furby and Pleo, the robotic baby dinosaur created by the company known as UGOBE:

> The company's unique products, known as Life Forms, intend to blur the line between technology and life. By integrating three disciplines-organic articulation with sensory response and autonomous behaviors-UGOBE aims to revolutionize robotics and transform inanimate objects into lifelike creatures. (UGOBE, n.d.)

The company's plans go far beyond toys:

> As [Creator Caleb] Chung sees it, the world is going to have more and more service bots, so they ought to be physically and emotionally pleasing. They ought to be as lifelike—and as lovable—as possible. (Thompson, 2007)

While there is resistance in the United States, the Japanese favor robots and even human-appearing androids—"they are in a headlong rush to welcome them into their lives as friends and personal assistants" (Jacob, 2006).

While technologies as simple as diaries, paintings, statues, photographs, and audio and video recordings provide a sense of closeness with those who have died, realistic androids of actual people (e.g., those by Osaka University's Hiroshi Ishiguro of NHK newscaster Ayako Fujii and of himself [Hornyak, 2006] and Hanson Robotics' recreation of science fiction author Philip K. Dick [Hanson Robotics, n.d.]) could represent an extreme way of using technology to create this sense of presence (Lombard & Selverian, 2008).

While regularly interacting with androids as if they are fully or nearly fully human (as characters interact with Data in *Star Trek*) is obviously a long way off if it ever happens, we seem to instinctively respond to all kinds of technologies as if they were living, social entities (Reeves & Nass, 1996; Turkle, 1984, 1995) and the business community is continually seeking the best ways to appeal to this human tendency in ways that will expand this intriguing telepresence phenomenon. (For more on telepresence, human-computer interaction and computer-mediated communication, see chapter 4, this volume.)

Health

Taking care of our health—both preventing illness and investigating, being treated for, recovering from, and coping with illness and injury—dominates nearly all of our lives at some point. Here again, telepresence offers great promise.

Health clubs and gyms have adopted a new generation of machines that provide real exercise in virtual settings (Kushner & Fleishman, 2008; Vierria, 2008): "From a snowy trail to Ancient ruins. Pick a place and hop on for a bike ride like nothing you've ever seen ... 'You can forget about your stressful problems and just really focus on the surroundings and the nature,' said Julie Marchenko, a virtual biker" (Stahl, 2008). At home, Sony's EyeToy, Microsoft's Xbox and especially Nintendo's Wii are getting video game players young and old off the couch and burning calories (Clark, 2008; Lanningham-Foster et al., 2006; Schmidt, 2007).

And virtual trainers and coaches like Maya in *Yourself!Fitness* (PC, PlayStation, Xbox) provide motivation and guidance:

> "She's my personal trainer," said Mr. Raphael, 38, a software engineer in San Francisco. "She just happens to live in my television." Each time Mr. Raphael begins a workout, Maya asks how he's feeling and the next time, remembers whether he said upbeat or sluggish. She also nags if he misses a scheduled workout, asking, "Where were you yesterday?" (Saint Louis, 2006)

Telepresence offers people around the world the prospect of better access to better medical care. In addition to various videoconferencing systems available for remote patient "visits," doctors are using mobile "remote presence robots" to "freely interact with patients, family members and hospital staff from anywhere, anytime" (InTouch Health, n.d.). Telerobotic technology "offers a surgeon the full sensory experience of conventional hands-on surgical procedures" and the potential to provide emergency and surgical care to anyone, anywhere (SRI International, 2006; see also BBC News, 2001). Virtual reality allows patients to experience war, natural disasters, air travel, public speaking, insects, and other sources of trauma and anxiety in a controlled, therapeutic environment (Bergfeld, 2006; Dotinga, 2005; Juan et al., 2006; Lyons, 2008; Moore, Wiederhold, Wiederhold, & Riva, 2002). VR also can help during physical rehabilitation, where Computer Assisted Rehabilitation Environments "[simulate] daily activities such as taking a walk in an urban environment, driving a car, hiking up and down a mountain or... steering a boat. The scenarios teach patients to stay balanced and react to situations they will face in the real world" (Stanek, 2006). Research demonstrates a variety of benefits of these technologies, including patient satisfaction (Hailey, Roine, & Ohinmaa, 2002; Keshner, 2004; Mair & Whitten, 2000; Petelin, Nelson, & Goodman, 2007; Rizzo & Kim, 2005).

Telepresence is also being used to ease our pain and anxiety during medical treatment. Hospitals are adding virtual windows and ceilings, "a combination of nature photography, computer and printing technology and special lighting equipment to simulate daylight" (Sagario, 2005) and thereby "reliably trigger an authentic experience of nature and the psychological and physiological correlates that accompany such an experience ... deep relaxation, freedom, and inner peace" (Witherspoon, 2005). Virtual worlds like SnowWorld, which was designed for burn victims, turn patients' attention away from their pain; its creators, David Patterson and Hunter Hoffman, "hope more virtual worlds will alleviate not only acute pain, but chronic pain, and expect worlds to be more widespread for acute pain such as wound care, childbirth and dental pain in only a few years" (Fisher, 2003).

Yet another form of telepresence technology likely to be a part of all of our health care, especially as we get older, is robotic pets and androids that respond to human voices and actions. "Japanese nursing homes are using realistic-looking robotic pets as companions for residents... Some have proposed taking that a step further by having androids take care of Japan's elderly population. Less humanlike robots already are being used to lift patients and give them baths. So far, the reaction has been generally positive" (Smith, 2007). It's not unreasonable to predict that we'll eventually have artificially intelligent technologies designed to serve, and which we'll treat, as close companions and providers of comfort and medical care.

We rarely consider them technologies that create "perceptual illusions of nonmediation," but just as with other telepresence technologies, eyeglasses and hearing aids modify the way we experience the world, and we quickly come to ignore their (very positive) roles in our perceptions. Advances in a range of technologies suggest the same potential for prosthetics for the many people each year who lose limbs to accident and disease. Richard Normann, a neuroscientist who has pioneered work in the field, says "It is not unreasonable to believe an amputee could have an arm that he will come to believe and use just like an existing arm" (Singer, 2007; see also Kotulak, 2004; Ortiz, 2007). And Brain-Computer Interfaces (BCIs), in which a computer is connected to the brain via sensors placed on the scalp or in the skull, allow people with damaged perceptual and/or motor systems (or anyone else for that matter) to interact with real or virtual worlds (Dornhege & Sejnowski, 2007). For example, Leeb et al. (2007) report how a paraplegic was able to use his thoughts to "move" down a street and interact with avatars of other people in a virtual environment.

The potential of all of these technologies to lighten the burden of the health and medical care we all do or will experience seems unlimited.

The Peril of Telepresence

While it is clear that current and future technologies promise to create many positive, and even startlingly positive, roles for telepresence in our everyday lives, as with nearly all technologies they can be used in ways that create harm as well. The following sections review some of these perils of telepresence.

Entertainment

A wide range of potential dangers are associated with telepresence and entertainment. Each medium since the written word has prompted cautions about likely costs that come with the benefits. The latest telepresence-evoking technologies are arguably able to reproduce nonmediated experience more vividly and accurately than ever before possible, which may both amplify the traditional dangers and create new ones.

As with all technologies, just because we can use telepresence technologies to do something doesn't mean we should. Often it's a matter of moderation, as with "addictive" video games and virtual worlds. Pergams and Zaradic (UIC, 2007) write about a less obvious example when they note that children are increasingly experiencing nature indirectly:

> Intrepid nature photographers now use high-definition photography to bring unparalleled images of wildlife and a 'you-are-there' experience approaching virtual reality to the viewer. It can be at once informative, thrilling and terrifying—and all from the comfort of your easy-chair or sofa.

Because direct experience with nature is a key contributor to positive attitudes and activism regarding the environment, they review diverse data to conclude that "virtual nature appears to directly compete with time previously allocated to the more beneficial, direct contact with the outdoors" and point to the "daunting prospect of today's children (tomorrow's parents) in a culture devoid of contact with the evolutionary driver and life-support system that is our natural world" (UIC, 2007, p. 142).

Other activities telepresence technologies permit seem problematic in any quantity or duration. A disturbing example is the installation of cameras in caskets before humans are buried and the webcasting of the images, as in the projects Death dot com (2004) and SeeMeRot.com (n.d.). Another example is virtual hunting (Parker, 2004; Vallis, 2004):

> Live-shot.com, selected by Fortune magazine as the worst technology product of 2004, would allow hunters to monitor animals through a Web browser connected to a video camera that is mounted on a hunting platform, along with a rifle, at [Texas rancher John] Underwood's 330-acre ranch. From his desk overlooking, say, Lake Eola in Orlando, the hunter can manipulate the camera, panning and zooming in on animals as they come into view. When he's ready, the hunter aims, fires and—voila! Trophy head soon to be delivered. (Parker, 2004)

A final example comes from Japan's NTT Communication Science Laboratories where a new technology allows users with remote control joysticks to control the equilibrium and thus the movements of a person wearing a headset: "The device originally was designed to add realism to video games and other virtual environments. But while technically impressive, the invention is viewed by some as ethically troubling—viewed, quite literally, as a new form of mind control" (Ortiz Jr., 2006).

A different set of concerns is raised as the technologies used to create our media experiences grow in sophistication and it becomes more difficult to determine what is "real" and what has been created or modified for us. Recording artists use autotuner technology to correct their pitch both in the studio and in concert, where they lip-synch and use prerecorded sounds (Nelson, 2004; Wei Chu, 2003). "Fakers" use image manipulation technology to create pictures of celebrities "in various stages of undress"—the best fakes "rise from the underground newsgroups and onto the hard drives of people who take them for the real thing" (Kushner, 2003). Kevin Connor of Adobe, the company that developed Photoshop software, says, "There's much more awareness and much more skepticism when [people] are looking at images....That's why we think that's something we need to get involved in. It's not healthy to have people be too skeptical about what they saw" (Jesdanun, 2008, February 24).

Law enforcement, the legal community, and news organizations are all seeking new techniques to detect digital image manipulation (Jesdanun, 2008, February 24). It's a particular problem in the area of virtual child pornography after a 2002 U.S. Supreme Court decision declared computer-generated images, rather than images of real children, protected by the first amendment; now prosecutors must spend millions of dollars each year to verify the authenticity of images to juries (Jesdanun, 2008, February 25). And distinguishing what is real and manipulated won't be limited to still images, as "movie makers and video game developers are getting closer to achieving the holy grail of animation: creating computer-generated actors that are visually indistinguishable from real people" (Johnson, 2008).

Strom (2006) expands the list of ways reality is blurring with virtuality:

We'll soon be seeing video games based on reality TV shows—you know, the shows that employ script writers to make sure the reality sounds real....Then there are people making real money by selling Second Life businesses that sell virtual goods to others inside their virtual world. There are others who auction on eBay virtual items that enable game players to advance to higher levels; these items are assembled by real low-wage workers who spend their days playing the games to accumulate them. There are fake Web pages for real people on MySpace, created by fans (or detractors). There are also real Web pages for fake people, some of which were created by advertising and PR people who want to push a particular brand or agenda....One of the most popular YouTube videos shows a lonely teenager talking about her life. But it turns out that lonelygirl15 is really an actress playing a part.

The confusion about what is real in mediated experiences extends (and may even contribute to) an opposite problem. Prompted by the first author's experiences as a journalist in Manhattan in the aftermath of the September 11, 2001, attacks, Timmins and Lombard (2005) documented a phenomenon they call "inverse presence," an "illusion of mediation" in which people misperceive "real" experiences as if they are mediated (indicated, for example, with comments such as "it felt like a movie"). They note potential negative consequences that include "disappointments and missed opportunities as reality that seems mediated turns out not to be as compelling and/or idealized as high presence mediated experiences" and the belief that "as in most mediated portrayals, the 'story' will all work out right in the end," leading to the failure to take actions to insure that they do.

Media scholars have long worried about the potential of media consumers to learn inaccurate and dangerous messages about the world. Ditton (1997) provided an early demonstration that telepresence may amplify this potential. She manipulated telepresence (perceptual and social realism) in an experiment in which participants watched clips from 15 films. She found that greater levels of telepresence were associated with greater changes in social judgments about topics addressed in the clips, despite participants' reported lack of awareness of using the fictional portrayals to make the judgments. Ditton's model holds that media users unintentionally blend memories of mediated and unmediated experiences and she concludes that "viewers' perceptions of the world will be even more distorted by the make-believe experiences they have through watching television as presentation technologies advance." (For more on telepresence and media effects, see chapter 8, this volume.)

Aside from the effects of high telepresence entertainment media on our judgments and behaviors, there's a related question of morality. Asher Meir (2007), research director at the Business Ethics Center of Jerusalem, considers

> virtual behaviors that are permitted by the rules (and physics) of the game space, but which simulate activities that are forbidden in RL [real life]—for example, the street gangs that reportedly are terrorizing some locations in Second Life. Is it ethical to mug someone in a virtual world? In my opinion, the answer is yes. The whole idea of these parallel universes is to enable people to do all kinds of things they fantasize about but don't care or dare to do in RL.

But media ethicists Thomas Bivins and Julianne Newton (2003) caution against this view:

> Virtual experiences become known to us through physical percep-
> tions of sight, sound, touch, taste, and smell and, therefore, cannot
> help but affect our so-called real selves. Hence, virtual exploration
> of an activity that might be deplorable in real life, such as rape or
> murder, cannot help but shift—for better or worse, minutely or
> grandly—the integrity of the actor's being. (p. 221)

It seems reasonable to conclude that the more perceptually and socially
realistic virtual experiences that evoke telepresence in the future will
amplify these shifts.

In extreme cases, entertaining telepresence may even cause serious
psychological problems. In normal parasocial interactions and relationships (Horton & Wohl, 1956), media users experience a (false) sense of
social interaction and connection with media personalities, but when
these experiences become too vivid for some people, they can become
obsessed with, stalk, and even harm the media personality (Dietz et al.,
1991; Giles, 2002). Timmins and Lombard (2005) point to extreme
cases in which inverse presence may have contributed to violence, such
as the 1999 Columbine High School tragedy in which the "Matrix kill-
ers" offered as a defense that they believed they were living in the film's
virtual reality and that therefore shooting people didn't really mean they
were being killed (Jackman, 2003).

Aaron Walsh, a programmer and instructor at Boston College, sees a
wider danger:

> Nobody knows exactly what impact insanely realistic, media-rich
> virtual reality will have on society. We're already dealing with early
> forms of immersive illness, such as addiction, alienation, mental
> schisms, and more, but today it's not a problem that affects a large
> percentage of users. We don't see massive problems today for a num-
> ber of reasons, including rather low-quality virtual environments
> and limitations on how much time we spend in these environments.
> But what happens when the visual and audio quality becomes
> indistinguishable from reality, the technology becomes truly main-
> stream, and a substantial portion of education takes place in such
> environments...? ... I'd estimate that the at-risk population can be
> calculate[d] by adding the percentage of people with addiction prob-
> lems to the percentage of society that suffer some form of mental
> illness. That's a big chunk of society. Is it all gloom and doom? Cer-
> tainly not, but it's a grand challenge we're not even remotely pre-
> pared for today. As with other disruptions society will eventually
> adapt, but I think we're in for a very rough ride. (Lamont, 2007)

Business

While some (e.g., see Ruffini, 2007) have proposed that a suitable "grand challenge" for the telepresence research community would be to "create a fully immersive system for meetings between people who are physically remote, yet feeling as they were together for real" (p. 3), they and others acknowledge that despite today's advanced technology, a system that reproduces all of the subtle social cues of face to face human communication (e.g., odors, eye gaze, skin tone variations, even haptics) is still far off. In the meantime, there's a danger that most users of telepresence systems will accept the more limited cues and act based on them, ignoring the absence or distortion of the normal, rich communication cues needed for mutually truthful and trustworthy interaction (Tompkins, 2003). More experienced users, and those who wish to deceive and conceal, may be at an advantage in such cases. In a related observation, Tompkins (2003) notes:

> The hypothesis that cues mindlessly trigger communication scripts may help explain why we have difficulty internalizing the fact that CMC [computer mediated communication] is public and not private communication. Common CMC practices are based on a presumption that messages are private and will not be forwarded, copied or researched. Yet, the public context of CMC allows for such practices. (p. 200)

With Cisco and others developing features that allow the recording of meetings in telepresence suites as other manufacturers express concern about privacy and security issues (Lawson, 2008), it's easy to see the real dangers of treating an experience supported and manipulated by technology as if it's a nonmediated, in person meeting around a conference table.

Another area of potential peril in the world of business concerns telepresence in advertising. There has long been concern about, and in many cases, regulation of, deceptive or false advertising, but the ability to provide consumers a vivid, interactive, technology-based experience that is claimed to reproduce the actual experience of using a product creates new opportunities for exaggeration and misrepresentation. As Lombard and Snyder-Duch (2001) note, "We hope to see these technologies used to provide users with a more enjoyable media experience and with more choices as consumers. We do not hope to encourage the use of presence-evoking interactive advertising to merely create the illusion of choice—a very undemocratic ideal." Educators, regulators, and consumer advocates may need to develop an ambitious set of new "media literacy" materials to keep up with the evolution of telepresence technologies used in advertising.

Education

There are two potential concerns in the area of telepresence and education. First, vivid, interactive, telepresence-evoking educational experiences that contain inaccurate representations of events, people, and objects may teach students inaccurate information (a complaint already made about the "docudrama" film and television genre; Rosenthal, 1999). In the case of skills training, where there is no actual danger or risk in a virtual environment in which scenarios can be reset and repeated, the inaccuracies may lead to overconfidence in the learner's abilities ("this is surely a concern for wannabe racing drivers who can achieve incredible lap times on a virtual track and think they are equally talented when it comes to driving a real car on the road"; Hawkins, 2004).

The second concern involves what is taught with high telepresence media. For example, the U.S. military uses high telepresence games at theme parks and malls (e.g., The Virtual Army Experience; Leland, 2009) as an education and recruitment tool, and more sophisticated training simulators elsewhere (Batey, 2008; Macedonia, 2002). But "[t]he military use of 'serious games' brings opportunities and risks... Do they desensitise 'players' to the consequences of firing at real human 'targets'? What are the ethics of learning to kill while playing?" (Hyland, 2007). Echoing concerns about inverse presence, Harmon (2003) notes that

> as video war games gain popularity throughout the armed forces, some military trainers worry that the more the games seem like war, the more war may start to seem like a game. As the technology gets better, they say, it becomes a more powerful tool and a more dangerous one.

Relationships

Many of the concerns about the implications of telepresence for our human relationships follow more general dystopian views of information technologies (DiMaggio, Hargittai, Neuman, & Robinson, 2001; Katz & Rice, 2002; Winner, 1997):

> Because we are citizens of cyberspace, even our next door neighbors do not matter all that much. We can stay in our rooms, stare at flat screens, surf the Internet, and be satisfied with simulacra of human contact....[A]ll-too-often becoming "wired" involves increasing isolation, discomfort, and even fear of the presence of other people. (Winner, 1997, p. 13)

While the evidence at this point is exploratory and ambiguous (DiMaggio et al., 2001; Katz & Rice, 2002), the idea that highly effective telepresent communication with family, friends, and others could cause us to spend less time and energy on, and even lose some degree of comfort and skill regarding, face to face interaction, is worth consideration.

Our relationships with social technologies from virtual pets to household robots raise some of the same issues. MIT professor Sherry Turkle asks, "Should we be creating robots just to make people feel good? Should we be making artificial companions? Isn't this a statement that we've given up on offering actual human companions?" (Thompson, 2007).

The dystopia portrayed in science fiction such as *Blade Runner* and *The Terminator* franchise, in which our robotic telepresence technologies turn on us, is fanciful. But at this writing several efforts are underway around the world to establish ethical policies and procedures for the creation and use of robots. The South Korea "Robot Ethics Charter" envisions "a near future wherein humans may run the risk of becoming emotionally dependent on or addicted to their robots" (Billings, 2007). How will we respond to and be changed by interactions with robots (and possibly androids) that function as surgeons, police officers, soldiers, and friends? Levy (2007) argues that we'll fall in love and have sex with robots in the future, which obviously would raise numerous questions and potential problems. Lombard and Selverian (2008) observe that in the not-too-distant future we may be able to create artificially intelligent android reproductions of ourselves for our relatives to have after we die, and they point to a variety of concerns including interference with healthy bereavement.

All of this suggests that, at a minimum, we should carefully consider the implications of the technologies we create and the relationships we develop with them.

Health

While some of the concerns about incomplete and distorted communication via technology, and, of course, security and privacy, apply in the context of telepresence and health, at least two other issues suggest different categories of potential danger in this area. One is the idea of artificially intelligent robots and androids that provide care and comfort to the elderly and those needing medical treatment. At a practical level, what happens when the human patient believes the caregiving machine understands what he says to it when it doesn't? Who is responsible when the technology provides inappropriate care? (Smith, 2007). More basically, in analyzing the ethics of caregiving robots Decker (2008, citing earlier work by Christaller et al., 2001) concludes that "People requiring care may not be made into objects by replacing staff with robots"

(Christaller et al., 2001, p. 221), and "In accordance with the formula for humanity [by philosopher Emmanuel Kant], caregiving should be carried out by humans. Robots are only acceptable as tools used, for example, in helping to lift patients" (p. 324).

A second area of potential danger in the health context concerns telepresence technologies designed to enhance human experience of the world. Eyeglasses, hearing aids, prosthetic limbs, and virtual worlds have been uncontroversial because they're non-invasive and designed to reproduce typical human perceptions and movements. But it is likely that sophisticated prostheses and neuroprostheses (devices including cochlear and retinal implants that function in place of damaged sensory organs) will eventually produce not just "typical" human perceptual and motor abilities for their users but "superior" ones, raising important questions and concerns. And as Wolpe (2007) writes, the advent of Brain-Computer Interfaces (discussed above) means "we are for the first time beginning to treat the human brain as 'wetware' that we can connect to other information technology systems. The social and ethical implications of such a development are vast," including issues of identity, privacy, autonomy, and more (pp. 128–129)

An Ethics of Telepresence

While telepresence technologies offer great promise to improve our lives now and in the future, and though it is clear that many of the perils of telepresence identified above are not of major concern given the level of sophistication of today's technologies, those who study, create, distribute, and use telepresence technologies need to be mindful of these perils. One step that we—as wide a community of experts and others as possible—should take now is to develop, adopt, and propagate a comprehensive ethical code of conduct regarding telepresence experiences. A detailed proposal is beyond the scope of this chapter, but first principles might include:

1. Individuals must be informed in advance about the existence and nature of telepresence illusions they will experience.
2. Detailed information about the operation of technologies that create telepresence illusions must be made available to the public.
3. Technologies which are or create the illusion of being independent social actors must be programmed to never harm people or property.
4. Scholars, creators, and distributors of technologies that evoke telepresence must consider the possibility of negative consequences of the technologies and take proactive steps to prevent them.

Conclusion

As with any technology or tool, telepresence technologies are neutral—they carry great promise to improve nearly every aspect of our individual and collective lives, but also to damage them. It is up to telepresence creators and scholars, and all of us who do and will use the technologies, to make sure they are used to fulfill their promise for positive outcomes (those discussed here and many more), and to minimize their potential for negative uses and impacts.

References

Allen, J. (2008, April 3). ezGear for Wii Boxing Gloves (Review). DailyGame. Retrieved April 2008 from http://www.dailygame.net/news/archives/007467.php

Associated Press. (2003, August 24) NFL, HDTV join forces. *Baltimore Sun*. Retrieved 2003 from http://www.sunspot.net/sports/bal-sp.hdt-v24aug24,0,5554359.story?coll=bal-sports-headlines

Associated Press. (2006, July 24). Virtual cockpit view promises safer air travel. *Technology Review*. Retrieved November 24, 2008, from http://www.technologyreview.com/read_article.aspx?id=17196

Associated Press. (2008, May 20). Philips demonstrates products in the pipeline including "3D TV" without glasses. *Technology Review*. Retrieved May 2007 from http://www.technologyreview.com/Wire/20808/?nlid=1087

Baard, M. (2007, July 9). Gadgets may help merge virtual reality with real life. *Boston Globe*. Retrieved November 24, 2008, from http://www.boston.com/business/personaltech/articles/2007/07/09/gadgets_may_help_merge_virtual_reality_with_real_life

Batey, A. (2008, December 13). Virtual hostility. *Financial Times*. Retrieved March 11, 2009, from http://www.ft.com/cms/s/0/e3ac2d58-c8b5-11dd-b86f-000077b07658.html

BBC News. (2001, September 19). Doctors claim world first in telesurgery. Retrieved October 2008 from http://news.bbc.co.uk/2/hi/science/nature/1552211.stm

BBC News. (2006, May 5). Air traffic simulator introduced. Retrieved November 24, 2008, from http://news.bbc.co.uk/2/hi/uk_news/4975974.stm

Bergfeld, C. (2006, July 26). A dose of virtual reality: Doctors are drawing on video-game technology to treat post-traumatic stress disorder among Iraq war veterans. *Business Week*. Retrieved October 2008 from http://www.businessweek.com/technology/content/jul2006/tc20060725_012342.htm?chan=top+news_top+news

Billings, L. (2007, July 16). Grappling with the implications of an artificially intelligent culture. *Seed*. Retrieved January 5, 2009, from http://www.seedmagazine.com/news/2007/07/rise_of_roboethics.php

Bivins, T. H., & Newton, J. H. (2003). The real, the virtual, and the moral: Ethics at the intersection of consciousness. *Journal of Mass Media Ethics, 18*(3&4), 213–229.

Blanchard, M. (2005, January 20). Pilots enter superjumbo virtual reality. *Canada's The Globe and Mail.* Retrieved November 24, 2008, from http://www.theglobeandmail.com/servlet/story/RTGAM.20050120.gttwsimulator20/BNStory/Technology

Block, R. (2005, May 12). Engadget visits NYU's ITP spring 2005 show. Engadget. Retrieved November 24, 2008, from http://www.engadget.com/2005/05/12/engadget-visits-nyus-itp-spring-2005-show/

Boyd, L. (2007, July 11). Virtual trainer keeps police safe. *The Cleveland Plain Dealer.* Retrieved November 24, 2008, from http://www.cleveland.com/news/plaindealer/index.ssf?/base/cuyahoga/1184142996146230.xml&coll=2

Brinn, D. (2004, December 19). Israeli technology creates American virtual cities. Retrieved October 2008 from http://www.israel21c.org/bin/en.jsp?enDispWho=Articles%5El865&enPage=BlankPage&enDisplay=view&enDispWhat=object&enVersion=0&enZone=Technology

Buffa, C. (2005, March 16). Hands-On: Nintendogs (DS). *Game Daily.* Retrieved November 24, 2008, from http://www.gamedaily.com/games/nintendogs/ds/game-news/hands-on-nintendogs/4059/8453/

Choi, Y. K., Miracle, G. E., & Biocca, F. (2001). The effects of anthropomorphic agents on advertising effectiveness and the mediating role of presence. *Journal of interactive advertising, 2*(1). Retrieved October 2008 from http://jiad.org/article17

Christaller, T., Decker, M., Gilsbach, J-M., Hirzinger, G., Lauterbach, K., Schweighofer, E., et al. (2001). *Robotik. Perspektiven fu ̈r menschliches Handeln in der zuku ̈nftigen Gesellschaft* [Robotics: Prospects for human action in the future society]. Springer: Berlin.

Cisco (2006, October 23). Cisco announces the Cisco TelePresence eeeting solution—A breakthrough "in-person" experience for real-time, remote, business communication and collaboration [Press release]. Retrieved November 24, 2008, from http://newsroom.cisco.com/dlls/2006/prod_102306b.html

Cisco (2008, May 8). U.S. troops in Iraq connect with family and friends via telePresence [Press release]. Retrieved November 24, 2008, from http://newsroom.cisco.com/dlls/2008/prod_050808b.html

Clark, R. (2008, September 28). Seniors trump barriers in Wii bowling tourney. New Jersey Online. Retrieved September 2008 from http://www.nj.com/sunbeam/index.ssf?/base/news-4/1222587621327110.xml&coll=9

Cook, L. (2006, November 26). Cuddly Webkinz the rage among tweens. *The Grand Rapids* (Michigan) *Press.* Retrieved November 24, 2008, from http://www.mlive.com/news/grpress/index.ssf?/base/features-1/1164527778165530.xml&coll=6

Crane, D. (2005, September 8). AGSS II Helo Gunner simulator: Super-realism for more enemy kills in battle. From DefenseReview.com (DefRev). Retrieved November 24, 2008, from http://www.defensereview.com/article785.html

Crowson, B. (2005, March 14). Virtually real. *Birmingham* (Alabama) *News.* Retrieved March 2005 from http://www.al.com/entertainment/birmingham-news/index.ssf?/base/entertainment/110795432190180.xml

Decker, M. (2008). Caregiving robots and ethical reflection: The perspective of interdisciplinary technology assessment. *AI & Society, 22*(3), 315–330.

Dietz, P. E., Matthews, D. B., Van Duyne, C., Martell, D. A., Parry, C. D. H., Stewart, T., et al. (1991). Threatening and otherwise inappropriate letters to Hollywood celebrities. *Journal of Forensic Sciences, 36,* 185–209.

DiMaggio, P., Hargittai, E., Neuman, W. R., & Robinson, J. P. (2001). Social implications of the internet. *Annual Review of Sociology, 27,* 307–336.

Ditton, T. B. (1997). *The unintentional blending of direct experience and mediated experience: The role of enhanced versus limited television presentations in inducing source-monitoring errors.* Unpublished doctoral dissertation, Temple University, Philadelphia. Retrieved January 4, 2009, from Dissertations & Theses @ Temple University database. (Publication No. AAT 9737933).

Dornhege, G., & Sejnowski, T. J. (2007). *Toward brain-computer interfacing.* Cambridge, MA: MIT Press.

Dotinga, R. (2005, January 27). It's not all in your head. *Wired.* Retrieved October 2008 from http://www.wired.com/news/medtech/0,1286,66408,00.html

Drive Square. (2004, November 01). Drive Square receives grant to develop portable vehicle [Press release]. Retrieved November 24, 2008, from http://www.businesswire.com/news/google/20041101005700/en

E-Health Insider. (2005, January 5). Computer generated brain surgery to help trainees. Retrieved November 24, 2008, from http://www.e-health-insider.com/news/item.cfm?ID=988

Fisher, B. (2003, July 23). Flying in a pain-free world. *University of Washington Daily.* Retrieved October 2008 from http://dailyuw.com/2003/7/23/flying-in-a-pain-free-world/

Flatman, D. (Producer) & Weiley, J. (Director). (1991). *Antarctica* [Motion picture]. USA: Museum of Science and Industry, Chicago.

Gardner, N. (2003, September 3). Study shows virtual demonstrations lead consumers to make real purchases. EurekAlert. Retrieved October 2008 from http://www.eurekalert.org/pub_releases/2003-09/uow-ssv090203.php

Giles, D. C. (2002). Parasocial interaction: A review of the literature and a model for future research. *Media Psychology, 4,* 279–305.

GoPets. (2005, September 15). GoPets running wild on the Internet; 100,000 and counting [Press release]. Retrieved November 24, 2008, from http://www.informationweek.com/showPressRelease.jhtml?articleID=X367611&CompanyId=3

Graham-Rowe, D. (2007, December 19). Virtual extras. *Technology Review.* Retrieved December 2007 from http://www.technologyreview.com/Infotech/19964

Greene, K. (2007, August 6). Better than high definition: New high-contrast displays could provide more-realistic images. *Technology Review.* Retrieved 2007 from http://www.technologyreview.com/Infotech/19141/?a=f

Hailey, D., Roine, R., & Ohinmaa, A. (2002). Systematic review of evidence for the benefits of telemedicine. *Journal of Telemedicine and Telecare, 8*(supplement 1), 1–7.

Hanson Robotics. (n.d.). Robots: The next step in human evolution isn't human. Retrieved November 24, 2008, from http://www.hansonrobotics.com/robots.html

Harmon, A. (2003, April 3). More than just a game, but how close to reality? *New York Times*. Retrieved January 5, 2009, from http://www.nytimes.com/2003/04/03/technology/circuits/03camp.html

Hawkins, R. (2004, June 11). Simulation software on test. *Infomatics*. Retrieved January 5, 2009, from http://www.infomaticsonline.co.uk/computeractive/features/2014020/simulation-software-test

Heingartner, D. (2004, June 3). Just like high-definition TV, but with higher definition. *New York Times*. Retrieved October 2008 from http://www.nytimes.com/2004/06/03/technology/circuits/03next.html

Hill, J. (2007, July 24). Feel the action. Message posted to http://blogs.theage.com.au/screenplay/archives/006845.html

Hopkins, C. D., Raymond, M. A., & Mitra, A. (2004). Consumer responses to perceived telepresence in the online advertising environment: The moderating role of involvement. *Marketing Theory*, 4(1-2), 137–162.

Hornyak, T. (2006, April 23). Android science. *Scientific American*. Retrieved November 24, 2008, from http://www.sciam.com/article.cfm?chanID=sa006&articleID=000E16B9-8ADE-1447-8ADE83414B7F0101

Hyland, T. (2007, June 17). Games give troops fighting chance, but are they right? *The Age*. Retrieved January 5, 2009, from http://www.theage.com.au/news/national/games-give-troops-fighting-chance-but-are-they-right/2007/06/16/1181414613167.html

IMAX Corporation. (n.d.). What is IMAX? Retrieved October 2008 from http://www.imax.com/ImaxWeb/imaxExperience.do?param_section=whatImax&param_subMenuSelect=whatImaxSelect

International Society for Presence Research. (2000). *The concept of presence: Explication statement*. Retrieved September 24, 2008, from http://ispr.info/

InTouch Health (n/d). Products. Retrieved March 11, 2009, from http://intouch-health.com/products.html

Jackman, T. (2003, May 20). Blame it on the Matrix. *Buffalo News*. Retrieved August 9, 2003 from http://www.buffalonews.com/editorial/20030520/1042361.asp

Jacob, M. (2006, July 15). Japan's robots stride into future. *The Chicago Tribune*. Retrieved November 24, 2008, from http://www.chicagotribune.com/technology/chi-0607150271jul15,1,1528949.story?page=1&ctrack=1&cset=true&coll=chi-technology-hed

Jafari, S. (2006, June 19). Mine simulators improve training. *The Louisville Kentucky Courier-Journal*. Retrieved November 24, 2008, from http://www.courier-journal.com/apps/pbcs.dll/article?AID=/20060619/NEWS0104/606190382/1008/NEWS01

James, R.W. (Producer) & Merrill, K. (Director). (1994). *Yellowstone* [Motion picture]. USA: IMAX.

Jesdanun, A. (2008, February 24). Researchers look to spot photo hoaxes. Retrieved January 4, 2009, from http://abcnews.go.com/Technology/WireStory?id=4336613

Jesdanun, A. (2008, February 25). Jury's quandary: Is porn photo fake? Retrieved January 4, 2009, from http://www.sfgate.com/cgi-bin/article.cgi?f=/c/a/2008/02/25/BUO2V6RVE.DTL

Johnson, S. (2008, December 31). Chips drive Hollywood closer to its most special effect. *San Jose Mercury News.* Retrieved January 4, 2009 from http://www.mercurynews.com/business/ci_11346361

Juan, M. C., Joele, D., Botella, C., Baños, R., Alcañiz, M., & van der Mast, C. (2006). The use of a visible and/or an invisible marker Augmented Reality System for the treatment of phobia to small animals. *Annual Review of CyberTherapy and Telemedicine, 4,* 33–38.

Kakesako, G. K. (2006, February 19). Schofield's new training center uses computer simulations to prepare soldiers for battle. *The Honolulu Star-Bulletin.* Retrieved November 24, 2008, from http://starbulletin.com/2006/02/19/news/story05.html

Katz, J. E., & Rice, R. E. (2002). Project Syntopia: Social consequences of internet use. *IT &Society, 1*(1), 166–179.

Keshner, E. A. (2004). Virtual reality and physical rehabilitation: a new toy or a new research and rehabilitation tool? *Journal of NeuroEngineering and Rehabilitation, 1,* 8.

Klein, L. R. (2003). Creating virtual product experiences: The role of telepresence. *Journal of Interactive Marketing, 17*(1), 41–55.

Kolb, D. A. (1984). *Experiential learning: Experience as the source of learning and development.* Englewood Cliffs, NJ: Prentice-Hall.

Kotulak, R. (2004, August 3). Considered science fiction neural technology is opening doors. *Centre Daily Times.* Retrieved October 2008 from http://www.centredaily.com/mld/centredaily/news/nation/9308539.htm

Kushner, D. (2003). These are definitely not Scully's breasts. *Wired, 11*(11). Retrieved January 4, 2009, from http://www.wired.com/wired/archive/11.11/fakers.html

Kushner, D., & Fleishman, L. (2008, November). Virtual fitness: Tomorrow's reality? *Men's Fitness.* Retrieved March 10, 2009 from http://www.expresso.com/pdf/recent_coverage/Expresso_MensFitness_11_08.pdf

Lamont, I. (2007, May 24). Virtual reality and higher education: Another perspective. Terra Nova [blog]. Retrieved January 4, 2009 from http://terra-nova.blogs.com/terra_nova/2007/05/teaching_in_vr_.html

Langlinais, J. (2008, May 13). First Lady Anita Perry to unveil TEXAS ON TOUR mobile marketing initiative during Texas Tourism Week. *PRNewswire.* Retrieved October 2008 from http://www.reuters.com/article/pressRelease/idUS237830+13-May-2008+PRN20080513

Lanningham-Foster, L., Jensen, T. B., Foster, R. C., Redmond, A. B., Walker, B. A., Heinz, D., et al. (2006). Energy expenditure of sedentary screen time compared with active screen time for children. *Pediatrics, 118*(6), e1831-e1835.

Lawson, S. (2007, September 6). Cisco bringing telepresence to the home. *PC World.* Retrieved November 24, 2008, from http://www.pcworld.com/article/id,136888/article.html

Lawson, S. (2008, November 13). Recording raises issues for telepresence. *PC World.* Retrieved January 1, 2009, from http://www.pcworld.com/businesscenter/article/153830/recording_raises_issues_for_telepresence.html

Lee, K. M. (2006). Presence, explicated. *Communication Theory, 14*(1), 27–50.

Leeb, R., Friedman, D., Muller-Putz, G. R., Scherer, R., Slater, M., & Pfurtscheller, G. (2007). Self-paced (Asynchronous) BCI control of a wheelchair in virtual environments: A case study with a tetraplegic. *Computational Intelligence and Neuroscience, 2007.* Retrieved January 2, 2009, from http://www.hindawi.com/GetPDF.aspx?doi=10.1155/2007/79642

Leland, J. (2009, January 4). Urban tool in recruiting by the Army: An arcade. *New York Times.* Retrieved March 11, 2009, from http://www.nytimes.com/2009/01/05/us/05army.html

Levy, D. (2007). *Love and sex with robots: The evolution of human-robot relationships.* New York: Harper.

Lichtman, H. S. (2006, August). Telepresence, effective visual collaboration and the future of global business at the speed of light. Human Productivity Lab. Retrieved October 2008 from http://www.humanproductivitylab.com/archive_blogs/2006/08/09/hpl_release_telepresence_effec_1.php

Lombard, M. (2008, October). *Using telepresence to communicate science in giant screen cinema.* Paper presented at Giant Screen Cinema Association Symposium, Jersey City, New Jersey.

Lombard, M., & Ditton, T. (1997). At the heart of it all: The concept of presence. *Journal of Computer-Mediated Communication,* 3(2).

Lombard, M., & Jones, M. T. (2004, October). *Presence and sexuality.* Proceedings of PRESENCE 2004, the Seventh International Workshop on Presence, Valencia, Spain. Retrieved from http://www.temple.edu/ispr/prev_conferences/proceedings/2004/Lombard%20and%20Jones.pdf

Lombard, M., & Jones, M. T. (in press). Defining presence. In F. Biocca, W. A. Ijsselsteijn, & J. Freeman (Eds.), *Handbook of presence research.* Hillsdale, NJ: Erlbaum.

Lombard, M., & Selverian, M. E. (2008). Telepresence after death. *Presence: Teleoperators and virtual environments,* 17(3), 310–325.

Lombard, M., & Snyder-Duch, J. (2001). Interactive advertising and presence: A framework. *Journal of interactive advertising,* 1(2). Retrieved October 2008 from http://jiad.org/article13

Lyons, J. (2008, September 10). Survivors confront the terror in their heads. *Sydney Morning Herald.* Retrieved October 2008 from http://www.smh.com.au/news/world/survivors-confront-the-terror-in-their-heads/2008/09/09/1220857547723.html

Macedonia, M. (2002, March). Games soldiers play. *IEEE Spectrum,* 32–37.

Mair, F., & Whitten, P. (2000). Information in practice: Systematic review of studies of patient satisfaction with telemedicine. *British Medical Journal,* 320(7248), 1517–1520.

Media Grid (2008, January 22). Immersive education initiative announces education grid and platform ecosystem at Boston summit [News release]. Retrieved November 24, 2008, from http://mediagrid.org/news/2008-01_Summit_Outcomes.html

Medical News Today. (2004, April 19). Simulator could substantially reduce operating room errors. Retrieved November 24, 2008, from http://www.medicalnewstoday.com/index.php?newsid=7423

Meir, A. (2007, August 16). Ethics at work: Virtual ethics. *The Jerusalem Post.* Retrieved January 4, 2009 from http://www.jpost.com/servlet/Satellite?cid=1186557468225&pagename=JPost%2FJPArticle%2FShowFull

Meltzer, A. (2007, May 29). Using telepresence to bridge the gulf in distance learning. Retrieved November from http://www.telepresenceworld.net/

articles/16/1/Using-Telepresence-to-Bridge-the-Gulf-in-Distance-Learning/Page1.html

Moore, K., Wiederhold, B. K., Wiederhold, M. D., & Riva, G. (2002). Panic and agoraphobia in a virtual world. *Cyberpsychology & Behavior, 5*(3), 197–202.

Mori, M. (1970). The uncanny valley. *Energy, 7*(4), 33–35.

MXR (n.d.). Mixed reality lab, National University of Singapore: Human Pacman. Retrieved November 24, 2008, from http://www.art.nus.edu.sg/index.php?option=com_content&task=view&id=42&Itemid=36

Naone, E. (2007, October 30). Making games physical: With a new vest, players can feel the impact of video games. *Technology Review.* Retrieved October 2007 from http://www.technologyreview.com/Infotech/19637/?a=f

Nelson, C. (2004, February 1). Lip-synching gets real. *New York Times.* Retrieved December 1, 2008, from http://www.nytimes.com/2004/02/01/arts/music/01NELS.html

New Zealand's Information Network. (n.d.) Bungy jumping sites: Kawarau Bridge. Retrieved October 2008 from http://www.newzealandnz.co.nz/bungy-jump-sites/kawarau-bridge.html

News-Medical.Net (2004, June 2). Virtual reality to help the diagnosis of back problems. Retrieved November 24, 2008, from http://www.news-medical.net/view_article.asp?id=2082

Ortiz, D. (2007, February 26). A virtual take on cutting-edge medicine. *Providence* (Rhode Island) *Business News.* Retrieved October 2008 from http://www.pbn.com/stories/23254.html

Ortiz Jr., S. (2006, March 10). A step toward remote-control humans. TopTech News. Retrieved December 1, 2008, from http://www.toptechnews.com/story.xhtml?story_id=02200000JR10

Parker, K. (2004, December 22). Lines between virtual and real killing blur. *New Hampshire Union Leader.* Retrieved December 1, 2008, from http://www.theunionleader.com/articles_showa.html?article=48650

Patch, K. (2004, June 16/23). VR tool re-creates hallucinations. *Technology Research News* (*TRN*). Retrieved November 24, 2008, from http://www.trnmag.com/Stories/2004/061604/VR_tool_re-creates_hallucinations_061604.html

Payne, Sr., D. (2003, November 2). Airmen fly in virtual world. *The Parkersburg* (West Virginia) *News* and the *Parkersburg Sentinal.* Retrieved November 24, 2008, from http://www.newsandsentinel.com/news/story/112202003_new02_simulator.asp

Pessoa, A. L. (2008). *When simple technology affords social presence: A case study for remote family member.* Paper presented at PRESENCE 2008, the Eleventh International Workshop on Presence, Padua, Italy.

Petelin, J. B., Nelson, M. E., & Goodman, J. (2007). Deployment and early experience with remote-presence patient care in a community hospital. *Surgical Endoscopy, 21*(1), 53–56.

Photonics.com (2007, September 14). BullsEye Laser Fire Extinguisher. Retrieved November 24, 2008 from http://www.photonics.com/content/products/2007/September/14/89022.aspx

Platoni, K. (2008, January/February). Seeing is believing: Maybe virtual reality isn't just a game anymore. Maybe it's a way to build a better you. *Stanford Magazine.* Retrieved March 13, 2009, from http://www.stanfordalumni.org/news/magazine/2008/janfeb/features/virtual.html

Playstation.com (n.d.). The eye of Judgment. Retrieved November 24, 2008 from http://www.us.playstation.com/PS3/Games/THE_EYE_OF_JUDGMENT

Polycom (2008, November 12). Students study climate change in Antarctica and visit NASA space centers during national distance learning week [Press release]. Retrieved November 24, 200, from http://money.cnn.com/news/newsfeeds/articles/marketwire/0451597.htm

Raths, D. (2008, March 27). Virtual worlds help public safety officials practice for real-life threats. *Government Technology.* Retrieved November 24, 2008, from http://www.govtech.com/gt/261426?topic=117693

Reeves, B., & Nass, C. (1996). *The media equation: How people treat computers, television, and new media like real people and places.* New York: Cambridge University Press.

Richards, J. (2008, August 18). Lifelike animation heralds new era for computer games. Times Online. Retrieved August 2008 from http://technology.timesonline.co.uk/tol/news/tech_and_web/article4557935.ece

Riebe, A. (2005, October 1). High-tech logging at VCC. *The Mesabi Daily News* (Virginia, Minnesota). Retrieved November 24, 2008, from http://www.virginiamn.com/mdn/index.php?sect_rank=1&story_id=204842

Rizzo, A., & Kim, G. J. (2005). A SWOT analysis of the field of virtual reality rehabilitation and therapy. *Presence: Teleoperators & Virtual Environments, 14*(2), 119–146.

Rogers, J. (2008, April 28). Trainer's death by bear mauling reignites a debate. *Philadelphia Inquirer.* Retrieved April 2008 from http://www.philly.com/inquirer/world_us/20080428_Trainer_s_death_by_bear_mauling_reignites_a_debate.html

Rosenthal, A. (Ed.). (1999). *Why docudrama? Fact-fiction on film and TV.* Carbondale: Southern Illinois University Press.

Roush, W. (July 2007). Second earth. *Technology Review, 110*(4), 39–48.

Ruffini, G. (2007). *A grand challenge for presence: Phase I: Presence 2007 panel.* Retrieved January 1, 2009, from http://www.starlab.info/peach/files/PGC-20071102.pdf

Sagario, D. (2005, July 5). People who spend hours in therapy look at gauzy clouds. *Des Moines* (Iowa) *Register.* Retrieved October 2008 from http://desmoinesregister.com/apps/pbcs.dll/article?AID=/20050705/LIFE02/507050303/1039

Saint Louis, C. (2006, February 23). Pop them in, and they're ready to push you. *New York Times.* Retrieved March 10, 2009, from http://www.nytimes.com/2006/02/23/fashion/thursdaystyles/23Fitness.html

Sandhana, L. (2005, June 6). Pacman comes to life virtually. BBC News. Retrieved November 24, 2008, from http://news.bbc.co.uk/2/hi/technology/4607449.stm

Sanstha, S. (Producer) & Melton, K. (Director). (2005). *Mystic India* [Motion picture]. India: Giant Screen Films.

Schlosser, A. E. (2003). Experiencing products in the virtual world: The role of goal and imagery in influencing attitudes versus purchase intentions. *Journal of Consumer Research, 30*(2), 184–98.

SeeMeRot.com. (n.d.). Retrieved on May 24, 2006, from http://www.seemerot.com

Selverian, M. M., & Hwang, H. S. (2003). In search of presence: A systematic evaluation of evolving VLEs. *Presence: Teleoperators & Virtual Environments, 12*(5), 512–522.

Severs, L. (2008, January 11). Virtual reality condos getting second look: Avatars allow buyers another way to check out products. *Business Edge* (Ontario, Canada). Retrieved October 2008 from http://www.businessedge.ca/article.cfm/newsID/16917.cfm

Singer, E. (2007, February 2). A prosthetic arm that acts like a real one: Patients use nerves left intact after amputations to control prosthetic limbs. *Technology Review*. Retrieved October 2008 from http://www.technologyreview.com/Biotech/18134

Smith, E. D. (2007, June 19). IUPUI professor one of the world's leading researchers in the study of androids. *The Indianapolis* (Indiana) *Star*. Retrieved October 2008 from http://www.indystar.com/apps/pbcs.dll/article?AID=/20070619/LOCAL18/706190366/-1/LOCAL17

Speetjens, P. (2004, April 15). The Gateway offers visitors to Jordan a whole new experience: Multi-million dollar tourist development set to become jewel in crown of Aqaba Special. *The Daily Star* (Lebanon). Retrieved October 2008 from http://www.dailystar.com.lb/article.asp?edition_id=10&categ_id=4&article_id=2100#

SRI International. (2006, April 20). SRI International completes collaborative demonstration of remote robotic surgical system aboard NEEMO 9 undersea space station; First extreme environment tele-robotic mission proves successful. *TMCnet* (Business Wire). Retrieved October 2008 from http://www.tmcnet.com/usubmit/2006/04/20/1590055.htm

Stahl, S. (2008, September 1). Health: Virtual biking. Retrieved March 10, 2009 from http://cbs3.com/health/expresso.bike.fitness.2.808043.html

Stair, M. J. (2005, September 20). Firefighters battle virtual fire. *The Wilson* (North Carolina) *Daily*. Retrieved November 24, 2008, from http://www.wilsondaily.com/Wil_region/Local_News/284286353387234.php

Standard-Times. (2005, April 18). UMD hosts drunk driving simulation. *The* (South Massachusetts) *Standard-Times*. Retrieved November 24, 2008, from http://www.southcoasttoday.com/daily/04-05/04-18-05/a05lo468.htm

Stanek, S. (2006, December 17). Virtual reality boosts rehab in Israel. Washingtonpost.com. Retrieved October 2008 from http://www.washingtonpost.com/wp-dyn/content/article/2006/12/17/AR2006121700601_pf.html

Steere, M. (2008, October 6). Scientist: Holographic television to become reality. CNN International. Retrieved October 2008 from http://edition.cnn.com/2008/TECH/science/10/06/holographic.television

Strom, D. (2006, October 9). Virtual reality or real virtuality? *TidBITS*, #850. Retrieved December 1, 2008, from http://db.tidbits.com/article/8701

Suellentrop, C. (2006, November 20). Wii is the champion. Slate. Retrieved November 2006 from http://www.slate.com/id/2154158

Swann, P. (2007, April 18). Hologram TV: Better than HDTV? TVPredictions.com. Retrieved 2007 from http://www.tvpredictions.com/hologramtv041807.htm

Taves, S. (2007, July 24). Do gadgets make gaming more fun? From guitars to Wii-motes, add-ons aim to make games more realistic. MSNBC. Retrieved February 2008 from http://www.msnbc.msn.com/id/23362935

Terdiman, D. (2007, December 10). New game controller: Your hands. CNET News. Retrieved December 2007 from http://www.news.com/New-game-controller-Your-hands/2100-1043_3-6222024.html

Thompson, C. (2007, January). It's alive! *Wired*. Issue 15.01. Retrieved November 24, 2008, from http://www.wired.com/wired/archive/15.01/alive.html

Thompson, C. (2008, June 30). New high-tech attraction tells Niagara Falls story. *San Jose Mercury News*. Retrieved October 19, 2008, from http://www.mercurynews.com/travel/ci_9744161

Timmins, L. R., & Lombard, M. (2005). When "real" seems mediated: Inverse presence. *Presence: Teleoperators and Virtual Environments, 14*(4), 492–500.

Tomitsch, M., Grechenig, T., & Mayrhofer, S. (2007). Mobility and emotional distance: Exploring the ceiling as an ambient display to provide remote awareness. In *Proceedings of the 3rd IET International Conference on Intelligent Environments (IE 07)* (pp. 164–167). London: The Institution of Engineering and Technology.

Tompkins, P. (2003). Truth, trust, and telepresence. *Journal of Mass Media Ethics, 18*(3&4), 194–212.

Trainmaster (n.d.). Trainmaster simulation platform. Retrieved November 24, 2008, from http://www.trainmaster.com/index.htm

Trotter, A. (2003, January 22). Simulated driver's ed. Takes virtual twists and turns. *Education Week*. Retrieved November 24, 2008, from http://www.edweek.org/ew/newstory.cfm?slug=19tech.h22

Turkle, S. (1984). The second self: Computers and the human spirit. New York: Simon & Schuster.

Turkle, S. (1995). *Life on the screen: Identity in the age of the internet*. New York: Simon & Schuster.

UGOBE (n.d.). Background: About UGOBE. Retrieved November 24, 2008, from http://www.ugobe.com/what/what_is_background.html

UIC. (May 31, 2007). Virtual nature via video raises concerns for conservation [News release]. Retrieved January 3, 2009, from http://tigger.uic.edu/htbin/cgiwrap/bin/newsbureau/cgi-bin/index.cgi?from=Releases&to=Release&id=1852&start=1172926272&end=1180702272&topic=0&dept=0

UIC. (2008, March 19). Practice makes perfect with 3-D dental simulator [News release]. The University of Illinois at Chicago. Retrieved November 24, 2008, from http://tigger.uic.edu/htbin/cgiwrap/bin/newsbureau/cgi-bin/index.cgi?from=Releases&to=Release&id=2121

University of Missouri System. (2008, October 29). University of Missouri announces plans to network four campuses with high-definition [News release]. Retrieved November 24, 2008, from http://www.umsystem.edu/ums/news/releases/news08102801.shtml

Vallis, M. (2004, November 19). In Texas, a mouse can kill a deer. *Chicago Sun-Times*. Retrieved December 1, 2008, from http://www.suntimes.com/output/news/cst-nws-mouse19.html

Vierria, D. (2008, July 27). Kids find the fun in working out. *Sacramento Bee*. Retrieved March 10, 2009 from http://www.sacbee.com/822/story/1108161.html

WCAU (2006, April 25). Simulator allows doctors to experience heart failure. WCAU/NBC10 Philadelphia. Retrieved November 24, 2008, from http://www.nbc10.com/health/8993719/detail.html

Wei Chu, S. (2003, August 25). Delivering perfect pitch. *Globe and Mail*. Retrieved January 4, 2009, from http://www.theglobeandmail.com/servlet/ArticleNews/TPPrint/LAC/20030825/SINGING/TPEntertainment/

Wen, H. (2008, August 12). When worlds collide. *The Escapist*. Retrieved November 24, 2008, from http://www.escapistmagazine.com/articles/view/issues/issue_162/5130-When-Worlds-Collide

Wendland, M. (2003, November 10). UP site trains high-tech lumberjacks. *The Detroit Free Press*. Retrieved November 24, 2008, from http://www.freep.com/money/tech/mwend10_20031110.htm

Wilson, E. (2007, March 15). Rehab center caters to technology-savvy generation [Press release]. Retrieved November 24, 2008, from http://www.army.mil/-news/2007/03/15/2269-rehab-center-caters-to-technology-savvy-generation

Winner, L. (1997). Technology today: Uutopia or dystopia? — Technology and the rest of culture. *Social Research, 64*(3). Retrieved January 5, 2009, from http://findarticles.com/p/articles/mi_m2267/is_n3_v64/ai_19952021/pg_1

Witherspoon, B. (2005, January/February). Using illusion to bring nature into imaging centers. *Radiology Business Management Association Bulletin*. Retrieved October 19, 2008, from http://www.theskyfactory.com/press/rbma-01_05.htm

Wolpe, P. R. (2007, February). Ethical and social challenges of brain-computer interfaces. *Virtual Mentor: American Medical Association Journal of Ethics, 9*(2), 128–131.

Wurst, E. (2008, January 25). The 'Guitar Hero' effect: Why the popular video game's success means more business to local music stores. *The Beacon News* (Aurora, Illinois). Retrieved January 2008 from http://www.suburbanchicagonews.com/beaconnews/lifestyles/757608,2_5_AU25_GUITAR_S1.article

Yee, N., & Bailenson, J. N. (2007). The proteus effect: Self transformations in virtual reality. *Human Communication Research, 33*, 271–290.

Zaradic, P. A., & Pergams, O. R. W. (2007). Videophilia: Implications for childhood development and conservation. *Journal Of Developmental Processes, 2*(1), 130–144.

Chapter 11

Popular Media and Telepresence

Future Considerations

Cheryl Campanella Bracken and Paul D. Skalski

The chapters in this book presented what is known to date about several areas of popular media and telepresence. As readers can probably tell, much is still undecided in the telepresence literature regarding issues such as terminology and methodology. Resolving these issues is beyond the scope of this volume, but several important considerations will be touched on in this chapter. These include: (a) definitional and conceptual issues, including the "types" of telepresence; (b) Methodological issues, including telepresence as a variable; and (c) Telepresence in the changing popular media environment.

Definitional and Conceptual Issues in Telepresence Research

Many different terms have been used to refer to telepresence experiences in this volume, including presence, telepresence, spatial presence, immersion, and even theatrical presence (see chapter 2, this volume). In one sense, this shows the complexity of telepresence experiences, but it also points to a potential conceptualization problem in the telepresence literature, chiefly overlapping concept labels. Lombard and Jones (2007) identify many different telepresence-related terms, including telepresence, tele-presence, (tele)presence, spatial presence, social presence, computers are social actors, copresence, co-presence, subjective presence, virtual presence, and sense of presence (p. 202). A number of these terms confusingly refer to the exact same thing, which may impede knowledge advancement. Future work should attempt to reduce these into a coherent set of concepts that captures telepresence experiences without redundancy.

A related issue concerns types of telepresence. Scholars have identified such distinct telepresence experiences as spatial presence, social presence, and self presence, among others. These terms refer to different forms of "the perceptual illusion of non-mediation" (Lombard & Ditton, 1997). While there is no clear consensus on types of telepresence, we strongly recommend that researchers clearly identify the type of presence they are interested in studying. We believe that the most commonly studied telepresence types are forms of either *spatial presence* or *social presence*, and the choice of one or the other has conceptual and measurement implications. If a study is looking at reactions to a mediated other, for example, then measurement items getting at spatial presence or feeling "in" the mediated environment do not make as much sense as items specifically addressing feeling "with" a mediated other. Incorporating the "wrong" type of presence raises validity issues in a study and may reduce the potential strength of statistical relationships. Another way to avoid this problem is by including multiple presence types in research, to parse out the relative contributions of each type and better understand how they relate. Ultimately, a formal telepresence "theory" could help unify types of presence or at least show how they relate to one another and to other concepts. Schubert (2009) recently addressed this type of issue in a re-conceptualization of spatial presence to arguing that it relates to both mediated and non-mediated environments, following similar work by Wirth et al. (2007) and Lee (2004). Much more can still be done along these lines.

Finally, there are concepts in Communication and Psychology that are closely related to telepresence, such as identification (Cohen, 2006), transportation (Green, Brock, & Kaufman, 2004), and perceived realism (Potter, 1988). These should also be reconciled with telepresence to help unify similar bodies of research and maximize the parsimony of the scientific literature as a whole. There has been some published scholarship attempting to accomplish this goal (e.g., Wirth et al., 2007) but more work is needed.

Methodological Issues in Telepresence Research

The chapters in this volume establish the importance of telepresence in media research, but methodological questions remain about the nature of telepresence as a variable. One consideration is whether telepresence is an independent or dependent variable. In much of the literature, telepresence is treated as a dependent variable. Many researchers are interested solely in how technology and user characteristics affect the perceptual illusion of non-mediation as an outcome. This has been the dominant approach in Computer Science, Engineering, and related fields, as exemplified by the articles in a typical issue of the *Presence: Teleoperators & Virtual Environments* journal. Other researchers, however, particularly those in Communication, Psychology, and other social/behavioral sciences, treat telepresence as an independent variable leading to further outcomes of interest in particular domains, such as entertainment and persuasion (see chapter 6 and chapter 7, in this volume).

The use of telepresence as both independent and dependent variables points to an additional consideration, the role of telepresence in multiple variable models of media effects. Is telepresence a mediator or moderator? Baron and Kenny (1986) define *moderator* as a variable that affects the direction and strength of the relationship between an independent and dependent variable, whereas a *mediator* accounts for the relationship between an independent and dependent variable. Moderators specify when certain effects will hold, while mediators indicate how or why such effects occur, according to Baron and Kenny. In the case of telepresence, it seems that the variable could be either a mediator or moderator. Treated as a moderator, telepresence would be a variable that interacts with other variables such as age, prior experience, and content to affect outcomes of media exposure. It seems plausible that telepresence could function in this manner, but given that telepresence is viewed primarily as a state (instead of a trait) driven by aspects of media form and content, we argue that telepresence should be treated more often as a mediator in multiple-variable models. That is, telepresence comes between technology and outcomes and explains why such effects occur. In this sense, telepresence functions as both a dependent and an independent variable. For example, in the case of video game effects, there may a relationship between video game play and enjoyment, and this relationship may be explained (at least in part) by adding telepresence as a mediator. As discussed by Tamborini and Bowman in chapter 5 of this volume, video game characteristics such as natural mapping make players feel more "in" the game, and this sense of presence in an exciting game world contributes to enjoyment. There is a likely direct path between video game play and enjoyment in this example, but if telepresence is added as a mediator, the paths leading to and from it should be stronger and account for more variance, as well as serving as an explanatory mechanism.

If there is a moderator in this type of relationship, it would likely be content or individual differences. Telepresence is a direct and logical outcome of technology exposure with an evolutionary basis (Lee, 2004), but it may be affected by content types and individual differences such as gender, age, and suspension of disbelief (see Oliver, 2002, for a detailed discussion of individual differences). Moderating variables like these can change the expected relationship between technology and telepresence. For example, exposure to IMAX movies should relate positively to telepresence, but if a viewer is not interested in the subject matter of the film, they may not feel a high sense of telepresence. In this example, content interest moderates the relationship between media exposure and telepresence. Moderators can reduce or increase telepresence, and as telepresence increases or decreases, the outcome that is mediated by it will respond accordingly (e.g., less or more enjoyment).

Another important methodological issue in telepresence research is measurement of the concept. Much has already been written on this issue, including discussions of measurement methods and specific scales (e.g., Insko, 2003; International Society for Presence Research, n.d.; Nunez, 2007). Here we would like to address the multidimensional nature of telepresence. Within the Communication literature, Kim and Biocca (1997) first presented telepresence as a two-dimension concept with Arrival and Departure factors. These dimensions describe audience sensations of transportation when viewing television. As a result of more recent work on the concept, there now seems to be general consensus amongst telepresence researchers that there are three dominant sub-dimensions: spatial or physical presence, engagement, and naturalness (Freeman, 2004). Freeman also identifies several measurement scales that include each of these three sub-dimensions in some form (see Schubert, 2009, for a fuller discussion of presence sub-dimensions). They include but are not limited to the ITC-SOPI (Lessiter, Freeman, Keogh, & Davidoff, 2001), Reality Judgment (Baños et al., 2000), and Measurement, Effects, Conditions (MEC; Wirth et al., 2007). Additional work has attempted to identify measurement dimensions of social presence (e.g., Biocca, Harms, & Burgoon, 2003). We are not advocating one scale over another at this time but recommend that researchers do not ignore the multi-dimensional nature of the concept. Furthermore, unless unidimensionality can be established, we recommend treating the dimensions of telepresence as separate in statistical analyses rather than summing to create an overall "presence" variable. One reason for this is that telepresence subdimensions may respond differently to particular experimental manipulations and other independent variables, as well as affecting outcomes in different ways.

Telepresence in the Changing Popular Media Environment

Entertainment and popular media are changing faster today than at any time in history. As communication becomes digitized, more of our media entertainment experiences are becoming mobile. In addition, media technologies are evolving into amalgams of popular media forms from the past and present, best exemplified by the Internet. There are more ways to exchange and experience entertainment than ever before. We know little about how much telepresence can be experienced when viewing new content types on YouTube or iPods or cell phones. Early research on screen size and video resolution would suggest that these formats should not lead to much telepresence, but newer research casts some doubt on this assumption. Bracken and Petty (2007) found that telepresence can be evoked by screens as small as 2.5 inches or 6.4 cm on the classic iPods. Others assert that mobile phones can elicit sensations of telepresence in media users (Jeffery, 2008).

Interestingly, Nielsen Company has begun to track the total use of screens in American's lives. They have dubbed television, the Internet, and mobile phones "the three screens" (Nielsen, 2008). According to Susan Whilting (vice chairperson for the Nielsen Company), "Americans keep finding more time to spend with the three screens. TV use is at an all-time high, yet people are also using the Internet more often—31% of which is happening simultaneously" (TV, Internet, 2009). The implications of this type of use from a telepresence standpoint remain uncertain.

We know even less about media user characteristics that are likely to impact sensations of telepresence. As Jenkins (2006) points out, media audiences are becoming increasingly active in shaping their experiences with media form and content, and these types of changes have important implications for how they will experience telepresence in coming years. Future research should attempt to identify and account for these and other individual differences influencing telepresence.

What does the future hold for popular media? All the predictions point to communication technologies that will heighten media users' experiences of telepresence. One area of discussion has been various uses of nanotechnology for entertainment purposes. For example, a "bionic" contact lens will allow people to view visual displays within their field of view (Jackson, 2008). This is one step closer to neurotechnology (or the integration of biological and computer systems), which one expert believes will become feasible within the next 10 years (Singer, 2006). Wearable technology is another area poised to become more popular in the near future, with applications in entertainment and health (Stevens, 2008). And augmented reality (AR), or the blending of the real and virtual world (McCall & Braun, 2008), is now being used in advertising (Schmitt, 2009)—MINI, for example, published a 2-D magazine ad that used webcams to provide readers with an interactive experience (TechnaBob, 2008). AR has other popular media applications as well and may eventually fulfill the promise that VR was never able to achieve. These are but a few examples of popular media on the horizon, most of which are going to be designed to create more compelling telepresence experiences than ever before. As a result, the importance of telepresence in research cannot be understated. It is central to our understanding of media in everyday life, now and (especially) in the future.

References

Baños, R.M., Botella, C., Garcia-Palacios, A., Villa, H., Perpiña, C., & Alcañiz, M. (2000). Presence and reality judgment in virtual environments: A unitary construct? *CyberPsychology & Behavior, 3,* 327–335.

Baron, R. M., & Kenny, D. A. (1986). The moderator-mediator variable distinction in social psychological research: Conceptual, strategic, and statistical considerations. *Journal of Personality and Social Psychology, 51,* 1173–1182.

Biocca, F., Harms, C., & Burgoon, J. K. (2003). Toward a more robust theory and measure of social presence: Review and suggested criteria. *Presence: Teleoperators and Virtual Environments, 12*(5), 456–480.

Bracken, C. C., & Pettey, G. (2007). It is REALLY a smaller (and smaller) world: Presence and small screens. In *Proceedings of the Tenth Annual International Meeting of the Presence Workshop, Barcelona, Spain,* pp. 283–290.

Cohen, J. (2006). Audience identification with media characters. In J. Bryant & P. Vorderer (Eds.), *Psychology of entertainment* (pp. 183–198). Mahwah, NJ: Erlbaum.

Freeman, J. (2004) *Implications for the measurement of presence from convergent evidence on the structure of presence.* Paper presented to the Information Systems Division at the annual meeting of the International Communication Association, New Orleans, LA.

Green, M. C., Brock, T. C., & Kaufman, G. F. (2004). Understanding media enjoyment: The role of transportation into narrative worlds. *Communication Theory, 14*(4), 311–327.

Insko, B. E. (2003). Measuring presence: Subjective, behavioral, and physiological methods. In G. Riva, F. Davide, & W. A. IJsselsteijn (Eds.), *Being there: Concepts, effects and measurement of user presence in synthetic environments* (pp. 109–119). Amsterdam: IOS Press.

International Society for Presence Research. (n.d.). *Tools to measure presence.* Retrieved May 15, 2009, from http://www.temple.edu/ispr/frame_measure.htm

Jackson, J. (2008, January 29). "Bionic" contact lens may create tiny personal displays. *National Geographic News.* Retrieved on May 19, 2009, from http://news.nationalgeographic.com/news/2008/01/080129-bionic-eye.html

Jeffery, R. (2008). Mobile forms of communication and the transformation of relations between the public and private spheres. In K. Ross & S. Price (Eds.), *Popular media and communication: Essays on publics, practices and processes* (pp. 5–23). Newcastle, England: Cambridge Scholars Publishing.

Jenkins, H. (2006). *Convergence culture: Where old and new media collide.* New York: New York University Press.

Kim, T., & Biocca, F. (1997). Telepresence via television: Two dimensions of telepresence may have different connections to memory and persuasion. *Journal of Computer-Mediated Communication, 3*(2). Retrieved from http://www.ascusc.org/jcmc/vol3/issue2/kim.html

Lee, K. M. (2004). Why presence occurs: Evolutionary psychology, media equation, and presence. *Presence: Teleoperators and Virtual Environments, 13,* 494–505.

Lessiter, J., Freeman, J., Keogh, E., & Davdioff, J. (2001). A cross-media presence questionnaire: The ITC-Sense of Presence Inventory. *Presence: Teleoperators and Virtual Environments, 10*(3), 282–297.

Lombard, M., & Ditton, T. (1997). At the heart of it all: The concept of presence. *Journal of Computer-Mediated Communication, 3*(2). Retrieved October 20, 2008, from http://jcmc.indiana.edu/vol3/issue2/lombard.html

Lombard, M., & Jones, M. (2007). Identifying the (tele)presence literature. *PsychNology Journal, 5*(2), 97–206.

McCall, R., & Braun, A-K. (2008). Experiences of evaluating presence in augmented realities. *PsychNology Journal, 6*(2), 157–163. Retrieved May 20, 2009, from www.psychnology.org

Nielsen Company. (2008). A2/M2: Three Screen Report. Available at: http://www.nielsen-online.com/downloads/3_Screens_4Q08_final.pdf

Nunez, D. (2007). *A capacity limited, cognitive constructionist model of virtual presence.* Unpublished doctoral dissertation, University of Cape Town South Africa. Retrieved January 10, 2008, from http://chomsky.uct.ac.za/dnunez/new/phdthesis/dnunez_clcc_model_phd.pdf

Oliver, M. B. (2002). Individual differences in media effects. In J. Bryant & D. Zillmann (Eds.), *Media effects: Advances in theory and research* (pp. 507–524). Mahwah, NJ: Erlbaum.

Potter, J. W. (1988). Perceived reality in television effects research. *Journal of Broadcasting & Electronic Media, 32*(1), 23–41.

Schmitt, G. (2009, May 5). Augmented reality: Can the 'Stars Wars' effect sustain engagement? *Advertising Age.* Retrieved May 19, 2009, from http://adage.com/digitalnext/article?article_id=136390

Schubert, T. W. (2009). A new conception of spatial presence: Once again, with feeling. *Communication Theory, 19,* 161–187.

Singer, E. (2006, May 21). The future of neurotechnology. *Technology Review.* Retrieved May 19, 2009, from http://www.technologyreview.com/read_article.aspx?id=16901&ch=biotech

Stevens, D. (2008). The emergence of cyberfashion. *Cybertherapy & Rehabilitation, 1,* 22–24.

Technabob. (2008, December 18). Mini augmented reality ads hit newstands. *Technabob.* Retrieved on May 19, 2009, from http://technabob.com/blog/2008/12/17/mini-augmented-reality-ads-hit-newstands/

TV, Internet and Mobile Usage In U.S. Continues To Rise (2009, February, 23). *Nielsen Wire.* Retrieved May 20, 2009, from http://blog.nielsen.com/nielsenwire/online_mobile/tv-internet-and-mobile-usage-in-us-continues-to-rise/

Wirth, W., Hartmann, T., Böcking, S., Vorderer, P., Klimmt, C., Schramm, H., et al. (2007). A process model of the formation of spatial presence experiences. *Media Psychology, 9,* 493–525.

Author Index

Subject Index